Archibald Wright Murray

The Bible in the Pacific

Archibald Wright Murray

The Bible in the Pacific

ISBN/EAN: 9783337099633

Printed in Europe, USA, Canada, Australia, Japan

Cover: Foto ©Lupo / pixelio.de

More available books at **www.hansebooks.com**

THE
BIBLE IN THE PACIFIC.

BY THE

REV. A. W. MURRAY,

AUTHOR OF "MISSIONS IN WESTERN POLYNESIA;"
"FORTY YEARS' MISSION WORK IN POLYNESIA AND NEW GUINEA,"
"THE MARTYRS OF POLYNESIA,"
AND "EMINENT WORKERS FOR CHRIST."

"The people who sat in darkness saw great light; and to them who sat in the region and shadow of death light is sprung up." MATT. iv. 16.

"Most wondrous Book! bright candle of the Lord!
Star of eternity! the only star
By which the bark of man could navigate
The sea of life, and gain the coast of bliss
Securely; only star which rose on time,
And on its dark and troubled billows still,
As generation, drifting swiftly by,
Succeeded generation, threw a ray
Of heaven's own light, and to the hills of God,
The eternal hills, pointed the sinner's eye."
—POLLOK.

PREFACE.

THE work now offered to the friends of Bible circulation and Christian missions originated with the Rev. H. T. Robjohns, B.A., one of the agents of the British and Foreign Bible Society for the Australian Colonies and New Zealand. An idea occurred to Mr. Robjohns, which, put into words, would be in substance as follows:—" Here we are on the borders of the great Pacific Ocean, on the islands and groups scattered over the bosom of which a work of Bible translation and circulation has been in progress for over half a century; how desirable it seems that, while we have amongst us men who have personally taken part in that work, steps should be taken for the production of a connected history of a work of such vital importance to the welfare of man, and the glory of the God of the Bible."

Mr. Robjohns mentioned his idea to my esteemed friend and fellow-labourer in the Pacific, the Rev. W. W. Gill, B.A. Mr. Gill, while highly approving of Mr. Robjohns' proposal that such a work should be undertaken, did not see his own way clear to undertake it, but suggested that I should be applied to. The thing was mentioned to the Committee of the New South Wales Auxiliary to the British and

Foreign Bible Society, and by them taken up warmly, and an application was made to me through the District Secretary of the Auxiliary, the Rev. R. T. Hills. After consultation with Mr. Hills I put my ideas in writing as to what should be the character of the proposed work. My letter was submitted to the Committee, and by them approved. They considered it due to the Committee of the Parent Society to refer the final decision to them. This was done, and with their sanction an arrangement was made by the Rev. Dr. Wright, the Editorial Secretary of the Society, with Messrs. James Nisbet & Co., Berners Street, London, to publish the work in the event of its being prepared.

And now it is completed, and with all my heart I thank God for having given me so congenial and important a work to do, and for having spared me and supplied the needful health and strength to accomplish it, and very earnestly do I pray that His blessing may largely rest upon it, and that the end of its publication may be answered in a very high degree. It records a vast amount of labour by men and women whose lives were consecrated to a work than which there is none nobler and grander in which man can engage. Many of the honoured men and women who did the work have long ceased from their labours and gone to their reward, but their work lives in its blessed results, and will live till the mystery of God shall be finished, and Jesus shall reign over a ransomed world; nor will it stop there, but in its influences and effects it will flow on and on throughout a limitless eternity.

I beg here to offer my warmest acknowledgments to all my beloved brethren who have assisted me in my work. In every instance, with a solitary exception, my application has met with a hearty response, and much interest has been expressed in the work, and many encouraging words have been spoken which have been highly appreciated. And while acknowledging obligations to helpers, I wish especially to name the valuable service which my life-long friend and fellow-labourer, the Rev. Dr. Turner, has rendered in editing the work as it has passed through the press, and which is the third service of the kind which he and Mrs. Turner have rendered me within a few years. To them therefore I owe a very large debt of gratitude. May the Master whom we serve amply recompense them. And to another esteemed brother, the Rev. S. M. Creagh, I am also under special obligations. He, in addition to furnishing information relative to translation work on the Loyalty Islands, has read over the manuscript with me, and in that way has rendered very valuable help.

The work is as complete as I have been able to make it. The information extends from the commencement of mission work on Tahiti in 1797 to the close of the year 1887, so the reader can ascertain what has been accomplished in the work of Bible translation, and what is the general state and prospects of any particular mission, by referring to the chapter which treats of that mission.

It may perhaps be thought that an undue amount of space is occupied with historical notices of the different missions; but it is to be borne in mind that Bible translation is an essential part of missionary work, that the rise and progress of the one is inseparably connected with the other, and so both are required to form a complete whole.

With these remarks, explanations, and acknowledgments, I send the book forth on its mission, again commending it to the blessing of Him from whom all blessings flow.

PETERSHAM, NEAR SYDNEY,
 NEW SOUTH WALES, *May* 1888.

CONTENTS.

EASTERN AND CENTRAL POLYNESIA.

CHAP.		PAGE
I. THE TAHITIAN VERSION		1
II. THE RAROTONGAN VERSION		20
III. THE SAMOAN VERSION		37
IV. BIBLE TRANSLATION IN NIUE		53
V. THE TONGAN VERSION		65
VI. THE FIJI VERSION		76
VII. ROTUMA		99
VIII. NEW ZEALAND		104

WESTERN POLYNESIA—THE NEW HEBRIDES.

IX. FOTUNA AND NIUA		124
X. THE ANEITEUM VERSION		132
XI. TANNA		146
XII. ERAMANGA		154
XIII. FATE OR SANDWICH ISLAND		168
XIV. NGUNA AND OTHER ISLANDS		182

WESTERN POLYNESIA—THE LOYALTY ISLANDS.

XV. MARE		189
XVI. LIFU		199
XVII. UVEA		208
XVIII. NEW BRITAIN		215
XIX. NEW GUINEA		225

THE NORTH PACIFIC.

XX. THE SANDWICH ISLANDS		238
XXI. MICRONESIA		255
XXII. THE MARQUESAS		277
CONCLUSION		291

EASTERN AND CENTRAL POLYNESIA.

CHAPTER I.

THE TAHITIAN VERSION.

In a record of Bible translation in the islands of the Pacific, the Tahitian version is clearly entitled to the first place. To this version an importance attaches greater than can be claimed for any other of our South Sea translations. The fact that the grand missionary experiment of modern times was made in the Tahitian group invests everything connected with that group with undying interest; and the translation of the sacred Scriptures, as one of the greatest achievements of the mission, stands pre-eminent.

To the translators of this version, all subsequent translators in the Pacific, especially in Eastern and Central Polynesia, owe a large debt of gratitude; and we feel sincere satisfaction in according to these brave pioneers of modern missions the praise to which they are so well entitled. They laboured, and we later missionaries in a measure entered into their labours. All that had been done to prepare the way for us was more or less directly traceable to their labours and sufferings. In their case, of course, there was no previous preparation, nor had they experience to guide them. All was new and untried. They were put down among a race of savages who had sunk to about the lowest level to which human beings can sink—a people without a written language, and of whose spoken language they knew not a word; a people whose character and habits were utterly loathsome, and who were addicted to the most horrid cruelties and the vilest practices, and who were wholly unable to understand their motives and to appreciate the sacrifices they were making in preferring to live amongst them to remaining in their own homes in the land of their fathers. Hence the wrongs and indignities they had to bear, and the self-denial involved in carrying out the enterprise in which they had embarked. Heroism indeed of the loftiest character and consecration of the highest order were demanded of them, and their example has been and will continue to be an inspiration and encouragement to missionaries in all parts of the world. When the *Duff*, after a short stay with them, took her departure in 1797, they were left alone on the dark and savage shore of the then little known Tahiti, with no human succour within thousands of miles, and no means of escape should their lives be in danger, and in utter uncertainty as to when they would have any communication with the civilised world. They were helpless and defenceless as lambs in the midst of wolves, having only one refuge to which they could betake themselves. Such were the circumstances in which the grand experiment had to be made, and a memorable struggle the experiment involved—a struggle extending over no less a period than twelve years. In due time, however—doubtless at the right time—the night of toil and tears came to an end, and a glorious day dawned upon Tahiti. When the faith and patience of both missionaries and their supporters had well nigh failed—had quite failed indeed in the case of many in England, and the question of giving up the mission was being seriously discussed by the faithful few—then at the critical moment, the darkest hour, the dawn appeared: God was pleased to affix the seal of His approbation to the toils and labours of His faithful servants. His arm was made bare in the sight of the heathen, and in the sight of an intensely interested few who looked on from afar. Events were brought to pass such as had not been witnessed since the primitive ages of Christianity. It is hardly an exaggeration to say that "a nation was born in a day."

A system of idolatry—a system of foul, cruel superstition, the growth of unnumbered ages, was swept away with a rapidity and completeness which confounded and silenced adversaries, confirmed the faith of wavering friends, and cheered beyond measure those who had all along held fast their confidence. In the course of two or three years from the time the dawn appeared, and the Spirit of God " broke the gloom of Pagan night," idolatry was completely subverted throughout the islands of Tahiti and Eimeo, and these two islands became the radiating point whence the light of life went forth to other islands and groups throughout the vast Pacific; and an impulse was given to the missionary spirit in every part of the Christian world, fraught with consequences the extent and importance of which the infinite mind alone can grasp. What glorious issues to the labours, sufferings, toils, and deaths of the pioneers! What a reward! How gloriously true is it that in due time faithful labourers shall reap if they faint not!

Amid the dark days, while the sowing in tears was going on, those of the labourers who had been able to abide at their post (a number had been compelled from various causes to leave the field of conflict temporarily or permanently) applied themselves to the study of the language, and when "the times of refreshing" came, they were in a position to meet the altered circumstances. The language had been reduced to writing, and a spelling-book had been prepared and printed in England. This reached the island in 1811. A smaller spelling-book, and a brief summary of the Old and New Testament, about seventy pages 12mo, had been printed in Sydney, so there was something ready at once to put into the hands of the converts; but there was urgent need for something more extended, and a vastly greater supply. The people, conscious of new wants, were longing to have these wants met. Hence the little books in print were sought after with the utmost avidity. From them many learned to read, and were hungering and thirsting for books to read. They had got the key of knowledge, but as yet there was little in their own tongue to unlock, and of course they knew no other tongue. In some cases the books they had had been wholly committed to memory, and in many families where all were learning to read there was only one book. Some, who had learned to write, had written out the whole of the spelling-book on paper of which they had managed to get possession, and others who could not obtain paper had prepared a substitute from the bark of a tree * on which they had managed to write out the alphabet with the spelling-book and reading lessons. And many had texts which they had heard preached from, and portions of Scripture with which they had become acquainted, written on scraps of paper which they had picked up, and these were regarded, not as charms, but as precious treasures, on which were inscribed portions of divine truth, which they had now learned to prize as beyond all price.

Such was the state of things in 1817 when the Rev. William Ellis arrived, and the first steps were taken towards printing the first gospel which ever saw the light in the "Ocean World." Mr. Ellis had a knowledge of printing and binding, and he brought with him a printing press, and a small supply of binding material. He

* Probably the paper mulberry.

was stationed on the small island of Eimeo, which is about eighteen miles distant from Tahiti, and enclosed within the same reef. With the least possible delay a printing office was built. The people worked with a will for the accomplishment of such an object, and the house, such as it was, was soon completed. It was a very primitive affair, of course, but it answered the end. Mr. Ellis mentions an incident connected with its erection which is worthy of especial note. It was partly paved with smoothed basaltic stones dug from the ruins of a heathen temple in a neighbouring marae. The maraes were sacred places, on which the temples and altars stood in the dark days of heathenism, in which, and on which, deeds of cruelty were practised with appalling frequency. The offering of human sacrifices held a chief place among the dark and cruel usages of idolatry throughout the whole of the Tahitian group, and these stones had no doubt been often stained with the blood of the wretched victims. How different the use to which they were put now, and how strikingly significant of the benign change already wrought by the gospel of peace and love!

Preparations for commencing printing were soon completed. Intense interest was aroused among the people, from Pomare the king downwards, and they flocked together from all quarters to witness the wonderful operations that were to issue in putting them in possession of the treasure they so longed to possess—a portion of God's own book in their native tongue. The king was intensely desirous of having a direct hand in producing the first sheets, and in this Mr. Ellis managed to gratify him. He so arranged everything, and so directed his majesty, that he succeeded in striking off the first three or four sheets. He was delighted beyond measure, and the people were scarcely less so, and well they might. When the consequences which have flowed to themselves, and to successive generations throughout the wide Pacific, from the introduction of the printing press are considered, it is impossible to overestimate the proceedings of that day. It was the 3rd of June 1817—emphatically a red-letter day in the annals of Tahiti and of the vast regions beyond.*

The spelling-book was the first thing printed, an edition of 2600 being struck off, and an edition of 2300 copies of the Tahitian catechism followed, and a collection of texts and extracts from Scripture, and then the great work of printing the Bible in the language of Tahiti was begun. The Gospel according to Luke had been translated by the Rev. Henry Nott, one of the first missionaries who arrived in the *Duff* in 1797. Mr. Nott had nobly stuck to his post, and he was honoured and privileged to have the chief hand in producing the first entire version of the sacred Scriptures in any language of Polynesia.

The printing of the gospel proved a formidable undertaking. The missionaries, Messrs. Ellis and Crook, by whom the work was chiefly done, worked eight hours and sometimes ten hours daily, and though they had instructed two natives, who relieved them of the more laborious part of the work, still the progress was slow. This was chiefly owing to the fact that "many things belonging to the printing materials and the accompanying apparatus were either deficient or spoiled." However, all difficulties were overcome, and in the beginning of 1818 the work was completed. During all the months the printing of the gospel was in progress the natives manifested the liveliest interest, and multitudes of visitors came from great distances to witness the operations, and ascertain the progress of the work; and when it was completed the eagerness to possess copies was such as can hardly be described. "When will the books be ready?" was the eager inquiry

* Full particulars may be found in Ellis' "Polynesian Researches," vol. ii. chap. x.

of every party. And when the printing and stitching of the sheets were completed the difficulties were by no means at an end—they must be bound in some fashion, and the supply of binding material was very limited. The first bound copy was sent to Mr. Nott, the translator, and the second to the king. The queen and principal chiefs were next supplied; and such preparations as the case admitted of were made to meet the general demand. Some of the natives had been taught the art of binding, and they were overwhelmed with work, and derived no small gain from their newly-acquired craft.

We must not attempt to describe particularly the various expedients to which the people had recourse to supply the lack of proper binding material. Substitutes for mill-boards were made from native cloth, a number of folds being beaten together. It was the work of the women to make the native cloth, and now they were set to transform it into stiff boards for the binding of the books; and on the men devolved the more difficult task of finding a substitute for leather. "Poor animals," says Mr. Ellis, "which had hitherto lived in undisturbed ease and freedom were hunted solely for their skins, and the printing office was converted into a tan-yard, to which the skins of goats, dogs, and cats were taken to be prepared for book-covers."

All the books hitherto circulated had been gratuitously distributed; now for this larger book the plan was adopted which has been followed almost universally throughout our South Sea Missions, that of requiring some equivalent suited to the circumstances of the people. In the present case the natives had no money, but they had no difficulty in procuring cocoa-nut oil, and a small quantity of that was demanded, and most cheerfully given. Cocoa-nut oil finds a ready market in any civilised land, and the proceeds of sales were remitted to the British and Foreign Bible Society, to which all our missions are so deeply indebted. We have only had to make our needs known to that noble society to have them promptly and liberally met; and though in most cases we have been able to refund the entire amount expended, yet it is a great boon to us to have the entire responsibility of printing, binding, and publishing taken off our hands by those who have every facility for accomplishing the work in a manner the most economical and satisfactory. With the furnishing of the paper for this first portion of the sacred writings began the relations of our missions with the British and Foreign Bible Society, which have been so harmoniously maintained throughout all the intervening years—now well nigh threescore and ten.

But to return. Mr. Ellis remarks that the months occupied in the printing and binding of the books was a most laborious time, yet it was one of the happiest periods of his life. The eagerness of the people to possess themselves of the precious treasure was cheering in the highest degree. Thirty or forty canoes were frequently lying along the beach, each of which had brought five or more persons, on no other errand than to procure copies of the gospel for themselves, and to convey to their friends, and sometimes they had to wait for five or six weeks before they could be supplied. And in other cases canoes would arrive bringing bundles of letters from others who were unable to come, written on plantain leaves, and rolled up like a scroll, begging that copies might be sent to them.

"Often," says Mr. Ellis, "when standing at my door, which was but a short distance from the sea-beach, as I have gazed on the varied beauties of the rich and glowing landscape, and the truly picturesque appearance of the island of Tahiti, fourteen or eighteen miles distant, the scene has been enlivened by the light and nautilus-like sail of the buoyant canoe, first seen in the distant horizon as a small white speck, sometimes scarcely distinguishable from the crest of the waters, at others brilliantly reflecting the last rays of the retiring sun, and appearing in bold and beautiful relief before

'The impassioned splendour of those clouds
That wait upon the sun at his departure.'

"The effect of this magnificent scene has often been heightened by the impression that the voyagers, whose approaching bark became every moment more conspicuous among the surrounding objects, were not coming in search of pearls or gems, but the more valuable treasure contained in the sacred Scriptures, deemed by them 'more precious than gold, yea, than much fine gold.' One evening about sunset a canoe arrived from Tahiti with five men on this errand." Mr. Ellis met them at the door of his house and asked them what they wanted. "Luka," they replied, "the word of Luka," holding up the bamboos of oil they had brought to pay for them. Mr. Ellis told them he had none ready, but if they would wait till the morning, they should have as many as they wanted. Mr. Ellis bade them good-night, and went inside the house, supposing they had gone to sleep at some friend's house, but on looking out in the early dawn, what was his surprise to see these five men lying on the ground, their only bed being plaited cocoa-nut leaves, and their only covering the large piece of native cloth they usually wear over their shoulders. On being asked why they did not go and lodge at some house as they had been directed, they replied: "We were afraid that had we gone away some one might have come before us, and taken what books there were to spare, and we should have been obliged to return without; therefore we determined not to go away till we had procured the books." The books were got ready for them as speedily as possible, each getting one. They begged two copies more, one for a mother, and another for a sister, for which they had brought payment. They wrapped the books carefully up in native cloth, each putting his own into his bosom, bade Mr. Ellis good-morning, and launching their canoe, and hoisting their sail, they started for their native island, rejoicing as they that find great spoil.

But we must not dwell longer on these interesting reminiscences of the olden time, but proceed to trace the progress of translation work as one portion after another was completed and put into the hands of the people. The Gospel of Matthew followed that of Luke in 1820, that of John in 1821, and the Acts of the Apostles in 1822–3. The Gospel of Mark was printed in 1827, and the Epistles of Paul, Peter, and Jude were printed at different dates, and they were issued in a well-bound volume, including all that had been previously printed, in 1828.

I am sorry I cannot ascertain the precise date at which the translating and printing of the New Testament were finished. It was probably in 1830. Before its completion, the Psalms and other portions of the Old Testament must have been in print; and in December 1835 the complete version of the sacred volume in the Tahitian language was finished.

"Several of the missionaries," Mr. Ellis informs us, "had translated parts of the sacred volume, but the work was ultimately accomplished by Mr. Nott and Mr. Davies. The whole, however, was carefully examined by each missionary before its final revision, and every possible care taken to render it as faithful as the capabilities of the language would admit. This great work certainly was not carelessly hurried over; and few translations into a newly formed language have probably been equally correct."

At the date mentioned above (December 1835), Mr. Nott informed his brethren that the translation of the entire volume of Divine Revelation was completed, and that the whole had been carefully revised for publication. The announcement was received with great joy by the brethren; and the venerated translator, who had made it his chief work for well nigh twenty years, was requested to proceed to England with the least possible delay to have it printed under the auspices of the British and Foreign Bible Society. Mr. Nott acceded to the wishes of his brethren; and on the 6th of February 1836 he sailed from Tahiti, and arrived in England on the 19th of June following. The Committee of the Bible Society readily undertook their part of the work. In August 1838 it was completed; and on the 18th of that month Mr. Nott sailed on his return voyage to his island home, bringing with him 3000 copies of the complete Bible, and an equal number of the New Testament. On September 1840 he reached his destination, and met with an enthusiastic reception. For his own sake his return to the scene of his lifelong labours was hailed by a grateful people, but the fact that he brought with him the treasure which multitudes so longed to possess—the complete Bible—awoke an interest and produced an excitement which can only be compared to what was felt and manifested when the nation renounced idolatry and embraced Christianity.*

And now the difficulty was to meet the demands that were everywhere made to possess the book. Money had

---

* The following testimony to the character and worth of Mr. Nott, from the pen of the late Rev. Samuel Marsden, of Sydney, New South Wales, is worth a place in this record. It is creditable alike to the writer and to the subject of his eulogy. Mr. Nott was in New South Wales, on his way to England to superintend the printing of the Tahitian Bible, and Mr. Marsden gave him a letter of introduction to a friend in England, from which the extract I am about to give is taken. After mentioning that Mr. Nott had been twenty-seven years in Tahiti, and that he had laboured and suffered with exemplary fidelity, he concludes as follows:—" I venerate the man more than you can conceive: in my estimation he is a great man; his piety, his simplicity, his meekness, his apostolic appear-

now come into circulation, and large numbers of the people had been hoarding up the needful amount, or depositing it with the missionaries, that they might secure copies as soon as they arrived. The supply brought by Mr. Nott was not nearly adequate to the demand, and this increased the eagerness of the natives on the one hand and the embarrassment of the missionaries on the other. They were carefully apportioned to the different stations, and immediately bought up. They were neatly and substantially bound, and they were sold at prices which must have been sufficient to cover the cost of printing and binding, and perhaps also incidental expenses. The complete Bible was sold for eight shillings, and the New Testament, I suppose, for half that sum.

The following extract from Mr. Ellis' History of the London Missionary Society will appropriately close our notice of the first edition of the Tahitian Bible:—"The acquisition of the entire Bible in the native language is undoubtedly one of the most auspicious events in the history of Tahiti, second only in importance and influence to the abolition of idolatry and the general profession of the gospel; and as long as any portion, however small, of genuine Christianity shall remain in the islands, it will be regarded, next to the arrival of the missionaries themselves, by whom, in harmonious co-operation with the Bible Society, it was conferred, as the richest gift the nation ever received." *

A second edition of the Tahitian Bible was printed by the British and Foreign Bible Society in 1845-6. It had been revised by the Rev. William Howe and the Rev.

---

ance, all unite to make him great in my view, and more honourable than any of the famed heroes of ancient or modern times. I think Mrs. Good will like to see such a character return from a savage nation, whom God has so honoured in his work. I shall leave Mr. Nott to tell his own story." The letter was addressed to Mr. John Mason Good.

* See Ellis' History of the London Missionary Society, p. 357.

Thomas Joseph, who, after between four and five years residence in the islands, returned to England in consequence of French aggression on Tahiti and Eimeo. Mr. Howe returned to the islands in 1847, having, in conjunction with Mr. Joseph, carried the revised Bible through the press during his stay in England. This edition was exhausted in a few years, and another was urgently required. The work again underwent a careful revision, perhaps the most thorough to which it had yet been subjected, and a very valuable addition was made to it in the shape of marginal references. The revisers were the Rev. W. Howe; the Rev. Alexander Chisholm, who had spent nearly seventeen years in the islands; and the Rev. John Barff, who supplied the marginal references. Thus the revisers were all well qualified, from their knowledge of the language, missionary experience, and other advantages, for their important work.

With reference to Mr. Barff, the following remarks from a letter of Mr. Chisholm in the Report of the British and Foreign Bible Society for 1861 will not be out of place in this record. "In the revision for this third edition," Mr. Chisholm writes, "the services of the late much lamented Rev. John Barff of Tahaa, tutor of the institution for training native evangelists, have been invaluable. Mr. Barff was born on the island of Raiatea, and was as familiar with the Tahitian language as with his own mother tongue, besides being in every other respect well qualified for the task. To the great grief of his venerable father, the Rev. Charles Barff, as well as of his brother missionaries, and thousands of poor natives besides, he only survived the completion of the revision a few weeks, when he was suddenly cut off in the midst of his years and usefulness. Indeed, there is reason to fear that the zeal and enthusiasm with which he prosecuted his work, leading him often to transgress the rules of prudence by sitting up late at night, when he could best spare time from his other onerous duties, were instrumental in hastening his death. But although he rests from his labours, his works remain to bless generations yet unborn. He being dead yet speaketh."

It is a touching fact that Mr. Chisholm did not long survive his fellow-labourer of whom he wrote so lovingly and appreciatingly. While engaged in carrying the Bible through the press, having advanced as far as the Gospel according to John, his life and labours were brought to a sudden close from acute disease of the heart, and he passed from his loved work on earth to serve in a higher sphere.

The remainder of the work was confided to the Rev. Joseph Moore of Congleton, formerly a missionary in Tahiti, and under his superintendence it was brought to a successful close. Five thousand copies were printed, and the first shipment of these reached the islands in 1864. In the meanwhile the man who would have been so rejoiced to receive them, the Rev. W. Howe, who had so long and so faithfully represented the London Missionary Society in circumstances of very great difficulty and self-denial, had also rested from his labours, and gone to his reward, and another had taken up his work and entered into his labours. This was the Rev. George Morris, who, in a letter to the British and Foreign Bible Society announcing the arrival of the books, wrote as follows:—"The long expected shipment of Bibles has at length reached the island, to the inexpressible delight of the Christian converts, multitudes of whom remain unshaken in their attachment to the Scriptures. The utmost excitement prevailed for some time as to the arrival of the precious cargo, and the people had their money in readiness to invest immediately in the purchase of a copy."

Mr. Morris further remarks: "Words cannot tell you how my heart is rejoiced at the arrival and sale of the blessed book. The tale of Tahiti's trials and sorrows is familiar to you; but so long as the Word of God is allowed to be freely circulated among her children, and is prized by them, so long will the enemies of their faith find it difficult, yea, impossible to overcome them. The Tahitian prizes the Bible. He knows its value, and feels it to be the only guide to the Sure Defence."

At a later date, Mr. Morris wrote on the same subject as follows:—" I rejoice that the sale of the Scriptures steadily keeps up. We cannot overestimate the value and importance of this, and I should tremble for the poor Tahitians if they had not the Bible. The Bible is their Magna Charta for time and for eternity. It has been the grand bulwark of their faith amidst many trials and temptations in days past; it is so now; and earnestly, most earnestly, do I pray that their attachment to it may continue firm, devoted, and faithful for days to come."

In 1870 the Rev. J. L. Green succeeded Mr. Morris at Tahiti; and in remitting a sum of money, the proceeds of sales of Bibles, bore testimony to the strong attachment which the natives continued to manifest towards the Bible, "which," he remarks, "constitutes their chief bulwark against the inroads of Papal superstition." He mentions the case of a woman who came to him to purchase a Bible, and on receiving it, she pressed it to her lips, and exclaimed as she kissed it, "Oh, the treasure of this book!" And Mr. Green adds, "There was so much of simplicity and godly sincerity in the act that it involuntarily brought tears to my eyes."

The demand continued steady, and as supply after supply reached the islands, they were bought up in a surprisingly short time. Under date January 21st, 1874, Mr. Green wrote as follows:—" I am glad that your Committee responded so promptly to our wishes in sending us a renewed supply of Bibles. The last consignment of

300, which arrived by our missionary ship *John Williams* last April, was exhausted in six weeks, and so completely too, that one which I had reserved for myself had to be given up, and yet it seemed that the supply only made the demand greater. In order also, in a few cases, to subdue the disappointment experienced by applicants, I was compelled to give away some old copies which had belonged to our early missionaries, and which I was keeping as a souvenir of our fathers in the field."

We must not further enter into particulars. The demand went on increasing year after year all over the group and islands beyond, wherever the Tahitian language is spoken. On the island of Raiatea, the District Committee applied to the Bible Society for 5000 New Testaments in 1874; and at that date the Rev. A. Pearce reported that during the four months preceding the date of his letter, he had sold more Bibles in that group (the Leeward Islands of the Tahitian Archipelago) than had been disposed of in as many years before.

In 1877 a new edition of 5000 copies was printed in London by the Bible Society, under the superintendence of the Rev. A. T. Saville. A few corrections forwarded by the District Committee were inserted, and maps were supplied, and the opinion was expressed by Mr. Saville "that the new edition was as nearly perfect as possible." The printing of this edition was specially opportune, as we find the Rev. J. L. Green reporting in the same year (1877) that during that year the sales had been greater than ever. "The actual sales last year," he remarks, "realised £266, 4s., an amount which seems almost incredible, when we consider the sparseness of the population, and the fact that the Bible has been possessed by the people for a generation past."

The reader will have noticed that except in one or two instances where I could not well avoid doing so, I have not mentioned particular remittances of money to the Bible Society. That omission will be met, I think, by the following striking fact, given in the report of the Society for 1880. The amount received at the Bible House from the South Sea Islands in payment for Scriptures for a series of six years, ending with March of 1880, was £6399, 3s. 10d. That fact needs no comment. It tells its own emphatic tale. A large proportion of the Christianised people of the South Sea Islands love the Bible, else they would not, year after year, part with their gold and silver to possess themselves of it.

In 1883, Mr. Green, while on a visit to England, arranged for the printing of a portable edition of the Bible. This was carried through the press during his stay, and we find in 1884 that he was again at his post, having brought with him 4000 copies; and the eagerness with which the people sought after these was not less than it had been on similar occasions in former years. Under date October 8th, 1884, Mr. Green wrote as follows: "You will be pleased to hear that the sales still continue active, although, of course, the first rush has somewhat abated. We sent 100 copies to Huahine three or four weeks ago, and they were all sold in a day. The Rev. E. V. Cooper, missionary of that island, has just returned from a visit here, and has taken three cases more, and I have no doubt they will soon disappear. News from Raiatea, to which island I sent three cases assorted about a month ago, reports: 'The Bibles are nearly all sold—a very few of the common binding left; but they will go presently.' I purpose visiting that island next month, D.V., and shall take some more down with me. My hope, expressed to you before leaving England, will be very nearly realised, viz., that of selling 4000 copies during the last five months of this year."

And here we must take our leave of Bible translation and Bible circulation in the Tahitian group; and in doing so, we note with special gratitude to God the fact that though seventy years have passed away since the first instalment of divine truth was printed and received with such avidity by the people, and more than fifty years have gone by since the arrival of the complete Bible stirred so deeply the hearts of the nation, and awoke such a widespread interest, yet the grand old book still retains its hold. Edition after edition has been printed and received with a large measure of the old enthusiasm, clearly evincing that the Tahitians are to a great extent what their fathers were, a Bible-reading and a Bible-loving people. And this is surely a matter calling for the deepest gratitude. What would the Tahitians of to-day have been, had they not through all the trying vicissitudes of their eventful history during the past forty years clung to the Bible?

The following testimony from the Rev. F. Vernier, of the Paris Missionary Society, who has been a number of years in Tahiti, possesses special interest. It is from a letter to the Bible House in London, written during the absence of Mr. Green in 1883. Mr. Vernier writes as follows: "It affords me much pleasure in writing you a few words about the sale of Bibles in this island. I am hoping to be enabled to testify to the permanent attachment of the dear natives of these remote islands for the word of God. They have bought from me since June £110 worth of Bibles, which has nearly exhausted my stock. The Bible has been and is still *the* book of the natives. They would not exchange a small part of it for all the books in the world. In fact it is the only book they care for."

The following remarks in the same Report, by the compiler, are also worthy of special note. "It is an interesting fact that while the natives of Tahiti have not been able to remain independent of the French flag, they insist upon the Roman Catholic priests allowing the perfectly free use of the Scriptures; and further, that the priests, seeing it quite hopeless to divorce the people from the Bible, are compelled, in order to retain their influence, to approve its circulation, and actually buy copies for their people from the Society."

CHAPTER II.

THE RAROTONGAN VERSION.

THE story of the planting of Christianity among the islands of the Hervey group, of which Rarotonga is the principal, is only second in interest and importance to that of the parent mission in the Tahitian group. There is a wide difference in the manner in which the end was gained. In the one case, the struggle was prolonged through many years; in the other, the contest between the powers of light and darkness was of short duration, but the results in both cases were the same, and they were of such a character as deeply to stir the hearts of contemporaries; and now, after the lapse of more than half a century, they are still fitted in a high degree to interest, stimulate, and encourage the friends of Christian missions.

The following are the main facts connected with the first missionary voyage to the Hervey Islands, which was made in the course of the year 1821.

The Rev. John Williams, by whom the voyage was made, had heard of the island of Aitutaki. Little was known about that island at that time, but Mr. Williams determined to make an effort to visit the island and introduce to it the gospel. With reference to this important matter, Mr. Williams writes as follows:—"By the remarkable success that had attended the introduction of the gospel to Rurutu, our own minds, as well as those of our people, were powerfully awakened to the importance of extending the benefits and blessings of the gospel; and under the excited and delightful feelings thus produced, we, with our native teachers, took an affectionate leave of our people and beloved colleagues, Mr. and Mrs. Threlkeld." Mrs. Williams accompanied Mr. Williams. They sailed in a vessel named the *Westmoreland*, intending to proceed on a visit to Sydney after calling at Aitutaki. On reaching that island the vessel was speedily surrounded by canoes filled with savages, whose appearance was anything but inviting or assuring. They exhibited all the wild features of savage life in perfection. Some were tattooed from head to foot; some were painted with pipe-clay and red and yellow ochre; others were all smeared over with charcoal. They shouted and danced, and exhibited the most frantic gestures.

Mr. Williams had an immense advantage in dealing with these wild people in being able to understand their language, and make himself understood by them, their language being so much akin to the Tahitian. Thus he and the natives of Raiatea were able at once to tell the wondering Aitutakians of the marvellous changes that had taken place in the Tahitian group—how paganism had been renounced, the idols burned, and a new religion embraced; and in conversation with the chief, Mr. Williams said to him, "I have brought two teachers to instruct you and your people in the knowledge of the true God, that you too may abandon and destroy your idols as others have done." The chief consented to receive the teachers, and they took up their abode among the fierce and savage Aitutakians. The names of the devoted men who were the pioneer missionaries to the Hervey Islands were Papeiha and Vahaputa, names which, especially the former, deserve to be held in everlasting remembrance.

In April 1822, Mr. Williams received letters from Papeiha and Vahaputa, giving an account of their difficulties and dangers, and partial success, and requesting that two more teachers might be sent, and conveying a message from the people to the effect that if Mr. Williams would visit them again they would renounce idolatry, burn their idols, and become worshippers of the true God. And the same vessel which brought the letters brought information of a very important character, which opened a new door of hope for the Hervey Islands. Some natives of an island called Rarotonga were reported as being in Aitutaki, and as having embraced Christianity, and being anxious to return with teachers to instruct their countrymen in the knowledge of the true God. Mr. Williams had heard before of an island named Rarotonga, it being mentioned in the legendary tales of the Raiateans, and on making particular inquiry he was satisfied that such an island existed; and after consultation with his fellow-labourers, Messrs. Threlkeld and Bourne, it was arranged that he and Mr. Bourne should visit Aitutaki, and go thence in search of Rarotonga, and should their search prove successful, endeavour to introduce to it Christian teachers.

Six teachers were selected for the enterprise, and on the 4th of August 1823 the party sailed in the *Endeavour*, a small vessel about eighty or ninety tons burden, and went forth on their important embassy. Five days' sail brought them to Aitutaki. As on the first visit, on nearing the shore they were speedily surrounded with canoes. But what a change had come over the Aitutakians in the meanwhile! Instead of being noisy, boisterous savages, they were now professing Christians, having destroyed or cast away their idols, and placed themselves under the instruction of the teachers. The missionaries found six natives of Rarotonga on the island; and after spending a short time in delightful intercourse with the now Christian Aitutakians, they started in search of Rarotonga. They went forth literally not knowing whither they went, but, as they hoped, in obedience to a call from the God of Abraham, and so under a safe conduct they took with them the natives of Rarotonga of course. The chief of Aitutaki also accompanied them, and they took Papeiha with them, that in the event of finding the island they might have the benefit of his experience in dealing with the natives.

After an unsuccessful search for Rarotonga for six or eight days, they steered for Mangaia, another island of the Hervey group, the position of which was known. Mangaia was found without difficulty, and an attempt was made to place teachers upon it. The chief and people expressed their willingness to receive the teachers, but when they got them in their power they treated them with such savage barbarity that they were glad to escape for their lives to the ship. Leaving Mangaia for the present, the party directed their course towards Atiu, another island of the Hervey group. This was found without difficulty, and the visit proved specially opportune. Two teachers had been sent to the island by Mr. Orsmond from Borabora, one of the islands of the Tahitian group, about three months before the present visit. They were found in a deplorable plight. The natives had robbed them of every article of property they possessed; they had suffered much from hunger, and were greatly discouraged. But the present visit met the case. It was as light in the darkness to the poor suffering teachers—God's opportunity meeting their extremity. The now Christian chief of Aitutaki bore his testimony as to what Christianity had done for him and his people, and persuaded the chief of Atiu to follow his example. The cast-off idols of Aitutaki which had escaped the flames were shown, and the folly and absurdity of idol worship was set before him, and the result was that he and his people determined to do as Aitutaki had done.

The missionaries found that the chief of Atiu was also the chief of other two islands of the Hervey group, Mauke and Mitiaro, and having induced him to agree to accompany them, they went in search of these islands, and having the chief as their pilot, they found them without difficulty, and succeeded in introducing Christianity to both of them. A teacher was introduced to each, and the people at once renounced heathenism and became nominally Christian. With reference to these three islands, Mr. Williams remarks: "Were ever three islands converted from idolatry in so short a time—islands almost unknown; and two of them never before visited by any European vessel?"

Cheered and encouraged, the missionaries resumed their search for Rarotonga. In this, however, their faith and patience were sorely tried. After being "baffled and perplexed" for several days, matters began to look serious, and it seemed as if the expedition would prove a failure. Early on the morning of the day on which the discovery was made, the captain of the vessel said to Mr. Williams, "We must give up the search, or we shall all be starved." Provisions were getting low, and there was the return voyage of 600 or 700 miles against a head wind to look out for. Mr. Williams replied that they would continue the search till eight o'clock that morning, and if no land was in sight at that time, they would relinquish the search and return to Raiatea. The hours which followed were to Mr. Williams a time of intense anxiety. Four times he sent a native to the masthead, but nothing was to be seen. It was within half an hour of the specified time when a native ascended a fifth time. Hope must have been well-nigh extinct. All the while, however, the object of their search was close at hand; and now the sun was clearing away the clouds which had concealed it from their view, and to the surprise and delight of all, the native who had gone aloft shouted out, "There is the land we have been seeking," and sure enough it was the land.

The clouds were speedily dispersed, and the lofty peaks of Rarotonga's beautiful mountains were revealed to the delighted gaze of the weary voyagers.

Mr. Williams speaks in glowing terms of the feelings experienced by himself and others on account of the successful termination of their search, while he devoutly acknowledges the guiding hand of Him who had led them by the right way. All were charmed with the beauty of the newly discovered land, and they had reason, for Rarotonga is one of the loveliest spots to be seen among the many gems which stud the bosom of the great Pacific. But what of the inhabitants of this fair isle? Alas! alas! a most revolting contrast did they present to the beautiful land on which they dwelt. They were savages of the most debased and ferocious type.

A boat was sent to the shore with Papeiha and the natives of the island brought from Aitutaki, to communicate with the people and ascertain their disposition as to receiving teachers. The reception was favourable. A multitude of people assembled, and listened no doubt with astonishment to the tale Papeiha had to tell of the renunciation of idolatry, and the wonderful changes that were in progress on other islands of the group; and when he told them that they had brought teachers to remain among them, they seemed delighted, and the chief, whose name was Makea, determined to go on board at once to bring the teachers on shore. The chief was greatly delighted, and, I suppose, surprised to see his own people, especially one of them, who proved to be a near relative of his own.

Everything appeared so promising that arrangements were at once made for commencing a mission on the island, and the teachers with their wives, and the natives who had been on Aitutaki, went with the chief to the shore. They had an enthusiastic welcome, and it appeared as if Rarotonga would prove as easy a conquest as other islands of the group. But first appearances among a savage people are little to be depended on. One hour they may seem innocent children of nature, and the next incarnate demons. The vessel stood out to sea for the night, while the teachers and their wives slept on shore. They passed a dreadful night, and when they returned to the ship on the following morning they had a shocking tale to tell of the treatment they had received. It was perfectly clear that teachers with their wives must not be left on the island in the state in which it then was, and the prospects altogether were so dark that the missionaries determined to leave the island for a time. But Papeiha took a different view, and with the zeal and heroism of a martyr he offered to remain alone among the cannibal savages of Rarotonga on condition that a fellow-labourer whom he named should be sent from Raiatea. The missionaries gladly accepted his offer, and this Christian hero, leaving his property on board, bade the missionaries and others an affectionate farewell, and returned to the shore alone, taking nothing with him but the clothes he wore, his New Testament, and a bundle of elementary books. What a bright example of Christian devotedness and lofty heroism! And this same man, a few years before, was a savage not much less debased than the Rarotongans. What a marvellous triumph of divine power and grace!

Papeiha had his reward. The natives who had been on Aitutaki remained steadfast and clung to Papeiha, rendering him invaluable help, and after an interval of about four months Tiperio, whom he had requested the missionaries to send, arrived, and in the meanwhile several other natives had joined him, and a considerable footing had been gained; and in little more than twelve months the whole population, estimated at 7000, had renounced idolatry and become professed worshippers of the true God. And thus was this important and populous island in a marvellously short time won to Christianity; and this before a white missionary had set foot upon its shores.

But I must not further pursue the history of the mission; and the following valuable paper from the pen of my esteemed friend and fellow-labourer, the Rev. W. W. GILL, B.A., renders it unnecessary for me to say anything with reference to the main subject of which this volume treats. Mr. Gill laboured on the islands for about thirty years, and is able to speak on every subject connected with them as no other living man can. Mr. Gill in his paper supplies the history of the translation of the sacred Scriptures into the language of the group, and gives other information respecting the islands and the natives of much interest and value. Mr. Gill's paper is headed "The Rarotongan Version," and is given here as it comes from his hand.

Almost in the middle of the South Pacific Ocean—between the parallels of 19° and 22° S. latitude, and 157° to 160° W. longitude—are seven small islands * known as the Cook or Hervey group. Six or seven hundred miles north and north-west of Rarotonga lie four low coral islands,† regarded as out-stations of the mission. The population of these eleven islands is somewhat less than 10,000; a pleasant, brown-skinned race. Seven dialects are still spoken by these islanders; from the commencement of the mission, however, the Rarotongan language alone has been used in printing. Doubtless, in time, this printed dialect will exterminate the rest. Already one dialect (the eighth), once spoken on Hervey's Island or Manuae, has disappeared. The only written specimens of this lost

* Rarotonga, Mangaia, Aitutaki, Atiu, Mauke, Mitiaro, and Hervey's Island or Manuae.

† Penrhyn, Rakahanga, Manihiki, and Pukapuka. The natives of Rakahanga and Manihiki are one people, speaking one dialect, and having the same traditions.

dialect* are three ancient songs in my possession, but not yet published.

The inhabitants of the Hervey group proper were formerly cannibals. In six out of the seven islands cannibalism only ceased with the introduction of Christianity. The natives of the northern atolls seem to have been of a gentler mould. War, murder, infanticide, and theft were, of course, rife in those northerly atolls as well as in the more southerly islands. In all of them the absolute power exercised by the priests in the name of their national gods was marvellous.

In 1827 the Rev. John Williams accompanied the Rev. C. Pitman to Rarotonga, and remained with him a year. The earliest attempt at the translation of the Scriptures into the language of the Hervey Islanders was then made by Mr. Williams, who (very imperfectly) rendered the Gospel of John and the Epistles to the Galatians and Hebrews from the Tahitian version into Rarotongan. Mr. Pitman being a good linguist, was soon able to co-operate with his friend in the work of translation. During subsequent visits to Rarotonga, Mr. Williams carried on the good work. The whole of the New Testament (except two books by the Rev. A. Buzacott) was translated by Williams and Pitman, the latter being responsible for its fidelity to the original.

In 1828 Mr. Buzacott became the colleague of Mr. Pitman at Rarotonga. For twenty years these good men toiled day and night at the translation of the Bible out of the original tongues into a language which had never previously been written. Mr. Pitman's profound acquaintance with the Hebrew proved invaluable. For years small portions of the New Testament were circulated

* In the Austral Group the original language of the islanders has entirely disappeared.

amongst the natives in MS., being either written on paper, or, when that ran short, on *tikoru, i.e.*, white native cloth made of the inner bark of the paper mulberry (*Broussonetia papyrifera*).

The first of Peter in Rarotongan was printed at Buna-auia on Tahiti. This was the earliest attempt at printing in the Rarotongan language. The Gospel by John and the Epistle to the Galatians were printed at Huahine. The remainder of the New Testament and most of the Old were printed and bound in numerous small volumes at Avarua on Rarotonga by the versatile and indefatigable Mr. Buzacott. Copies of the original editions of the Scriptures in Rarotongan may be seen in the library of the Bible Society, and in the museum of the London Missionary Society.

The first complete edition of the Rarotongan New Testament (every verse of which had been repeatedly compared with the Greek original) was carried through the press in England at the expense of the British and Foreign Bible Society by Mr. Williams during his visit to this country (1835-8). The entire cost of the 5000 copies then printed was refunded to the society by the ready sale of the book amongst the Hervey Islanders.

The manner in which the Rarotongan New Testament was received is deeply interesting. "The eagerness with which they received it would have cheered your heart could you have been eye-witness to the scene. The countenance of a successful applicant glistened with delight while he held up his treasure to public view; others hugged the book; many kissed it; some sprang away like a dart, and did not stop until they entered their own dwellings, and exhibited their treasure to their wives and children; while others jumped and capered about like persons half frantic with joy. Many came with tears in their eyes, begging and beseeching that they might have one; and if Mr. Buzacott said, 'You cannot read,' the reply was, 'But my son or my daughter can, and I can hear and understand them.' When some came whose character was such as to cause a little hesitation, their appeals were pointed and affecting. 'Do let me have a Testament; do let me have the good word of God; perhaps by reading it my heart may be made better.' Others pleadingly said, 'We did not know that our eyes would ever have beheld such a sight as this in Rarotonga; we shall neither eat, drink, nor sleep, if you do not give us the good word of God.'" (Life of Rev. J. Williams, p. 541.)

The first edition of the entire Bible was carefully edited by Mr. Buzacott during his prolonged stay in England (1847-1851), at the request of the British and Foreign Bible Society. Five thousand copies were printed and disposed of in three years. The printing was done slowly, and with the utmost care. This Bible was at once accepted by the brethren as the basis of all future editions. Well does it deserve this honour.

The writer will never forget the unbounded enthusiasm with which this priceless boon was received by the islanders. At Mangaia a case of Bibles was taken into the church; after a short thanksgiving service copies were given to those who had some time previously paid for them. At a Friday exhortation meeting, held at break of day, a venerable native, named Tenio,* said that he had secured a copy of the Bible, but could not sleep until he had finished reading the entire book of Job, which had never before been seen in a Rarotongan dress. Lifting up the sacred volume before the entire congregation, he concluded his address in these memorable words:—"This is my resolve; the dust shall never cover my Bible; the moths shall

---

* Named after the son of Kaiara, whose pathetic story is related in my "Historical Sketches of Savage Life in Polynesia," pp. 130-135.

never eat it; the mildew shall never rot it. My light! my joy!"

Until 1852, the books of Ezra, Nehemiah, Esther, Job, and the Minor Prophets had never been in the hands of the natives. It was no ordinary privilege to expound to an eager auditory books absolutely new to all present but oneself. The natives seemed never weary of asking the meaning of these novel portions of Scripture.

In 1855 the Rarotongan Bible was reprinted, with a few alterations, under the supervision of the Rev. William Gill and Dr. Mellor. Five thousand copies were struck off.

In 1872 the Bible Society issued a third and greatly improved edition of 5000 copies. It was edited by the Revs. E. R. W. Krause and George Gill (brother of the editor of the second edition). Marginal references were added, and numberless words of foreign origin exchanged for purely indigenous expressions.

In 1884 I was requested by the Committee of the Bible Society to prepare a standard edition with a view to its being stereotyped. Innumerable printers' errors were corrected; the article (*a*) before all proper names in the nominative when they follow the verb (having, strangely enough, been dropped out in the edition of 1872) was everywhere restored; out of the various renderings given by preceding editors, that which seemed to be the most faithful representation of the original was finally selected; many terms of natural history derived from the English Revised Version have been inserted (in their native form) in the text or side-notes of the Old Testament. In regard to the italics, I have followed the rule laid down by the Revisers of the English Bible. It is for others to say whether I have succeeded in a difficult task, conscientiously carried out. If my work is a success, it is due mainly to the untiring aid of *Taunga*, who for more than forty years has been a faithful preacher of the Word in the

Western Pacific, in Samoa, and latterly in Rarotonga—the land of his birth. Taunga, the pupil and beloved friend of Pitman, is acknowledged to be the best living authority on the Rarotongan language. In 1852 I heard the Rev. W. Howe remark that the Tahitian brethren found by experience that no one could beat "Noti" (the Rev. H. Nott's version). Even so the unexpected result of the several revisions of the Rarotongan Bible has been to prove conclusively that, overlooking the serious blemish of words of foreign origin, the work of the original translators is beyond all praise for idiomatic purity, nervous strength, and beauty. And well it is for the islanders that it is so, as throughout the Eastern Pacific the various dialects are rapidly deteriorating, by admixture from various sources, native and foreign. I subjoin a single illustration of the grip which the early translators possessed of the Rarotongan language. In the edition of 1851 the phrase in Zechariah v. 3, "on the *face* of the earth," is correctly rendered "i te *tua* enua." The translator is compelled to reverse the figure. It is no longer "the *face*," but "the *back*," broad and strong, of the earth-parent. A subsequent editor, scandalised at the alteration of the figure, to solve the difficulty dropped out the clause. Of course the original translation (the only possible one) is now restored.

Having daily used the Rarotongan Bible for thirty-seven years, I may be pardoned for saying that I regard it as an admirable rendering of the original. Many of the improvements found in the Revised English Version have been anticipated. As in all the other Pacific and New Guinea Versions, the sacred name "Jehovah" is transliterated, never translated, thus adding immeasurably to the force of the contrast between the ever-living God and the objects worshipped by the heathen. The English rendering of 1 Kings xviii. 21 is tame indeed in comparison with the Rarotongan.

The original translators of the Rarotongan Bible caught the real genius of the language and gave it a permanent embodiment whilst it was as yet utterly untouched by outside influences. The rendering of the patriarchal portions is simply perfect, the language of the islanders being so well adapted for the purpose. Indeed, Polynesian life, at its best, is strictly patriarchal. The gospels lend themselves very readily to translation; but in the epistles a difficulty was evidently felt by the translators in obtaining exact equivalents for the key-notes of the Christian system. Too great praise cannot be given to the Rev. H. Nott of Tahiti and his coadjutors, who, in making the Tahitian translation, unconsciously fixed the theological terms for several other groups.

In the Rarotongan version the translators use "akavangakau" = "heart-judge," for "conscience." In preaching or rapid speaking we simply say "ngakau" = "heart," * which is beyond question the strict equivalent in the Eastern Polynesian dialects, "heart-judge" being an invented phrase, but now current. "Faith" (akarongo) is "*to listen* to God speaking," the native preacher being always careful to add "with the ear of the heart." "Trust in God" is "*leaning* on God." The pious are those "who dwell in the shadow of God." "Heaven" is "the day, or light of God."

In a literary point of view it is remarkable that it should be possible with an alphabet of thirteen letters only to render faithfully the Word of God into the language of savages. In transliterating proper names a few other letters are used; but in the language proper, as above stated, only thirteen. No book speaks to the heart of man—whatever be his race, home, or speech—as the Bible. Its voice is sure of an echo from the human heart.

* Literally "the bowels." These islanders, like the Hebrews of old, place the seat of the affection and intellect in the bowels.

The islanders in reality possess but one book; hence the anxiety of the brethren to make it a perfect image of what its Divine Author intended. Each edition issued by the British and Foreign Bible Society has been a distinct advance upon the preceding in regard to clearness of sense.

The educational power of the Bible is great. Portions of the sacred volume that to *us* are of little interest may be most attractive to savages listening perhaps for the first time to Bible story. I never cared much for the genealogical portions until my own converts put me to shame by evincing an intimate acquaintance with them. In Polynesia, other things being equal, the chief with the longest pedigree is the most respected. These pedigrees usually carry with them lands and titles. The stories contained in Joshua and Judges, &c., exercise a marvellous fascination over the minds of brave savages, who are astonished above measure to find that their most famous war-stratagems were long ago anticipated in far-off lands. The awful vengeance exacted upon whole families and tribes is the exact counterpart of what they practised themselves in times of war. The native intellect is interested in tracing the striking parallel which exists between numerous Mosaic institutions and the unwritten laws of *tapu* in Polynesia. It is probably on this ground that all the Christian Polynesians I have met with believe themselves to be Shemites. The histories of Elijah, Elisha, Daniel, and Jonah are of undying interest. After all, the great point is to give to the natives the entire New Testament, the Psalms, and Proverbs, with Genesis, Job, and Isaiah. The lesson of my missionary life is this—I would give to every race, if practicable, the entire Bible. But if this may not be, I would omit as little as possible. There are races that can never hope to get more than the New Testament and the Psalms. Others must rest content with the four gospels. Let no tribe, however, be entirely without a loving message from the Father of Spirits.

At first the heroic portions of the Scriptures tell most upon a warrior race emerging into the light; then the miracles and parables of the New Testament captivate. But as the spiritual life deepens, interest is centered in the character and work of Christ and the teaching of His apostles. The Bible is read, studied, and quoted by the Polynesians of to-day in place of the heathen songs and myths of bygone ages. In fact it is moulding the lives and characters of the entire race.

I subjoin a few specimens of idioms used in the Rarotongan Scriptures:—

"The life we live;" "the sin we have sinned;" "the death we die," &c., &c., &c. For (Rom. xii. 8) "he that sheweth mercy, with cheerfulness," we have (instead of "cheerfulness") "with the heart in touch."

In 2 Cor. iv. 15, for "abundant grace," we have "grace great (even) running over." So in 2 Cor. viii. 2, for "abundance of joy," we have "joy running over."

Colos. ii. 2, "knit together in love," becomes "fitting into one in love."

"For ever and ever" (1 Pet. iv. 11) is "time on, on, still on."

The Rarotongan of Heb. xiii. 5 has four negatives: "I will never leave thee nor forsake thee; no, never—on, on, on!" How many dying Hervey Islanders have been comforted by these beautiful words, the final clause showing that the negation goes on for ever.

In Polynesian, as in Greek, the definite article is always placed before "God" (Atua). In Rarotongan for "saying" six words are needed (i te na ko anga mai), and for "I write" (1 John ii. 12, &c.) eight words are required (te tata atu nei i te tuatua); but "you and I" are expressed by a single word (taua), &c. So that after all the Rarotongan Bible is about the size of the English of the same type.

CHAPTER III.

THE SAMOAN VERSION.

As in the case of the Tahitian group, Samoa is now so well known that little need be said in a work like the present with reference to the country and the people. Since 1830, when the Rev. John Williams and the Rev. Charles Barff conveyed the gospel to its shores, it has been coming more and more prominently before the friends of Christian missions and Bible circulation, and for a number of years its commercial value and importance have been growingly developed, and it has even become an object of interest to the "Great Powers," who, under God's overruling providence, control the destinies of the world. It is universally admitted to be one of the richest and most beautiful of all the islands and groups scattered over the great Pacific Ocean. The French navigator La Perouse, who visited it in 1787, described it as "one of the finest countries in the universe," while he branded the natives as "atrocious savages, whose shores ought not to be approached." His impression as to the character of the natives was not unnatural, under the circumstances, but it was entirely wrong. It was owing to a hasty inference drawn from the fact that a serious quarrel took place between the natives and a watering party from his ships who landed at the island of Tutuila, and in a skirmish which arose eleven of his people, including his fellow commander De Langle and some scientific gentlemen, lost their lives, a number of the natives being also killed. The affair arose from a petty act of theft which was committed by a native belonging to a party who called at the ships while the watering party were on shore. The thief was fired upon and wounded, mortally it was said. This exasperated the natives, and they went straight to the shore where the Frenchmen were and reported the treatment they had received, and a rush was at once made upon the foreigners, and a fight ensued, with the result above mentioned.

The truth is the Samoans were not by any means exceptionally ferocious. Shocking cruelties were sometimes practised in their wars, but on the whole they were heathens of a milder type than those found on any other group or island, so far as my knowledge extends, in any part of Polynesia. Cannibalism was never practised among them; human sacrifices had no place in their religious observances; their children were loved and cherished; the aged were respected and reverenced; the sick were, as a general rule, carefully tended; and women were almost, if not quite, on an equality with men. And those redeeming traits in their character and customs entitle them to rank much above the ordinary South Sea savage. Perhaps they came nearer the idea of the guileless, innocent, gentle savage, as he has been pictured by visitors—who, after coming in contact with him for a few days, or it may be hours, go and report that they have found a race almost angelic—than any other heathen tribe yet discovered. Alas, however, the Samoans, with all their comparative mildness and amiability, were unmistakably partakers of the nature common to all the children of Adam, and so needed the gospel equally with the more deeply sunken Tahitian and the more ferocious Fijian.

Samoa occupies a central position among the islands of the Pacific. It is about 3000 miles to the east of Australia, and lies in W. longitude from 168° to 173°, and in S. latitude from 13° to 15°. The islands are all of volcanic origin. They are covered with the richest vegetation from the shore to the mountain tops. The mountains rise to the height of 2000, 3000, and 4000 feet. The principal islands are Savaii, Upolu, Tutuila, Manono, and Tau, commonly called Manua, but Manua is really the general name of a small group of three islands, of which Tau is the largest. Besides the four principal islands there are six small ones, all of which are inhabited.

The first census was made by the missionaries aided by native teachers in 1843, when, as nearly as could be ascertained, the population was 33,900. Since that time there has been a slow but steady increase, and when the last census was made, over ten years ago, the total population of the group was 35,184. That includes 204 Europeans and Americans; Polynesians from other islands, 236; imported labourers, 475; and 4 Asiatics. The probability is that there has been a considerable increase of the native population since the above census was taken, and also that there has been a considerable addition to the foreign settlers and residents. The natives are a fine noble-looking race, closely resembling the Malays, to which race I have no doubt they belong.

As already intimated, Christian teachers were introduced to Samoa in 1830; and in 1836, six missionaries, of whom the writer was one, arrived, and commenced missionary operations on a scale somewhat adequate to the extent of the field. The Samoan mission was a direct offshoot of the Tahitian. Mr. Williams and Mr. Barff were Tahitian missionaries, and the pioneer teachers, with the exception of two or three from the Hervey Islands, were natives of the Tahitian group. Down to the time of our arrival the mission was considered an out-station of the Tahitian mission; and when we arrived we found the Rev. George

Platt from Raiatea, and Mr. Samuel Wilson, son of the Rev. Charles Wilson of Tahiti, who had been sent to assist the teachers and superintend the mission till we might arrive. They had been about eighteen months on the group, so they had gained a considerable acquaintance with the language, which is closely allied to the Tahitian, and had done not a little to prepare the way for us. They had prepared a few hymns, a spelling-book and catechism, and Mr. Wilson had translated the Gospel according to Matthew. The translation was necessarily very imperfect; still to us and the people it was a precious boon. Settling among a people of whose language we knew nothing, it was an immense advantage to have a gospel in print a few months after our arrival; and perhaps no portion of the sacred Scriptures was more joyously welcomed both by ourselves and the natives than the "Mataio," and certainly around none do more interesting and touching reminiscences cling in the review of the long past.

Our brother, Mr. Barff, who had come with us to assist us in entering upon our work, kindly undertook to print it and the other little things which we found ready for the press. He returned to his own station at Huahine by the same vessel that conveyed us to our destination, taking the MSS. with him, and early in the following year (1837) we received one thousand copies of the Gospel of Matthew as far as the twenty-first chapter, and some time later in the same year a second thousand reached us with the remaining sheets of the first thousand.

We had entered upon our work with a deep conviction that to give the people to whom we were sent the Bible in their own tongue must be kept before us as an object essential to the fulfilment of our mission; and this conviction led us, the first band of missionaries to the group, on our arrival in 1836, before we separated to go to our respective stations, to take a step which is perhaps worth recording. Before leaving the *Dunnottar Castle*, which for eight months had been our home, we apportioned the New Testament, each agreeing to take certain books, and do his best to translate them as soon as his knowledge of the language and other engagements would allow. Our object in taking this step was that each brother, knowing the parts assigned to him, might direct his studies accordingly, and so prepare himself for the work he had undertaken. Our views with reference to the importance of giving the Scriptures to the natives with the least possible delay were fully shared by our brethren who from time to time were added to our mission; redistributions of work were made, and we all worked harmoniously together for the accomplishment of the great object. The prominence we gave to Bible translation and Bible teaching gave rise to our being called " Bible missionaries" after Romish priests had gained a footing on the group, a designation of which we were in no way ashamed.

Before attempting the work of translation proper with a view to publication we made an effort to meet the pressing needs of the mission by drawing up and having printed what we called "A New Testament Scripture History." This consisted of an abridgment of the Gospels and the Acts of the Apostles. It was a makeshift, but it was of great use to the natives; and to ourselves the preparation of it was profitable as a sort of initiation to the more important work of out-and-out translation. So far all our printing had been done by our brethren Barff and Buzacott of the Tahitian and Hervey Islands' missions. Most cheerfully did they serve us in this respect, and their kindness was fully appreciated and acknowledged, but the growing requirements of our mission were such as could only be met by our having a printing establishment of our own, and a man with a competent knowledge of printing and binding to take charge of these departments of work, and this was now on the eve of being met.

Towards the close of 1838 an ever-memorable event occurred, which was hailed with great joy both by ourselves and the natives. This was the arrival of the missionary brig *Camden* with John Williams and a large reinforcement of missionaries for our different fields. Only three of these were appointed to our mission, but one of the three, Mr. J. B. Stair, was a printer. Mr. Stair came furnished with all necessary appliances for carrying out the special object of his mission, so we were now in a position to meet the growing demand for books all over the group. We did our best to turn to account this important trust. A number of books, some of them not very small, which it would not be in keeping with the design of this work to particularise, were printed in the meanwhile; and as soon as circumstances allowed the printing of the sacred Scriptures was proceeded with.

The first portion we ventured to print was the Gospel according to John. This was in 1841, and other portions followed at longer or shorter intervals as we were able to overtake the work of translation and revision. We spared no labour to secure accuracy. We acted on the principle that only in cases of necessity should the work of translating the Word of God into a foreign language be left to a single individual, whatever may be his qualifications. Of course where there is only one person available there is no choice; he must just do his best with the aid of native pundits; but in cases like our own, where a number of brethren are associated on one group, throughout which one language is spoken, it seems clearly desirable that some such plan should be adopted as that which we followed, and which I think has been substantially acted upon in all our South Sea missions.

With us it was a standing rule that after the translator

had done his best his manuscript must be submitted to a committee of not less than three of his brother missionaries, appointed at a general meeting of the mission, the translator, wherever practicable, making a fourth, or being one of the three; and as the committee became responsible for the fidelity and accuracy of the translation, it devolved upon them to compare every word with the original, and alter or amend the renderings as the majority might decide. The work was tedious and laborious, but it was pleasant and interesting work notwithstanding; and its importance was such as could not be overestimated. Some of the most precious recollections of my missionary life are associated with our revision meetings, when, in conjunction with brethren beloved, almost all of whom have "gone before," we pondered over the word of life, striving to give it in its purity to those for whose souls we watched, as those who must give account.

We, with our native pundits, used to sit about nine hours daily, except on Saturdays, when we took half a holiday to recruit a little and prepare for the Sabbath services. Whether at home at our own stations or elsewhere there was always a demand for preaching when the Sabbath came round. Our sittings extended over two, three, and sometimes four, or even five weeks, according to the length or difficulty of the book we had in hand, but we used to feel that three weeks were about long enough for a continuous sitting. We were pretty well furnished with critical helps, and versions were of service to us. The Septuagint, the Vulgate, and our South Sea versions which had preceded our own—the Hawaiian, the Tahitian, the Rarotongan, and the Tongan—always were on our table. Boothroyd's English version also, and of course the authorised version, and English commentaries, were all laid under contribution. Rosenmüller's commentaries on the Old Testament were of great use, as were also those of

Dr. Henderson on the prophetical books. We adhered strictly to the rules furnished by the British and Foreign Bible Society for the guidance of translators. As we had been having help from the Society, and were depending upon it to continue its help in the future, we made it a matter of conscience to abide by its rules.

All our meetings were begun and closed with prayer, one of ourselves leading in English in the morning, and one of our native pundits in the evening. At the commencement of a book our progress was generally slow; sometimes we did not get beyond five or six verses for the first day or two, but as we proceeded, and became accustomed to the style of the author, we would get through from twenty to forty or more verses. When we could not agree on any point it was settled by the majority of votes; and in cases of unusual difficulty the question was reserved for the united deliberation of the whole mission at a general meeting, or sometimes a circular was sent round the mission to afford time for more careful deliberation. When sitting in committee, our usual mode of procedure was for one member of the committee to read the verse to be considered in the original, then the translator or some one in his stead read the proposed rendering, and generally, I think, the verse was also read in English from the authorised version, and then it was taken up and considered clause by clause and word by word.

After the New Testament was completed and printed at our press, and bound in pamphlet form, each of the Gospels and the Acts being bound separately, and the Epistles in groups according to their size, the members of the mission divided themselves into four committees for a further revision of the whole; and when this was completed the entire version was rewritten and the manuscript sent to London to the British and Foreign Bible Society with a request that an edition of 15,000 should be printed.

The Committee responded promptly to our application, and in 1849-50 this second edition of our New Testament was carried through the press under the supervision of our former printer, Mr. Stair, who had been obliged some time before to leave the mission field on account of Mrs. Stair's health.

In July 1850 we received the first instalment of the books, and though the natives had long had the entire New Testament in their hands, the arrival of the new edition, neatly bound in one volume, was welcomed with great interest, and in a few years the entire edition was sold at two shillings and sixpence per copy, and the whole amount at which it was invoiced to us, £1388, 13s. 6d., was remitted to the Society, and a balance was left to meet incidental expenses.

We went on with the books of the Old Testament in the same manner as we had done with those of the New, and in due time these were completed. They too were printed at our own press and issued in separate parts. Thus the entire Bible was printed on the spot, under English superintendence of course, but the bulk of the work was done by natives, all the paper having been supplied by the Bible Society.*

The work was finished towards the close of 1855, and great was the satisfaction felt both by ourselves and the natives on the occasion. It formed an era in the history of our mission, and the event was celebrated throughout the group with a heartiness and enthusiasm befitting its importance. Public meetings were held in all the principal villages, and a great amount of interest was awakened,

---

* The brethren who superintended and directed the printing of our Bible were Mr. J. B. Stair, the Rev. J. P. Sunderland, and the Rev. S. Ella. The New Testament and Psalms were printed while Messrs. Stair and Sunderland were in charge of the press, and the printing of the entire Old Testament, except the Psalms, was superintended by Mr. Ella.

All the main points in the history of our mission, linked as they were more or less intimately with the translation and circulation of the sacred volume, were brought vividly before the mind, and great were the joy and gratitude felt in view of what God had wrought. The results already realised were such as called for the devoutest thanks, while bright visions of the future rose before us of a work widening and extending throughout successive generations, bearing down every obstacle, and conferring untold blessings, temporal and eternal, without limit and without end. The interest awakened by the meetings did not cease with the passing hour. The Bible had been much valued by the people generally before, and there had all along been an encouraging demand for it, but that increased greatly after the celebrations. And the translators, of course, were deeply grateful that they had been spared to bring to a close their great and difficult task; and great was their satisfaction to think that their mission was now placed upon an immovable rock. Men come and men go—each does his allotted work and passes away; but the Word of the Lord abideth, and once get a fair rendering of that Word into the vernacular of any people, and a foundation is laid against which the gates of hell shall never prevail.

And now steps were taken preparatory to a final revision and a new edition of the entire Scriptures to be printed in one volume—the first was in four volumes, five, indeed, for the Psalms were bound in a volume by themselves. And to prepare for this final revision, as we then regarded it, the whole was divided into eight parts for corrections and suggestions from individual brethren; and to secure uniformity as far as possible we appointed two of our brethren, the Rev. George Pratt and the Rev. Henry Nisbet, afterwards Dr. Nisbet, to go over the whole and give to the work the finishing touch. These brethren had had nearly twenty years' experience; they were located on the same island, and Mr. Pratt, under favouring circumstances, had expended a great amount of labour in collecting material for the final revision. Hence they were regarded as peculiarly eligible for the important work. For three hundred and thirty-one days they plodded afresh through the entire Bible. Dr. Turner and myself were referees in cases of difficulty, and these were pretty numerous, and involved a considerable amount of work; and for three months we took it in turn to sit with them while they were occupied with the more difficult books. Special difficulties were again, as in the former revision, referred to the entire mission.

The work was completed towards the close of 1859, and at that time Dr. Turner was about to proceed on a visit to England, and to him the manuscript was entrusted. He was requested to supply marginal references, an arduous, but a most useful work; and to apply to the British and Foreign Bible Society to print an edition of 10,000. The Bible Society undertook their part of the work with all readiness, and carried it out to our entire satisfaction; and the accuracy that was attained reflected the highest credit on our painstaking brother Dr. Turner and his estimable wife, who lent most valuable help throughout the great undertaking. And the outcome was the Samoan Bible complete in one handsomely bound volume. Part were bound in sheep and were marble-edged, and part in calf, gilt-edged. The former were sold at seven shillings per copy, the latter at nine shillings. It would have been better if all had been in superior binding, as the natives only took the inferior, as a general rule, when they could not get the other. The higher price was no consideration, and it was cheering to see how readily they parted with their property in order to gain possession of what they regarded as a priceless treasure.

Money had not yet come largely into circulation, so we

had to a great extent to receive cocoa-nut oil instead, and so great was the rush for some time that a man had to be employed at some of our principal stations whose chief occupation it was to receive and measure the oil, so the missionary had nothing directly to do with the "unclerical work of oil-measuring." He had only to be certified that the required amount had been received for one or more copies, and to hand them to purchasers.

They were forwarded to us in instalments of 3000 or 4000, and in less than seven years the entire edition of 10,000 was sold, and the amount at which it was invoiced to us, £3114, 4s., was remitted to the Bible Society.

Before this edition was sold out arrangements were made for the printing of another.

At a general meeting of the mission, held in September 1867, it was resolved that an application should be made to our never-failing friends at the Bible House to print us a stereotyped edition; and it was further resolved that there should be another revision, and the carrying out of that was confided to Mr. Pratt and myself, Dr. Turner and the Rev. S. J. Whitmee being appointed referees in cases of difficulty. So the entire Bible was again gone over. For three years, with longer or shorter intervals, we had the work in hand. It was begun in March 1867, and finished in July 1870.

In the meanwhile it was considered desirable to ask the British and Foreign Bible Society to print an edition of 5000 copies of the New Testament and Psalms in large type, to meet the case of those who, from failing sight, were unable to read the complete Bible that was in use. The Rev. T. Powell was about to proceed to England on a visit at the time, and should the Society comply with the request, it was to be printed under his superintendence. All was carried out according to the wish of the Mission Committee, and in 1869 the books reached the islands.

They seemed to be all that could be desired as regards type and binding. They were bound in calf, but there was one defect, they did not stand the climate; hence they did not sell so readily as was expected. Still large numbers were sold at four shillings per copy, and certainly, but for a mistake made in the Bible House in not naming the contents of some cases containing them, all would have been sold long ere now; but some years after it was supposed that all were sold about 1000 copies were found in cases which it was thought contained complete Bibles; hence a number still remain unsold. These it is hoped will yet be sold at reduced prices. Of course there will be a succession of elderly people who will be likely to purchase them.

While the work of revision for the stereotyped edition of the Bible was in progress Mrs. Turner's health failed, and it became necessary that she and the Doctor should make another visit to England, so we were able to secure our brother's valuable services to superintend the printing of this edition as he had that of the former.

Dr. and Mrs. Turner sailed for England on the 13th of December 1869; and so much of the copy as was ready was placed in the Doctor's hands, that the work of printing might be proceeded with as soon as the necessary preliminaries could be arranged after they reached their destination. The remainder of the manuscript was forwarded in detached portions. The stereotyping and printing were carried out by the Bible Society with all practicable despatch. The edition consisted of 15,000, and in 1883 only 2000 copies remained unsold.

A third edition, the fourth including that printed in the islands, still further improved,* was printed again, under the superintendence of Dr. Turner, who a few years since was compelled by the failure of health to relinquish his

* It was printed from an entirely new set of plates.

much loved work in the islands and retire to England. That edition is now in the course of sale, and is being purchased with equal readiness as former editions have been.

And the last thing we have to note in connection with the Bible in Samoa will form a cheering and appropriate close to this record. In a letter from Dr. Turner, dated February 7th, 1887, he communicates the intelligence to which I refer. In October 1886, the printing of a small edition of the Samoan Bible was commenced, and the work of printing was being pushed forward with such vigour that at the date of Dr. Turner's letter the middle of the book of Job had been reached, and if the work continued to advance as rapidly as it had done so far, it would be completed in six months from that date. "It will," Dr. Turner remarks, "be a precious boon to Samoa. We shall be able to sell it well bound in whole skin basil for two shillings, and in coloured basil, gilt edged, for two shillings and sixpence. I expect the Samoans will all be for the latter. The edition is 20,000, and if it get to be used generally in the schools they will soon melt away. It will be very convenient too for the natives in travelling, and a thousand other ways. May the good Lord greatly bless it for the more extended reading of His precious word."

And so we close the record of Bible translation and Bible circulation in Samoa—a record which to the writer possesses an interest which the reader cannot be expected fully to share. To all lovers of the Bible, however, it must possess an interest for the emphatic testimony it bears to the transcendent excellence of the sacred Book.

In 1830 Samoa was a heathen land. With all its natural beauty and loveliness it was a land of darkness and the shadow of death, and its people, comparatively mild and amiable as they were, and surrounded with all that is needful to meet their temporal wants, were without God, the present life being a dreary monotony, and the future a blank. Now the darkness is past and the whole land is covered with light, even as the waters cover the sea, and to a great extent the people have received the light and walk in the light—not a single heathen remains. Every village has its house of prayer and its native pastor, and every child, except perhaps a few who belong to Popish parents, is being educated, and a fair proportion of the people give credible evidence that they are on their way to a better life.

And what has wrought the mighty change? The Bible has done it, God's own Book has done it. Man's part has been a very subordinate one. He has only drawn aside the vail, if we may so speak, and instrumentally caused the Light to shine which has wrought the marvellous transformation. God be praised for the Bible! Ever may the Samoans continue to be a Bible-loving and a Bible-reading people, so shall their future be growingly bright and happy, and in increasing numbers they will pass on to that land where even the Bible will be no longer needed, for the Author of the Bible Himself is the all-sufficient and the everlasting light. To His name be all the glory, world without end. Amen.

Since this chapter was written, I have had the high privilege of making a visit to Samoa, after an absence of seventeen years. A lengthened notice of my visit would be out of place here, so I shall only refer in a few words to what has a direct bearing on the subject treated of in this volume. During my stay on the islands, I applied to the Rev. Arthur E. Claxton, the present treasurer to the mission, for information as to the amounts received from different districts throughout the group on account of sales of Bibles during the past few years. His statement shows that during the seven years ending in December 1887, he had received $17,496, representing 8748 Bibles, or 1093 copies per annum. The largest number sold in any single year of the seven was in 1887 (last year), when the sales reached 1623.

The small sized edition has not yet reached the islands. When it does, there will surely be a rush upon it. Every boy and girl among the 30,000 Protestants of the group who is able to read will wish to possess a copy, and will be likely to give their parents no rest till they get one. So the demand for the Word of Life continues in Samoa, and is likely to continue—a pretty satisfactory proof that it is in constant use. God grant that the Samoans may not only be a Bible-reading but a Bible-practising people—that their characters may be formed in accordance with its holy precepts, to the glory of His name, and their own present and eternal well-being.

CHAPTER IV.

BIBLE TRANSLATION IN NIUE.

This island, though small, and not of much account, either from a commercial or scientific point of view, has a missionary history of much interest. It is a low unpretending looking spot, with no land nearer than Tonga and Samoa, Tonga being about 200 miles to the west, and Samoa about 300 miles to the north. From these two groups it has, no doubt, been peopled, as the language spoken by the natives is to a great extent a compound of Tongan and Samoan. It is about forty miles in circumference, and has a population of about 5000.

The natives are a fine, robust, noble-looking race, but in their heathen state, they were the wildest and rudest of all the tribes of uncivilised men with whom it has been my lot to come in contact. This, I suppose, was owing in a great measure to the fact that they had been almost entirely cut off from intercourse with the outside world from time immemorial.

When a ship touched at the island their excitement was such as broke through all restraint. Such scenes I have witnessed in early days on board our mission ships as no language can adequately describe. They were fierce, ungovernable savages, and their appearance was quite in keeping with their behaviour. Many of them wore long hair, which hung down loose upon their shoulders; clothing they dispensed with as a useless incumbrance.

They adorned, perhaps rather disfigured themselves, with what they considered ornaments, consisting of feathers of various colours, and arranged in different modes, and weapons of war appeared in profusion on all occasions, and altogether they presented a finished specimen of the untamed barbarian. Such they were, and such they continued to be, just what Captain Cook found them, till they were tamed and civilised by the gospel of the grace of God.

The missionary history of the island dates from 1830. In June of that year Messrs. Williams and Barff called on their way to Samoa, and made an unsuccessful effort to introduce Christian teachers. Many similar attempts were made from Samoa in subsequent years, but it was not till 1849 that our efforts were crowned with success. In October of that year, Paulo, a Samoan teacher, and his wife took up their abode among the fierce and savage people of Niue. We need hardly remark that in so doing they placed themselves in extreme peril. Their danger was enhanced by a cruel practice which prevailed among the natives owing to the dread they had lest disease or some other calamity should come upon them if any foreigner were allowed to live on the island—hence any hapless stranger falling into their hands was invariably put to death, even their own countrymen were not spared, for any one leaving the island and returning shared the same fate as a foreigner whenever an epidemic broke out or any great calamity visited the island. Thus the teacher and his wife were in constant danger during the early years of their missionary life, but the eye of the great Preserver was upon them, and notwithstanding the many plots that were formed for their destruction they were safe in His keeping.

The Niueans did not readily yield to the claims of Christianity. On the contrary, the great bulk of them clung to heathenism for several years. The teacher, however, plodded on, and in due season the reaping time came, and a glorious harvest was gathered in. The mission was reinforced from time to time, and in 1861, when the Rev. W. G. Lawes settled on the island, there were five teachers stationed at different points, and at convenient distances, so as to be easily accessible to the whole population.

Mr. and Mrs. Lawes arrived in August 1861, and entered upon their labours in circumstances intensely interesting. A brief extract from a letter written by Mr. Lawes after they had been about two months on the island will convey a clearer idea of the state of things at that date than any mere general description. "We landed," Mr. Lawes writes, "on the 20th of August. We were heartily welcomed by the people, who had been expecting their promised missionary. The landing-place was crowded with hundreds of men and women, who were so eager to shake and smell our hands that it was with difficulty we reached the teacher's house. The people are very lively and energetic, and no doubt fully merited the name which Captain Cook gave them. We could not help contrasting the two landings—the present and the past. Now they are all clothed, joyfully welcoming their missionary—then they were naked savages rushing down like wild boars upon their visitors. We found a good house ready for us, which our female friends soon made a comfortable home. As soon as the excitement of our landing had subsided a little, a joyful sound broke upon our ears in the stillness of the evening hour. It was the voice of praise and prayer ascending from the family altars of a people who fifteen years ago were degraded savages. Although there was not much poetry in their hymns, or music in their psalms, it was a joyful sound to us; no Christian heart could hear it and remain unmoved.

"As soon as our good ship had gone, and I was able to look round upon my field of labour, I was amazed at the extent of the work already done. So far as I have been able to ascertain, there is not a vestige (outwardly) of heathenism remaining; all has crumbled away beneath the power of God's Word. There are five good chapels on the island; one of them will hold 1100 people, but it is too small. They are fine specimens of native ingenuity; they have been built, of course, without European oversight; except in the doors there is not a nail in the buildings—all is firmly tied together with cinnet. The teachers seem worthy men, and God has manifestly been with them in their work. Of course their knowledge is very limited, and the work to be done great and arduous. I am appalled when I think of the great work before me. May I not hope for help? The Word of God has to be translated, and all this land cultivated for Christ."

The Rev. George Pratt and Mrs. Pratt of the Samoan mission accompanied Mr. and Mrs. Lawes to their field of labour, and remained with them some ten or twelve months, rendering them and the mission very valuable help. Mr. Pratt was the bearer of a priceless treasure—the Gospel of Mark in the language of Niue. How this came about Mr. Pratt explains as follows:—"The Samoan Pastors in Niue translated the Gospel of Mark from the Samoan. They met together and discussed the translation verse by verse, and after thus making it as perfect as they were able they sent it to Samoa to be printed at the mission press. The MS. was handed to me to examine with the aid of a Niue student at Malua, and when printed I took it to Niue, accompanied by Mr. Lawes, who had been appointed to labour on that island. A day or two after landing I took an evening walk, and came upon a native sitting at the door of a nice new-plastered cottage, and reading aloud, according to native custom, from Mark's Gospel. That was enough reward for all the labour bestowed on the preparation of the book." That was the first portion of the Word of God printed in the Niue language, and it was translated by Samoans; nor were the efforts of these worthy men in the way of Scripture translations confined to a single gospel. "I remained," says Mr. Pratt, "the best part of a year with Mr. Lawes, and during that time I revised the remaining three Gospels and the Acts, all translated by the Samoan Pastors, and I translated Philippians and the three Epistles of John." These, Mr. Lawes tells us, "were printed in Sydney by the New South Wales Auxiliary to the British and Foreign Bible Society, and we received them bound in cloth in 1863. Never before had Niue possessed so large and precious a book. To both missionary and people that was a joyous day. Sleep that night was out of the question for many of us. In the meantime I had acquired enough of the language to be able to go on with the work of translating the remaining books of the New Testament. In 1866 these were finished and sent to Sydney with a revision of the printed portions. The Auxiliary there at once printed them for us, and in the following year Niue received the New Testament of our Lord Jesus Christ complete. There was great joy on the island. A large number were paid for in advance to insure receiving some of the first copies. As soon as the cases arrived we were besieged with applicants, and obliged to open them there and then, so eager were the people for the Word of Life." The edition consisted of 3500 copies.

The book of Psalms followed. It was also printed in Sydney, and was received in 1870. "By which time," Mr. Lawes continues, "the translation of the books of Genesis and Exodus was completed. While on a visit to Samoa in that year my old friend and helper, the Rev. G. Pratt, urged upon me the importance of a thoroughly careful revision of the New Testament, to be printed in England in the event of my visiting the fatherland in

1872. The first translation was necessarily very imperfect, and the first edition was almost exhausted.

"I went very carefully through the whole several times. In this work of revision I had the help of my brother, the Rev. F. E. Lawes, who had joined me on Niue three years before. Many thousand corrections and improvements were made towards bringing up the translation to our knowledge of idiomatic Niuean at that date.

"Gratefully would I acknowledge God's great goodness in permitting me to bring this work to a conclusion so far at least as the New Testament is concerned. I felt from the first day of my residence on Savage Island that if the people's faith was to be established on a firm basis, and their spiritual growth to become strong and vigorous, they must have the Word of God, the New Testament at least, in their own tongue. To the realisation of this object as much of my time as could possibly be spared from other missionary work has been given during the past twelve years. They have been years of constant plodding work, but such glorious work that it has brought with it its own exceeding great reward. It may be helpful to others to know our *modus operandi* in the translation and revision of the Scriptures. I have, of course, translated from the originals, both in the New and Old Testaments, following the Textus Receptus in the former, and Van der Hooght's Hebrew Bible in the latter. In critical helps to the right understanding of the text the following have been of the greatest use:—Alford's Greek Testament (particularly the marginal references), the Critical English Text, Ellicott on the Epistles, Lightfoot, Trench on Miracles, &c., Lange on Genesis, Kiel and Delitzsch, Hengstenberg and Alexander on the Psalms, the Englishman's Greek Concordance, and also the Hebrew and Chaldee, and Bishop Wilson's Hebrew Concordance, have been invaluable. In the Old Testament I have constantly consulted the Septuagint. For difficulties in translating into the Niue dialect other versions have been of greatest service. On every difficult passage I have consulted the New Zealand, Tahitian, Rarotongan, Tongan, Fijian, and even the Malagasy version with great advantage; but I am most indebted to the Samoan version, with which every verse of the Niuean has been carefully compared. I believe the Samoan to be one of the most correct and faithful translations of the Scriptures extant. The Rev. George Pratt, who has had so much to do with that translation, and who has some knowledge of the Niue dialect, has kindly examined every portion of my work as it has been done, so that our translation has had the benefit of his long experience and scholarly attainments. In our present revision we are indebted to him for many suggestions and criticisms. Every portion has been submitted to intelligent natives, and I have found it an excellent plan to give the MSS., after they are quite finished, to the young men of my teachers' class for their careful perusal.

"Twelve years ago Niue had no portion of God's Word in print, and but few readers on the island. Now the New Testament and book of Psalms are in their hands, and a new revised edition, together with the books of Genesis and Exodus, will soon be completed for them. The New Testament is in every house on the island, and in every house are those who can read its blessed truths. Twelve hundred Savage islanders, out of a population of 5000, have made a personal profession of their faith in Christ, and are living in accordance with the teaching of God's Word. Many have died resting peacefully on that Saviour it has revealed to them.

"Instead of darkness and cruelty we have light and peace. Where superstition and fear reigned, intelligent faith and joyful hope now prevail. Commerce and civilisation too are found where a few years ago no man dared to land. Instead of the desert we have a garden; instead of death, life: all resulting from the Word of God in the hands of a few simple-minded, believing, prayerful men. Truly the Word has not lost its power, but is as potent as ever to raise the fallen and save the lost. Savage islanders show their appreciation of the sacred volume by paying for it, and doing what they can to send it to others. During the last ten years they have paid upwards of £500 to the Bible Society for the New Testament and portions printed in Sydney, and they have raised £2300 as contributions to the Missionary Society, that heathen islands beyond may enjoy with them the blessings of the gospel through the teaching of God's own Word of life and peace. I had hoped to go on with this great work on Niue, and fully expected to return there, but now the Master seems calling me to New Guinea. I hope I may, by God's grace, be able to do something towards giving that immense island the Word of God which is able to make wise unto salvation. We have need of the sympathy and prayers of all Christians."

The above record needs no comment. It tells its own marvellous tale of conquest, effected not by might, nor by power, but by the Spirit of God working through and by His own Truth; and it supplies a fresh earnest of the complete subjugation in due time of all nations, tribes, and tongues to the dominion of the Prince of Peace.

According to the expectation which Mr. Lawes mentions at the close of the above extract, he did not resume his work on Niue, but on his return from England he and Mrs. Lawes proceeded to New Guinea, where they arrived near the close of 1874, and where, with two or three short intervals, they have worked on till the present time.

After the departure of his brother, the sole charge of the mission devolved upon the Rev. F. E. Lawes, and with the exception of some eighteen months or so, during which he and his family visited England, he has remained at his post, and with his estimable wife has laboured on for the consolidation of the work of God on Niue. And in addition to other missionary duties, he has gone steadily forward with the translation of the Old Testament Scriptures. In the month of April 1878 he wrote to the Bible Society as follows:—" You will be gratified to know that these Ninean Scriptures (referring to a consignment that had recently been received) were mostly purchased by young people, children many of them, boys and girls who have only lately acquired the art of reading; we are glad to find in our schools now a good many little children who can read. There are more readers on the island now than there have been at any former period, and few if any are without Testaments. The Bible, so far as we have it, is the literature of the land—school-books, class-books, church-book, geography, history, and biography. It is in the hands of the young and reckless, and by the couch of the sick and dying. The gospel has lost none of its power on the hearts of the Savage islanders. Its later triumphs are less observed by man than its earlier, yet they are seen and acknowledged by God.

"A very few of the leading men who received and protected the early teachers now remain. A goodly number of them died during the year 1877. It may be said of them that the Word of God was a light unto their feet during the latter part of their lives, and their consolation and hope in death. One of these worthies was my brother's pundit in all his translation work, a shrewd, intelligent old man, formerly a great warrior, latterly using all his influence, which was great, for the good of the land, and to advance the work of God. Eight of our teachers have gone to New Guinea. Of these two have died, and one has returned home. Four more young men with their wives are now awaiting the *John Williams* to take them to South Cape, China Straits."

From the Report of the Bible Society for 1880, we find that the edition of the New Testament, with the books of Genesis, Exodus, and Psalms, sent to the island in 1872-3, had been sold out, and that £700, proceeds of sales, had been remitted to the Society. It is also announced in the same report that at that date (1880) Mr. Lawes was on his way to England, and that on his arrival other portions of the Old Testament would be put to press. Accordingly, during his stay in England, the complete Pentateuch was printed, and at a later date, some time after his return, we find him writing as follows:—"The people are very pleased with the Pentateuch, three of the books being new to them. The delight with which they receive book after book of the Old Testament, giving the account of God's earlier dealings with mankind, is very pleasant to contemplate."

The latest intelligence relative to the progress and present state of Scripture translation on Niue which I am able to give is from a letter from the Rev. F. E. Lawes, dated October 19th, 1887. I should have had the information at a much earlier date but for the fact that a letter which I wrote asking Mr. Lawes' help, dated December 30th, 1886, did not reach him till August 18th, 1887. After referring to the printing of the Pentateuch mentioned above, Mr. Lawes proceeds as follows:—"We have in manuscript not yet printed the books of Joshua, Judges, Ruth, 1st and 2nd Samuel, 1st and 2nd Kings, also the prophecies of Isaiah, and the book of Jonah. These we are anxious to get printed, but think of translating Jeremiah first, in order to make the book a little more complete."

It appears that during his stay in England a new edition of the New Testament and Psalms was also printed.

"Of each of these" (including the Pentateuch), he tells us, "we have sold a thousand, and are now into the second thousand. The Niueans pay in full the cost of printing and binding their books, and moreover indulge in the luxury of gilt edges and morocco binding. The present edition of Scriptures has not sold so rapidly as the former, but that is chiefly owing to the greater number of books in circulation, and not from lack of interest in the sacred volume.

"As to the value put upon the Word of God, it is doubtless treasured up in the hearts of a great many in Savage Island. We are often cheered by an apt quotation from those from whom we did not expect it. We have this year lost an unusual number of church members by death, and so far as I know in every instance they were found prepared for the Master's summons. One man, a newly appointed deacon, after only a few days' illness, died of pneumonia. Just before his death, he arose and took his spectacles and New Testament out of his box, and read aloud John xiv. 1, 2; he was too exhausted to read more, and almost immediately departed to occupy the place prepared for him in the house of many mansions. In the same village an old man named Jeremiah died in July last. He was one who helped to protect John Williams on the occasion of his visit to Niue in 1830. He early made the acquaintance of Paulo, the first teacher, and his name stood first in the church book. He wished to be buried on the very spot where Paulo stood to preach the gospel on his first visit to his village; it is a lovely spot on the top of a hill overlooking the sea. His relations have made a pretty grave for the old man surrounded by flowers. It is a bright testimony to Jeremiah's delight in the gospel. He was a dear friend of my brother (the Rev. W. G. Lawes of New Guinea), and not less dear to us. He was always ready for every good work. His influence and help were always on the right side, and we mourn for him as a faithful friend and invaluable helper. I might give other instances, but you will say, what about the living? The gospel is undoubtedly moulding the lives of the people, not rapidly, but slowly and surely. It is delivering them from the bondage of Satan and introducing them to the liberty of the sons of God. We have many discouragements, yet we cannot shut our eyes to the fact that God is with us, working by His Spirit in the hearts of men, women, and children."

So ends our notice of Bible translation and Bible circulation on Niue, and surely the record is such as calls for devout gratitude to God, and supplies the highest encouragement to the friends of the Bible and of Christian missions. One more conquest has been achieved, one more island won for Christ, and one more earnest given of the final triumph when He shall reign without a rival over a ransomed world.

CHAPTER V.

THE TONGAN VERSION.

The history of the Tongan mission dates from the year 1797, the same year in which the Tahitian mission was commenced. The group was discovered by Tasman in 1643, and it was visited by Captain Cook in 1773; and owing to the kind reception given him by the natives, and the friendly intercourse he had with them, he gave it the name of the Friendly Islands. The group lies between 170° and 178° west longitude, and between 18° and 20° south latitude, about due south from Samoa, and southeast of the great Fiji group, these three groups forming one great cluster of islands separated by channels of from 250 to 400 miles in breadth. There are three principal islands in the Tongan group, named respectively Tongatabu or Sacred Tonga, Habai, and Vavau, and there are a great number of small islands. Captain Cook speaks of over sixty, but many of these must be mere islets without settled inhabitants. The population at the present time is about 22,000. The natives are a fine race of people of the Malay stock, not excelled, I think, by any of the tribes of Eastern or Central Polynesia. In their heathen state, however, they were a savage race, daring, fierce, and cruel, not quite so bad in some respects as the Fijians and Maoris, but just about upon a level with the Tahitians, Rarotongans, and other natives of Eastern Polynesia.

Ten of the first band of missionaries, sent by the London

Missionary Society in the ship *Duff* in 1796, were commissioned to endeavour to commence a mission on Tongatabu; and after the missionaries appointed to Tahiti were landed at their destination, the vessel proceeded to Tonga, and on the 10th of April 1797, anchored in the centre of the bay on the northern shore of Tongatabu, near the now well-known town of Nukualofa. The missionaries were favourably received, and on the fourth day after their arrival the *Duff* sailed, leaving them at the mercy of the then savage Tongans.

About four months after their settlement the *Duff* returned to ascertain how they were being treated, and to afford an opportunity of leaving the island should any or all of them wish to do so. The commander, Captain Wilson, had the great satisfaction of finding them all alive, and all in health with a single exception. So far the natives seem to have behaved kindly towards them, but they had suffered much insult and annoyance from three white men of most abandoned character, who by some means had found their way to the islands about eighteen months before their arrival. The *Duff* remained with them about a month, and when the time for her departure came, they all, with the exception of Mr. Nobbs, who had been ill most of the time since their arrival, determined to continue at what they regarded the post of duty. Their names were Bowell, Buchanan, Gaulton, Harper, Shelly, Veeson, Wilkinson, Nobbs, Kelso, and Cooper. The saddest perhaps of all the trials that came upon them was the defection of one of their own number. Soon after the vessel left, Veeson withdrew from them, and became to all appearance an apostate—a solemn warning to all who are desirous of engaging in mission work to count the cost, and to all on whom it devolves to select and appoint men to the office of Christian missionaries to exercise the utmost caution, though, of course, it is nothing to marvel at. The wonder is, all things considered, that defections are so rare as they have been hitherto.

Some time after the departure of the *Duff*, an American ship, named the *Mercury*, called at the island, and put on shore seven of its crew, and these proved even more vicious and abandoned than those who had preceded them. They took every opportunity of annoying the missionaries, extorting or stealing from them tools, clothing, or other things as inclination prompted or opportunity served, and spreading among the natives the most false and malicious reports, and more than once seeking their destruction. And naturally enough the natives were not slow to follow their example. Thus they were in peril from their own countrymen, and they were in peril from the heathen, with no human protection against either. About a year after their settlement on the island a civil war broke out, and brought their troubles to a climax. They refused to take part in the war; those who had hitherto befriended them to some extent now gave them to understand that no further protection would be afforded them. Thus they were exposed to all the horrors and dangers of war in its most appalling forms. Their houses were plundered, their very wearing apparel was taken from them, some of them being able to secure nothing beyond a piece of native cloth, and their lives were in constant peril. They wandered from place to place in search of a safe retreat, suffering much from hunger and thirst, and cold and nakedness. Literally, they wandered in deserts and in mountains, and in dens and caves of the earth.

At length their trials culminated in the murder of three of their number, Bowell, Harper, and Gaulton; and a seaman named Burnham who had attached himself to them was also killed. These first martyrs of Polynesia were all comparatively young men. Harper, the eldest, was 29 years of age, Bowell was 25, and Gaulton was still younger.

It is painful to think of their brief and chequered course and its sad termination, but doubtless all was wisely ordered. "Precious in the sight of the Lord is the death of His saints." We may not be able to trace the results of their labours and sufferings, but it does not follow that they were fruitless, yea, may we not rather confidently conclude that they were in some way instrumental in preparing the way of the Lord, and that, as in the case of martyrs of other lands of early and later date, the blood of the martyrs of Tonga proved the seed of the Church in Polynesia as elsewhere.

The situation of the remaining missionaries continued to be wretched in the extreme. They were exposed to constant insult, and their lives were in peril by night and by day; no visible impression was being made upon the natives, and at length they felt constrained to come to the conclusion that should an opportunity of leaving the island offer it would be their duty to embrace it. The war was not ended; another fearful struggle was impending. A hurricane swept over the island, making terrible havoc among bread-fruit trees, bananas, and cocoa-nuts. An earthquake shook the island, causing the sea to overflow a large part of the low land, and destroying the little produce which had escaped the devastations of war, and thus a dire famine must follow. And at this juncture, which was emphatically "man's extremity," God appeared in a very marked manner. On the 21st of January 1800, a ship called off the island. She was an English privateer with a Spanish vessel as a prize. The captain had called at Tahiti, but did not intend to touch at Tonga. He had an errand however to Tonga, and to Tonga he must go. The storm that had wrought such desolation on the land had carried the ship a long way to leeward of the island. The storm was followed by a calm, during which a strong current carried it back, and thus an opportunity was afforded for the escape of the missionaries. When the captain was made acquainted with the circumstances he generously offered them a passage to Port Jackson, with the best accommodation his cabin afforded. The offer was thankfully accepted, the missionaries were soon on board, and on the 24th of January 1800 the ship weighed anchor and stood out to sea, and so ended the first attempt to plant Christianity in Tonga.

Many years passed before the mission was resumed. After a long "night of toil" in the Tahitian group a morning of joy had gladdened the hearts of the toilers, and placed them in circumstances to extend help to other lands beyond, and in the course of the year 1823 three native missionaries were sent from the church at Porapora, two of whom were married, and some time after two others were sent from the church at Papara in Tahiti. They were well received and kindly treated, and in 1827 they were able to report that four members of the chief family had embraced Christianity. A chief woman also had sent a letter written by a native expressing a desire to be baptized. And in the course of the same year tidings reached Tahiti that the whole population of the district in which the teachers resided had placed themselves under instruction, and were professedly Christian. The success which crowned the efforts of these poorly qualified labourers was doubtless largely owing, under God, to the wonderful tale they had to tell of the triumphs of Christianity on Tahiti and other islands of that group, of which they themselves were living witnesses.

At this stage of the mission's history it passed into the hands of the Wesleyan Church. The Rev. John Thomas, a Wesleyan missionary, arrived, and the teachers cordially united with the people in inviting him to settle among them, and take charge of the mission and carry forward the work which they had begun.*

For two or three years Mr. Thomas appears to have laboured alone in conjunction with the Tahitian teachers, but in March 1831 a strong reinforcement arrived, consisting of the Rev. Nathaniel Turner, the Rev. James Watkin, and Mr. W. Woon, a printer. And now a want which had been sorely felt was met. Hitherto all the natives had in their hands from which to learn to read were small things in manuscript;† now there was a printer, and a printing press. Of course no time was lost in getting printed school-books, select passages of Scripture, a hymn-book, catechisms, &c.

The delight and astonishment of the natives when they saw the press in operation were similar to what was felt by the Tahitians, and the same eager desire to possess the books was manifested by the Tongans. But what we have chiefly to do with is the translation of the sacred Scriptures, and matters directly akin to that.

With reference to these subjects, the Rev. W. G. R. Stephinson, President of the Australian Wesleyan Conference for the present year, has kindly favoured me with a paper from which the information that follows is largely derived. Mr. Stephinson was himself a missionary in Tonga about fourteen years, so he is well acquainted with everything connected with the mission.

The missionaries, he tells us, entered upon the work of translation as soon as their knowledge of the language allowed, and of those who had the principal share in the

---

* A full account of the early history of the Tongan mission may be found in Mr. Ellis' History of the London Missionary Society, p. 70 onwards.

† That is, all in their own language, for doubtless the Tahitian teachers brought copies of such books as were in print in their languages at the time they left on their mission to Tonga. The differences in the language spoken throughout Eastern Polynesia are only dialectic, not radical. Hence the natives of one island or group learn the language of another very readily.

work he mentions the following, viz., the Revs. Messrs. Cross, Turner, Tucker, Rabone, Wilson, West, Adams, Daniel, Davis, and Amos. Mr. Thomas, he says, was most indefatigable, and all gave years of earnest and painstaking attention to the work, often rising at four and five o'clock in the morning, and continuing their work during most of the day. First portions of the Gospels were printed in leaflets, and used in both adult and children's schools, and afterwards the Acts of the Apostles and the Epistles were in like manner used and circulated among the people. By daily teaching in the schools and conversing with the people the missionaries became increasingly familiar with the language, errors were corrected, and the editions one after another improved. It was arranged that the translation of a book or an epistle should be passed by the translator to other missionaries for corrections and suggestions; and this plan, Mr. Stephinson remarks, though under the circumstances it was the best that could be adopted, was attended with serious risk. The only way of sending from island to island was by canoe, and that was very hazardous. On one occasion, when several manuscripts were being sent from one island to another, a violent storm arose, the canoe was overturned, and the precious documents, on which years of labour had been expended, were lost, and the work had to be done again.

The Old Testament was translated in the same careful manner, and for years the different books were printed at the mission press. A few of the natives had been taught the art of printing, and doubtless also of binding, so the work of the missionary would be very much lightened and expedited.

The first complete edition of the New Testament was printed at the mission press in 1849, and after undergoing another revision it was sent to London, and an edition consisting of 10,000 copies was printed by the British and

Foreign Bible Society. The books reached Tonga in 1853, and, according to the Rev. Thomas West, they were of "incalculable value as enabling the missionaries to extend very widely the use of the Scriptures in the schools, and thereby to render futile and fruitless in almost every place the untiring efforts of Romish emissaries." "I am quite sure," Mr. West adds (he was addressing the Bible Society), "from my intimate knowledge of the native character, that the reception of the entire Word of God, through the liberality of your Society, will be esteemed by them as the highest national blessing they could receive."

The translation of the entire Bible into the Tonguese language must have been completed in 1859, as we find that in 1860 the Bible Society had undertaken to print an edition of 10,000, and that at that date the work was passing through the press, under the superintendence of Mr. West.

The following extracts from Mr. West's letter, referred to above, show how carefully he and his brethren strove to produce a correct and idiomatic version of the sacred volume. They evidently went about their work with a deep sense of its importance, and spared neither pains nor labour. "The separate books," he remarks, "were assigned to different brethren, who in turns have mutually and critically examined each other's work, and where that has been impracticable the translations have been read and revised by an examining committee. That having been done, every such complete portion has been submitted to the final supervision of one of the missionaries appointed by the translators themselves, and upon him devolved the responsibility of carrying it through the press.

"Again, the translation of the entire Bible in Tonguese, now in the course of publication, is not a new and untried version. With the exception of the historical books from 1st Kings to Esther inclusive, all the other books have passed through large and repeated editions at the mission press, subject at all times to the course of critical examination before specified.

"These editions have extended over a period of many years, some portions having been in circulation for upwards of twenty years. Hence every part of the translation has come under the review and criticism of intelligent natives, independently of each other, and at various times. The whole therefore may be safely regarded as thoroughly faithful and idiomatic. I need not state here what my own share in the translation department has been, but I may just say, in reference to the present revision, entrusted to my care, that I have closely compared every part with the Fijian version, and with several kindred Polynesian translations which have received the sanction of your Society, and also, as far as I am capable, with the original text."

Mr. West makes special mention of the Rev. Thomas Adams as having rendered great service in revising and carrying through the press several portions of the Old Testament, and also of having prepared to some extent the revised copy of the New Testament, already mentioned as having been published by the Bible Society. With reference to the estimation in which the Bible is held in Tonga, Mr. West says—"It is the book of the people, that it is venerated and loved, that it is generally and carefully studied by the people, and that it is the grand daily text-book in the numerous mission schools throughout the islands."

With reference to the same subject, Mr. Stephinson remarks—"Nothing could exceed the pleasure with which the people received the complete Bible. With the greatest eagerness the edition was bought up till all were gone, and further editions had to be printed. The amount for the purchase of a copy would be brought to the mission-house, and left there till the following year, as the natives said, 'to secure one of the first copies, and to make sure of it,' and in hundreds of cases the last shilling would be given to secure the precious boon. In this way the Word of Life found its way to the houses of the people throughout the entire group, exerting everywhere a most blessed and salutary influence." Mr. Stephinson continues: "With the utmost diligence the people not only learned to read, but devoured the Scriptures. For many years the Bible was almost the only book they possessed, and like the Bereans, they searched it daily to see whether these things were so, and large portions were committed to memory. In temptations peculiar to their circumstances they were fortified against the attacks of the enemy, and repulsed his assaults with, 'It is written;' and when in later days they were assailed by the emissaries of Rome, the knowledge of the truth gave them an advantage over the advocates of tradition, and made them more than conquerors. The Bible is still their delight, the guide of their youth, and the comfort of their declining years, the light in the chamber of sickness, and their guide in the dark valley of the shadow of death, conducting them to fairer worlds on high."

Mr. Stephinson closes his paper with the following information:—"By a resolution of the Wesleyan District Meeting in Tonga, the Rev. James Egan Moulton was sent to England in 1878 to revise the New Testament, and to carry it through the press. Mr. Moulton was specially qualified for the work, and has rendered valuable service by the manner in which he has executed the task committed to him."

Owing to Mr. Moulton's failing to comply with the rules of the Bible Society, his version was printed by a private firm. It bears date 1880, and I suppose reached the islands during that or the following year. It was warmly welcomed by the natives, and by them pronounced superior to all former versions, and such being the case it met with a ready sale.

In 1883 an Education Act was passed by the Tongan Government which enacted that the Word of God should be the text-book in all Government schools, and that the version used should be that of the British and Foreign Bible Society.

All the Bibles and Testaments which the Society had in stock were required to meet the increased demand, and a small edition of the existing version was printed by the Society to meet the emergency.

The revision of the Old Testament is now in progress, but I suppose the work is being retarded by the sad calamities that have recently come upon the mission, and there seems much reason to fear that a considerable time must elapse before any definite steps can be taken towards the printing of a new edition. In the meanwhile it is matter for great satisfaction that the people have the complete Bible in their hands, and that very large numbers of them are grounded and settled in the truths which it teaches. A lengthened reference to the fiery trials through which the mission is now passing would be out of place here. The main facts are before the world. The whole affair is deplorable in the highest degree. The persecuted people and the sorely tried missionaries who remain faithful to their trust have strong claims upon our sympathy. Speedily may He who executeth righteousness and judgment for all that are oppressed appear for His suffering people in Tonga, delivering them from the power of their oppressors, and restoring to them the peace and prosperity of years gone by.

CHAPTER VI.

THE FIJI VERSION.

The Rev. Thomas Williams, for many years a missionary in Fiji, and now residing in Victoria, Australia, has kindly furnished me with a very valuable paper on the translation of the Bible into the language of that group. I regret that want of space compels me to omit much that is valuable and interesting in Mr. Williams' paper. I have no choice, however, in the matter.

Fiji and its people are now so well known that I shall say nothing directly with reference either to the one or the other, but will come at once to the deeply interesting story of the movement which has effected such a change as has few parallels in the history of our race.

Nowhere, so far as my knowledge extends, has Christianity more clearly demonstrated its power than in Fiji. It is scarcely possible to conceive of human beings in a more deeply debased, more thoroughly brutalised, and demonised condition, if I may so say, than were the Fijians in their heathen state; and we may assert without fear of contradiction that the power which has transformed the Fijians of fifty years ago to the Fijians of to-day has proved itself adequate to meet the case of man in every conceivable condition.

The movement which has issued in this mighty transformation had a very small beginning. Two missionaries, the Rev. William Cross and the Rev. David Cargill, M.A., who had had a few years' experience of missionary life and work in the Tongan group, were commissioned by their brethren, under the sanction of the Wesleyan Missionary Committee in London, to attempt the commencement of a mission in Fiji. Mr. Williams speaks of Messrs. Cross and Cargill as being well fitted for their perilous undertaking, and he notes particularly that "they were no strangers to translation work, having made their first essays therein in the Friendly Islands." In the month of October 1835 they landed on Lakemba, the most easterly island of the Fiji group which lies nearest to Tonga, being only about two hundred and fifty miles distant. "Here," Mr. Williams remarks, "they were brought face to face with a very mild type of the population of cannibal Fiji. Here also they were met by a number of Tongans with whose language they were familiar. Many of these settlers spoke Fijian, and materially assisted the missionaries in acquiring it." As soon as their knowledge of the language allowed they applied themselves to the work of translating the Scriptures. "First," Mr. Williams tells us, "they translated verses, and then Scripture lessons were translated consisting of portions of the Gospels."

The first things *printed* in the Fiji language were a school-book of four pages, and twenty-four pages of the Gospel according to Matthew. These were printed at the mission press in Tonga, and were a precious boon to the missionaries, and they were eagerly welcomed by a few of the natives, who even at this early stage of the mission seem to have been possessed by an earnest desire after the Word of Life.

"The days of dependence on the Tongan press," Mr. Williams tells us, "were not of long continuance." Early in the year 1839 a printing press was added to the Lakemba establishment. It was brought out by two missionaries, Messrs Jaggar and Calvert, both of whom were acquainted with the art of printing. "The press was looked upon by the Lakembans with breathless astonishment, and although it was not worked at the rate of two hundred sheets per hour, the productions were deemed miraculous, and many of the onlookers said 'it was a god.'"

Mr. Williams continues—"The few natives who at this stage of the mission truly waited for the law of the Lord were soon made glad by having the Gospel of Mark placed in their hands. That Gospel was the first complete portion of the *Vola Tambu*, Sacred Book, translated and printed in the isles of Fiji. Impelled by a sense of duty, intensified by compassion for men whose spiritual necessities were so great, both the translators, Messrs Cross and Cargill, and the printers, applied themselves diligently to their respective departments with encouraging results. Increasing light was chasing before it the darkness from the minds of those who professed the new faith, and these gladly communicated their newly acquired knowledge to their countrymen."

Mr. Williams makes some interesting remarks on the difficulties which the student of the Fiji language has to encounter at the outset, which want of space compels us to omit. He refers especially to the peculiarities of the pronouns, which present especial difficulties to the learner, and demand great care in their use. Similar peculiarities are found in all the dialects of Eastern Polynesia, and also in some of the languages spoken in the New Hebrides. In Fiji, however, there may be greater complications. There is a dual form in all the eastern dialects, and there is also an inclusive and exclusive form; and in some of the islands of the New Hebrides there is a triplicate form. Hence very great care is required in the use of pronouns to avoid very serious mistakes. "A misused inclusive pronoun," Mr. Williams remarks, " would make the missionary and his associates more vile than cannibals; or it might place the God of all good in the category of the vilest sinners."

With reference to the progress and extension of the mission, Mr. Williams proceeds as follows:—"An accession to the staff of missionaries was naturally followed by the occupancy of new stations, and a first step on the part of those occupying them was to operate on the darkness and ignorance of the people around them by the establishment of schools. Only less primitive than the 'Irish hedge' schools were these first schools in Fiji, yet by the help of these, conducted without noise or show, a work of overthrow and recovery was commenced which has proved itself to be as effective as it was unpretentious."

These schools led to the discovery of a very unwelcome fact, viz., that wide dialectic differences existed in the language as spoken in different parts of the group. No less than fifteen were found to be in use, so it was obvious that some comprehensive plan must be adopted—some one dialect must be selected to which the others would in course of time become sufficiently assimilated to form the common and standard language of the Fijian nation. In the meanwhile twelve pages of the book of Genesis were printed in three other dialects besides that of Lakemba.

After due deliberation the Mbau dialect was selected as having the strongest claim to be the recognised language of the group. The dialectic differences do not appear to have been so great as to cause any very serious inconvenience.

With reference to translation work and kindred subjects, Mr. Williams writes as follows:—"In the year 1843 the missionaries in District Meeting assembled resolved to attempt the translation of the entire New Testament, to be printed at the mission press. As a preliminary certain books were allotted to the missionary or missionaries at each station, with instructions that they were to be translated into the dialect spoken at the station where the missionary or missionaries resided. Some time after this the Old Testament was similarly apportioned. This plan did not succeed to the extent that had been hoped for, although it had its advantages, and was decidedly helpful in attaining the desired end. Out of it too grew a feature of these times—a number of 'Quarterlies' were called into existence, and because of the rarity of intercommunication, these manuscript serials found great favour. No leading journal of Europe or the colonies was welcomed more warmly than the 'Lakemba Nole' or the 'Viwa Letter,' the 'Somosomo Quarterly,' &c. In the pages of these papers the missionaries wrote criticisms on each other's translations, made suggestions, endeavoured carefully to balance the claims of various renderings, &c., &c.

"However, this polyglot method of preparing and publishing the sacred Book was cumbrous, and after it had received a fair trial its continuance was voted to be unadvisable." Again the subject was fully discussed at a general meeting of the missionaries, and a resolution was passed that henceforth the Scriptures should be printed in the Mbau dialect only. "From the time this decision was arrived at," Mr. Williams continues, "the work of translation was virtually given into the hands of the brethren stationed at Viwa, a small island nigh to Mbau, on which the dialect of that island was spoken. The Rev. John Hunt, the chairman of the district, had so grown into the confidence of his co-workers that he naturally occupied the position of translator-in-chief. The Rev. R. B. Lyth was associated with Mr. Hunt, and the work done by Messrs. Hunt and Watsford was submitted to him for examination before it went to press."

"Mr. Hunt," Mr. Williams tells us, "commenced at once the special and congenial work assigned to him with a resolved heart." Of Mr. Hunt's qualifications for translation work, Mr. Williams speaks as follows:—"Of Mr. Hunt, one who knew him well says, 'He was a thoroughly good translator. He had a fair knowledge of the Greek and Hebrew; he was a most careful and diligent student of God's Word, and he was a good Fijian scholar.'"

The Rev. John Watsford, Mr. Williams writes, has supplied the following details:—"In 1844-5 Mr. Hunt translated Matthew, Mark, and Luke, and I translated John. Mr. Hunt sent all his translations to me, and I went carefully through them with a native, made notes, and returned them. I also sent my translations to him, and he revised them.

"In addition to the Gospels already named, Mr. Hunt translated the remaining portions of the New Testament, and the whole of the translations underwent a careful scrutiny from Mr. Lyth, a work for which he possessed special qualifications. The translation prepared with so much solicitude was given into the hands of brethren as competent as they were anxious to produce the sacred volume in a style thoroughly creditable. Stray portions had found their way into the hands of a few of the Christian natives, and they with their friends were on the tiptoe of expectation. At length the glad day was greeted, the long-looked-for boon was secured, and the missionaries with their numerous converts rejoiced with exceeding great joy." The New Testament was complete in the language of Fiji.

Mr. Williams was himself in the field when the happy event occurred. One of the first two, if not the first copy, was sent to him, and he mentions the delight he experienced in comparing the new version with the renderings in portions already in print, and remarks that its publication "sent a thrill of gladness through the heart of Christianised Fiji." As an illustration of this Mr. Williams mentions the following incident. One of the missionaries wrote to him as follows:—"I had walked home one day from your house, a young teacher, named Samson, accompanying me. He was thoroughly tired when we reached home, and crawled away to his bed. When I went into my house I found a parcel of New Testaments for me. I thought, one of these will please Samson. I took it out and said, 'Here, Samson, is the *Vola tabu* come for you.' He sprang to his feet and danced for joy. I don't think I ever saw a man happier than he seemed. 'The lame man was made to leap as the hart.'"

It is painful to read what Mr. Watsford tells us with reference to a native pundit named Noah who had rendered him and his colleagues most valuable help. "Noah's work at the translations was very great—Mr. Hunt's and mine. He assisted us both. He worked hard. His mind, as you know, gave way. The strain was too great. He became a wreck for life. Truly the sight of that man, who had rendered such signal service to the mission, wandering over the isle demented was a singularly sad one."

I know of a case precisely similar to that of Noah. It occurred in the New Hebrides. Such cases should be a warning to missionaries to guard against overtaxing the powers of their native pundits. Especially is this needful in the islands of the Pacific, where the previous habits of the natives have not been such as to fit them for bearing continuous mental strain to anything like the extent that men brought up in civilised lands can undergo without inconvenience or risk. Poor Noah! Doubtless he was not forgotten by Him whom he served so faithfully while the power for work remained, and the award of the faithful servant as surely greeted him when his course was ended as it did or will do those whose labours he shared.

The first edition of the New Testament consisted of one thousand copies, and towards the expense of printing that and portions previously printed the British and Foreign Bible Society contributed £300.

The printing of the complete edition of the New Testament was followed by the printing of three thousand copies of the Gospel of Matthew, and the same number of the Epistle to the Romans, and the Epistle to the Philippians, these being regarded as specially fitted to be "antidotes to Popery."

As soon as the first edition of the New Testament was out of hand, steps were taken towards preparing for a second; and "it was resolved that additional pains should be taken in preparing for it." The work of revision was interrupted for some time by the absence of Mr. Watsford from the mission on account of domestic affliction; but on his return in 1852 he was appointed to revise the whole, and see it through the press. In carrying out this work in 1852–3, he had the assistance of the best native help obtainable. His most efficient helpers were three Mbau chiefs, all men of superior intelligence.

About this time, Mr. Calvert, who was still in charge of the press, obtained most valuable help in the printing department in a very remarkable way. A young man, a Frenchman named Edward Martin, who had been for some time in the United States of America, was wrecked on one of the islands of the Fiji group in a hurricane, and this young man, by some means which God was pleased to employ, had his eyes opened to see his need of a Saviour, and was brought to a saving acquaintance with the gospel; and this "trophy of redeeming love," Mr. Williams remarks, "became a devout and devoted labourer in missionary work. He learned the art of printing and bookbinding that he might assist in the work of the printing office, taught these arts to several of the natives, and as an evangelist he added greatly to the value of his services."

With reference to the second edition of the New Testament, Mr. Williams supplies the following interesting information:—"All concerned in bringing out this second edition were most laborious in their efforts to make it superior to the first, nor did they fail." As evidence of this, Mr. Williams states that the Viwa edition, as it is called, "is regarded both by missionaries and natives at the present time as the best they have."

Of this edition 3000 copies were printed at the mission press, and some time afterwards 5000 were printed in London by the British and Foreign Bible Society, and reached the islands at a specially opportune time. "The munificent gift of the Bible Society," Mr. Williams remarks, "reached the islands at a time when the requirements of the mission were such as greatly to enhance the value of the gift, and it is gratefully spoken of to the present day."

The following summary, furnished by Mr. Williams, shows at a glance what had been accomplished in the way of Scripture translation and publication prior to the date we have now reached (1854):—

1. Selected portions for school lessons or other purposes, printed in Tonga in 1836.
2. Similar portions with the Gospel by Mark, printed in Lakemba in 1840.
3. The Gospel of Matthew and the Acts of the Apostles, printed in 1843.
4. The first edition of the New Testament complete, printed in Viwa, consisting of 3000 copies, in 1847.
5. And the second edition of the New Testament carefully revised, 5000 copies, printed in London in 1854.

Shortly after the translation of the New Testament was completed, steps were taken towards the accomplishment of the still greater and more difficult work of rendering the Old Testament into the language of Fiji. At a District Meeting held in 1847 or 1848, Mr. Hunt, who had done such valuable service in connection with the translation of the New Testament, was appointed by his brethren to undertake the translation of the Old. He agreed to do his best to carry out the wishes of his brethren, and without delay set himself with characteristic heartiness to the great work to which he was called. The book of Genesis had been translated by another hand whose name is not mentioned, and after careful examination by Mr. Hunt it was adopted by him, but in some unaccountable way the MS. was lost, and of course the book had to be translated again. But Mr. Hunt went on with Exodus, and from that passed to the Psalms, and he had just reached the close of the 46th Psalm when he was seized with an illness which in a short time brought to a close his beautiful and eminently useful life. Of him we may say with perfect truth and singular appropriateness, "he was a burning and a shining light." His removal was an incalculable loss to the mission, but God had prepared another man who, Mr. Williams tells us, was singularly fitted to take up the work which he had laid down. This was the Rev. David Hazlewood, "a born philologist," as Mr. Williams describes him; and his attainments, evinced by the services he had rendered to the cause of Fijian literature, seem to justify this description of him. He had prepared a Fiji Grammar, and a Fijian and English, and an English and Fijian Dictionary—all said to be of marked excellence; and in addition to these works he had made other valuable contributions to Fijian literature. It seems natural therefore that his brethren should have turned to him as the fittest man among them to succeed Mr. Hunt. From the time of his joining the mission he had applied himself diligently to the study of the Hebrew language, and now the opportunity was afforded of turning his knowledge to account. He was a remarkably modest and unassuming man. He did not shrink, however, from the work to which he believed himself called, and he applied himself to it as one who realised its supreme importance, determining virtually to do "one thing."

Several books of the Old Testament had been translated by Mr. Williams and Mr. Hazlewood under the earlier translation arrangements, and thus Mr. Hazlewood's work was somewhat lightened now. How long Mr. Hazlewood was engaged in his great work I am unable to ascertain, as the date on which he entered upon it is not given, but under date May 11, 1853, he wrote—"Sixteen pages remain to finish the translation of the Old Testament into Fijian." Ten days later he wrote—"There remain forty-six verses of the Old Testament to be translated. These I expect will be done before you receive this letter, so that if you think it worthy of note, you may note that on the 23rd of May 1853 the translation of the entire Scriptures of the Old and New Testament into the Fijian language was completed. I have nevertheless a few words noted which require attention, and I should be very sorry to have less than a year or two for revision, but I feel as though I were losing a burden. This is the day I have long desired to see, and thank God, I see it. To Him alone be the glory." Mr. Hazlewood's wish to be spared to revise his translation was repeated in another letter, and the reason he assigned for this wish was that he had accumulated considerable material towards revision which no one could use so well as himself. In connection with the completion of the translation of the Old Testament, Mr. Williams mentions what he designates as "another generous act of the British and Foreign Bible Society, a grant of one hundred reams of paper to facilitate the printing of the Old Testament."

In the course of 1853 declining health compelled Mr. Hazlewood to leave the mission field. He retired to New South Wales, and after remaining a short time at Parramatta, he settled at West Maitland, and there he was permitted to carry out his cherished wish. He revised the entire Bible, and had proceeded with a second revision as far as the fifth chapter of Zechariah, when he was called to lay down his pen and rest from his labours. Happy man! "Blessed is that servant whom his Lord, when He cometh, shall find so doing." "Like the heroic martyr Tyndale," Mr. Williams remarks, "he worked at the task to which he had devoted his life face to face with death, his companions being his Hebrew Bible, Hebrew Grammar, and Dictionary, and laid down his pen to die. Shortly after his death an agent of the Bible Society stated at an annual meeting held in Victoria, that a few days previously he had seen the last page of MS. revised by Mr. Hazlewood, and on it was the impress of his hand made by the enfeebling perspiration from it—the augmenter of his weakness and the harbinger of his dissolution." Mr. Hazlewood passed to his rest and reward on the 30th of October 1855, in his thirty-sixth year. He was about the same age as John Hunt. Their lives were short as numbered by years, but they were crowned with faithful earnest work, which will live and yield precious fruit to the latest generations. Referring to Messrs. Hazlewood and Hunt, Mr. Williams remarks:—"These two names to the end of time must take foremost rank in relation to Bible translation in Fiji. To their united sanctified labours is mainly due a version of the Scriptures that the Fijian can love and revere."

The Bible Society's edition of the New Testament, received in the islands in 1854, gave great satisfaction both to the natives and the missionaries, and the latter were unanimous in their wish that the Old Testament should have the same advantage as it had had in being revised by the superintendent of the translating and editorial department of the Society; hence arrangements were made for securing this object. And in the meanwhile, to meet the pressing demand, 5000 copies each of Genesis, Exodus, and the Psalms were printed at the mission press; and an application was made to the Bible Society, which met with a ready response, to undertake the printing of an edition of the complete Bible.

The Rev. James Calvert was proceeding to England after an absence of eighteen years, and under his superintendence an edition of 5000 Bibles and 10,000 New Testaments was printed. But in the meanwhile, to meet the earnest cravings of the Fijian converts for divine truth, the Committee of the Bible Society ordered an edition of 5000 copies of the New Testament to be printed and forwarded at once to the islands.

In June 1856 Mr. Calvert arrived in England with Mr. Hazlewood's translation of the Old Testament. Towards the expense incurred in the preparation of the work the Committee of the Bible Society voted the sum of £500, and £400 for the support of Mr. Calvert for two years while engaged in assisting to revise and correct the manuscript under the superintendence of the late Rev. T. W. Meller of Woodbridge.

In the Report of the Bible Society for 1857 the commencement of the work is thus noted:—"The arrival in this country of the Rev. James Calvert has enabled the Committee to take the necessary steps for giving effect to a resolution some time since adopted which authorised the printing of a revised edition of the Fijian Scriptures. The entire Bible is translated and has received the best energies and laborious toil of the devoted missionaries of the Wesleyan Church. The work is being carefully passed through the press under the joint supervision of the Rev. Mr. Calvert and the editorial superintendent.

From a later Report of the Society—that for 1863—we learn that the work of printing had been interrupted for a time. "The Committee," the Report states, "have resumed the printing of the Fiji Bible from the point at which the work was relinquished by the Rev. James Calvert, who was under the necessity of returning to the islands before the completion of his editorial labours. The unfinished portion of the text from Job to Malachi has been placed by the Wesleyan Missionary Society in the hands of the Rev. R. B. Lyth, who is versed in the language, and has after careful examination prepared the entire MS., and will, with the aid of the Rev. T. W. Meller, editorially superintend the printing."

In the meanwhile the desire of the Fiji Christians to possess the Scriptures seems to have been insatiable. Mr. Calvert wrote about this time (1863) as follows:—"The 4000 copies of the New Testament are nearly all bought up, and the demand is constant. The supply will be exhausted long before we can have more sent out. Will you please complete the 10,000 copies, and send them out as soon as possible."

At length the great work was completed. In the Report of the Society for 1865 the fact is thus stated:— "The Committee can at length announce the completion of the entire Bible in the language of Fiji, a work upon the preparation of which a vast amount of care and anxious study have been expended."

The first instalment of the precious treasure was forwarded to the islands without delay, and the testimonies of the missionaries as to the reception given to it by the natives are in the highest degree interesting, as showing what a marvellous work of grace had been wrought among the Fijians. The Rev. Joseph Nettleton, tutor of one of the theological institutions, gives the following touching incident:—"Paul Vea, who has been a most successful pioneer preacher and pastor for thirty years, has been with us four weeks afflicted with palsy. He was near death. I gave a copy of the whole Bible into his hand to look at it before he died, and kissing it, he said, 'Lord, now lettest

Thou Thy servant depart in peace, according to Thy word.'"

The Rev. F. Tait wrote—"On the 5th of December 1864 I saw the first copy of the entire Scriptures in Fijian. I intend to keep that copy as mine for ever. Great was our joy and that of the natives. On the following day I went to Bau to preach, and never shall I forget the joy and excitement of the teachers when they knew that I had arrived, and that I had with me a copy of the Holy Scriptures. They left their work in the town and ran up the hill to the mission house to see it. Oh! how their eyes sparkled with unmistakable pleasure. Old Joel Bulu, the most laborious and eminent of all our native missionaries, and now nearly worn out in the service, snatched it from my hand, and placing it upon his head in token of the highest respect, his eyes beaming with pleasure and excitement, said, 'How blessed are our eyes that see this glorious sight!'"

Another missionary, the Rev. Mr. Langham, wrote— "How the natives rejoiced at the sight of the complete Bible! On receiving them, being greatly excited myself, I walked through Bau with a copy. I took it to the school, and the king's house, followed by a troop of youngsters, who shouted as we went along, 'Here is the Bible complete! Look at it! look at it!' On showing it to the king he asked if we had plenty. I told him we had sufficient for all the preachers in Fiji. 'But,' said he, 'what about us chiefs who can read, and wish to have the whole book, can we not get a copy?' When I told him he should have one, he was satisfied."

In 1866 Mr. Calvert again visited England, and on his departure from Fiji, the following resolution was adopted by the District Meeting:—"That all documents with respect to the late revision of the Scriptures be placed in the hands of the Rev. James Calvert, and that he be requested to get the New Testament reprinted as soon as possible." Mr. Calvert reached England in due course, and applied, as instructed, to the Bible Society, and the Committee at once agreed to the request of the District Meeting, which was that 3500 copies of the New Testament in octavo, longprimer, should be printed, and 3000 in a different type and style of binding.

In the meanwhile the Scriptures were not only being bought and read in Fiji, but they were proving the power of God unto salvation to many—bringing poor benighted souls out of darkness into light, from death to life. The following testimony from the Rev. J. Horsely, one of the missionaries, is intensely interesting:—"In 1865 it fell to my lot to examine twenty-eight young men who were recommended by our native ministers as candidates for the office of local preachers. While listening to the accounts of their conversion, I was struck with the oft-repeated mention of the New Testament as having been the only means used by the Holy Spirit to convince them of their danger and lead them to 'the Lamb of God who taketh away the sin of the world.' Since that time I have carefully noted such cases whilst engaged in my missionary labours. From conversations, examinations, and written documents I have ascertained that more than two-thirds of our two hundred catechists, lay-preachers, and schoolmasters have been aroused to a sense of their danger whilst living in sin and have afterwards obtained peace solely through the reading of their Testaments, without having received any counsel, admonition, or spiritual instruction from any one. And when it is remembered," Mr. Horsely adds, "that we have 4260 in society with us in this circuit alone, and 432 upon trial, what a blessed fact is here brought out to the glory of God!"

Mr. Horsely gives a number of illustrative cases which want of space compels us to omit. "Many of these men," he remarks, "were wild degraded cannibals, but they have been transformed by the power of God attending the quiet perusal of His Word; and where in the wide world can there be found a more astonishing transformation? Here is not only a miracle, but a miracle of power to prove the divinity of the Scriptures; these once bloodthirsty cannibals are made meet to be partakers of the inheritance of the saints in light."

The printing of the edition of the New Testament referred to above appears to have been completed and an instalment forwarded to the islands in 1869. Further supplies followed, and the demand continued year after year, and the influence exerted upon the natives was deepened and extended as time went on.

In the Bible Society's Report for 1872, a very valuable and interesting letter is given from the Rev. Lorimer Fison, from which we can only find space for a single extract. It relates to the closing scene in the life of a singularly exemplary Christian, and is as follows:—

"I should like to tell you more about this simple-hearted Christian man, for I loved him, and it does me good to think about him, and talk about him; but if I should begin to tell you his history, I should have to tell it all, and it is both long and wonderful: therefore I give this only as to the end of it. When he lay dying, the teacher in charge of his island asked him whether he were going to heaven? 'William,' said he, 'where else should I go? Have I not been going thitherwards throughout all these years? And do you think that now I am standing before the gates of the City, I am going to turn aside to the right hand or to the left? No, William, I shall enter in through the gates into the midst of the City.' And when he had spoken these and other good words, not forgetting a farewell word to the missionary whom he loved, and who loved him so well, he went through the gate into the midst of the City." Blessed scene, and blessed gospel which can accomplish such wonders!

In successive numbers of the Annual Report of the Bible Society, we find notes of large sums of money, £200 at one time, £300 at another, and so on, remitted on behalf of the Fiji mission. It would be tedious to notice these remittances particularly. We may remark once for all, that the reader may safely conclude that as in the case of Tonga, Samoa, and other groups, the entire amount expended by the Society in printing and publishing the Fijian Scriptures will be refunded by the grateful Fijians.

Year after year the demand continued unabated. In the Report of the Bible Society for 1881, the Rev. A. J. Webb, in a letter to the Committee, wrote as follows:—" Your last consignment of New Testaments has all disappeared, being bought up as soon as the cases were opened. The demand in fact for Testaments seems never to cease. Scarcely a day passes here at Levuka without one or more applicants for the Word of God. From the provinces the demand is large; incessant are the applications for Testaments. Planters apply for them on behalf of Fijians who work for them, and stipulate that part of their pay shall be in that form. A planter who openly vaunts his disbelief in God, the Bible, and a future life, wrote for a Bible for one of his Fijian labourers, and afterwards offered to receive a number of copies, and supply the natives with them. I have known scores of children go to work for the settlers in squads in anticipation of the arrival in their district of a case of Testaments. When it was landed, the young folk came in files with their money in their hands, and the case was soon emptied."

Mr. Webb goes on to remark that the Fijians not only possess themselves of the Word of God, but read and prize it. The matron of the hospital, he says, has on more than one occasion remarked to me " how much the Fijian patients read the Word; they are a people of one book." He mentions also a visit made to the gaol. No white prisoner wished to see him, so he went to the Fijians. They had no intimation of his visit, so it was the more gratifying to find several of them sitting with the Bible open near them. He was warmly welcomed, and conducted a service with them, into which they entered with great apparent heartiness. A half-caste warder said to him that he was in the habit of talking with the Fijian prisoners, and found much religious feeling amongst them.

In the Report of the Bible Society for 1883, we find the following intimation:—"At the request of the missionaries, conveyed through the Wesleyan Missionary Society by Mr. Calvert, your Committee have agreed to reprint the Bible of 1864–66, it being thought that a revision of the text is at present premature." This was carried into effect without delay, and in the Report for 1885 the missionaries acknowledge the receipt of a large consignment, adding, that this much-needed supply will shortly be disposed of, and begging for an edition of 5000 copies to be at once printed. This request was also promptly complied with.

Mr. Williams supplies a few facts illustrative of the knowledge and appreciation of the Word of God by the Fijians:—" One native agent" (teacher or pastor, I suppose) "writing respecting another, recently dead, describes him thus: 'Even as the man spoken of in the first Psalm, whose delight is in the law of the Lord, and in His law doth he meditate day and night. Such a one was Daniel Tofale. He was constant in prayer, and in thinking of the Holy Book, whence his sermons were full of faith and fire.'"

"A student in the Training Institution, James Havea by name, was asked by his companions to prepare a paper on the evils of strong drink. He did so, justifying his statements by the following strikingly apt quotations —Eph. v. 18; Isa. v. 11; xxxiii. 7, 8; Gal. v. 21; 1 Cor. vi. 10; Luke xxi. 34; Prov. xxxi. 4, 5—evincing his acquaintance with his Bible and the correctness of his judgment by the appropriateness of his selections; and he had no Fijian Cruden to assist him."

Another case which Mr. Williams gives is that of a young man whom he visited on his death-bed. He found him reading his New Testament. "What part are you reading?" he inquired. "The 32nd verse of the 8th chapter of Romans," he replied. Mr. Williams asked, "What he supposed the 'all things' mentioned in the verse comprised." He replied, "The lesser gifts now needed by myself—patience in my affliction, and grace to support me to the end of it." He went on to say, "I have peace with God, my mind dwells on Him for whose sake I have this peace. His Word is more to me than my food. I like to meditate upon it; it is very sweet." Four days after this conversation the young man died. Mr. Williams was with him at the time of his death, and made a remark to the effect that he was near his end. To this he replied, "Near my rest, sir;" "and into his rest he calmly entered with the praises of God upon his lips."

The dying testimony of an old man to Mr. Williams as he lay on the brink of eternity was—"I am old and weak; my time to die is come, but I am not afraid of death; through Jesus I feel courageous to die. His word is my food. I think upon it and lean entirely on Him."

Another aged man on the eve of his departure said— "To-day I shall look with mine eyes on the things which I believed though I saw them not; now I am going to possess them."

Mr. Williams furnishes some very interesting particulars relative to the later years of Thakambau, the late king of Fiji, a man whose name will be prominent in Fijian history in all time to come. He was beset with trials towards the close of his life, and happily his afflictions appear to have been instrumental in leading him to turn to God, and seek in Him a friend who never faileth those who put their trust in Him. He chose as his companion a poor blind lad named Shem. When he was free from business engagements he would say, "Now, Shem, I am disengaged; let us retire, that we may hear what the Lord will speak." The king was the reader, and poor blind Shem the expositor; and when they came upon truths which he was unable to explain, the king would say, "Well, Shem, though we don't understand this we can believe it, for it is God who speaks, and His word is truth." With reference to this scene, Mr. Williams remarks—"With a knowledge of Thakambau from 1841 to the time of his death, I know of no scene so deserving of the artist's pencil as the warrior king and his blind mentor in that humble oratory on the isle of Mbau."

In concluding his paper, Mr. Williams speaks strongly as to the importance of vigorously following up the labours of past years by keeping an adequate staff of European missionaries in the field, and taking care that the demand for the sacred Scriptures is fully met. "In certain directions," he remarks, "the dangers to which native Christians are exposed are seriously increased by Fiji becoming a Crown colony. At no previous period of the mission's history has the duty of supplying the Bible and efficient Bible instructors been more urgent than at the present. The native agents are as bravely resolute to prosecute the work as ever they were before, but enemies of whom they had no thought and of whose subtilities they were ignorant are appearing in the field, and they have not the ability to oppose them effectively. Supply therefore the help the native churches need by the supervision of European missionaries, and the printed word, FOR IT IS THEIR LIFE."

In September 1885, a deputation representing the Wesleyan Church in New South Wales, Victoria, and New Zealand, went to Fiji to take part in the celebration of the jubilee of the mission. The deputation consisted of the Rev. Thomas Williams of Victoria, the senior member of the party; the Rev. Dr. Kelynack of Sydney, New South Wales; and the Rev. Alexander Reid of the Three Kings' Institution, New Zealand. On his return to Sydney, Dr. Kelynack reported that the triumphs of the Gospel as seen in the islands "was simply marvellous, and that it would delight every lover of the Bible to see how the precious book is prized;" and Mr. Williams supplies the following testimony:—"At the jubilee and other services held during my three months' sojourn, renewing my acquaintance with old friends and old scenes, many opportunities were afforded of hearing native ministers, students, and other agents preach and address public meetings; and in simple justice to those whom I heard I must record the pleasure derived as I noted their extensive knowledge of Scripture, and the appropriateness of passages quoted readily and accurately, the chapter and verse of each being given with as much ease as the name of the book in which they occurred."

From the Report of the mission for 1887, we copy the following figures. At the date of that Report there were in the field 10 European missionaries, 55 native ministers, 987 teachers in charge of districts, 2526 school teachers, 1910 local preachers; in full membership, 27,097; on trial, 4264; Sabbath schools, 1425, and teachers, 2679, with 42,041 scholars; day schools, 1765, with 40,718 scholars; and attendants on public worship numbered 101,150. And in the balance-sheet of the Report, read on the 24th of January 1887, we find the Fiji auxiliary credited with the large sum of £3324, 3s. 10d.

And now in closing our account of Bible translation and

circulation in Fiji, we are at a loss for words to express the feelings which arise in the mind in view of the marvellous work that has been accomplished in that group. Comparing the Fiji of to-day with the Fiji of fifty years ago—what a contrast do we behold! The lion changed into the lamb, the vulture to the dove—we might almost say incarnate demons changed into sons and daughters of the Lord Almighty. And by what mighty instrumentality has this most marvellous change been wrought? Two plain men—just average missionaries—led the way, and commenced an assault against this veriest stronghold of Satan, and with no other weapons than those which the Gospel supplies. What a wild project it seemed to the eye of sense!—how tremendous the odds against them; yet they conquered, for the Lord of Hosts was with them. The struggle indeed was long and fierce, and terrible were the trials through which the honoured men and women who from time to time joined the mission were called to endure, but by God's grace they were enabled to stand fast and quit themselves as heroes and heroines in the holy cause. They were indeed men and women of the loftiest type of Christian consecration, and to them the Church of God owes a large debt of gratitude; still they were only instruments, and sure we are that they would be foremost in ascribing all the praise to the Great Conqueror. He made them what they were, He sustained them during the conflict, and He gave them the victory. It is meet and right therefore that He should bear the glory.

May His presence and blessing be vouchsafed in continually increasing measure to those who remain in the field. There is still a struggle to maintain, a warfare to wage, but with His effectual help, guaranteed by His great promise, "Lo, I am with you alway," there is nothing to fear. So we take our leave of Fiji, gratefully and hopefully. God bless Fiji!

CHAPTER VII.

ROTUMA.

ROTUMA is a small isolated spot occupying a central position in the South Pacific Ocean. It lies in south latitude about 12°, and is about 300 miles to the north of Fiji. It is a beautiful little island about twenty miles in circumference, and having a population estimated at 3000. It is of volcanic origin, and it is rich in all the productions common to such islands in the Pacific.

The natives are a fine race, not surpassed, I think, in any part of Polynesia. They trace their origin to Samoa. Their tradition is that on a certain day, a god, whom they call Raho, with his wife Koa, came from Samoa to the spot on which the island stands walking on the water. Raho had a basket of earth which he commenced scattering about, and all at once the island sprang up, and on it they took up their permanent abode.* It seems altogether probable that their ancestors did come from Samoa. A party of Samoans losing their way at sea, near their own group, would be very likely to make the island, as the south-east trade winds, which blow steadily during many months of the year, would carry them directly in its track. It is only about 600 miles distant from Samoa, and from 2° to 3° further to the north. There is one thing, however, that seems to cast a shade of doubt on the question of their origin—their language is not pure Eastern Polynesian.

* See Dr. Turner's "Nineteen Years in Polynesia," p. 358.

Throughout all the eastern and central groups there is one thing common to all the dialects spoken. There are no double consonants, every word and every syllable ends in a vowel, whereas on Rotuma this rule does not hold; but this may be accounted for by supposing that at some remote period a party from some other land may have been cast upon it, and become amalgamated with the descendants of the Samoans.

Christian teachers from Samoa were introduced to the island by John Williams while on his way to the New Hebrides in the brig *Camden*, in November 1839, and this was the last service but one that he was permitted to render to the cause of Christian missions.

In April 1845, the writer, in company with the Rev. Dr. Turner of the Samoan mission, made a visit to the island in the first *John Williams*. Our errand was to remove the teachers left by Mr. Williams, pursuant to an arrangement entered into by the directors of the London Missionary Society and the directors of the Wesleyan Missionary Society, and to pass over our interest and influence in the island to the agents of the Wesleyan Church, who had been placed on the island some time after the teachers of the London Missionary Society were introduced to it by Mr. Williams, and from that date it has been occupied by them in connection with the Fijian and Tongan missions, and all the Bible translation work that has been done on the island has been done by Wesleyan missionaries. A number of years passed before an English missionary was stationed on the island; but in 1857 the Rev. Joseph Waterhouse, with the assistance of a Fijian teacher named Eliezer, managed to translate the Gospel of Matthew, the 19th Psalm, and the 13th chapter of 1st Corinthians. These, with some other books, were printed at Hobart, Tasmania, and conveyed to the island by Eliezer, and no doubt were received with great joy by many among the natives.

At an earlier stage of the mission, the Rev. R. B. Lyth, of the Fiji mission, had, with the assistance of a native of the island, arranged an alphabet and translated a Scripture catechism on "Faith and Duty," and "Rules of Society," by the late Rev. John Hunt of the Fiji mission; and these seem to be all that the people had in print in their own tongue till they received the important addition above described. It is very likely that many of them may have learned to read from Tongan and Fijian books, and may have acquired a considerable knowledge of these languages from teachers from these groups who had been stationed among them. At the time of our visit we were surprised to find a number of them speaking the English language more correctly than any natives of Eastern Polynesia could have done. Many young men had made voyages in English and American ships, and on board these they had picked up the English language, and had learned a good deal besides of which it would have been better if they had remained ignorant.

In 1864, the Rev. William Fletcher, B.A., a cultured and scholarly man, who had laboured seven years in Fiji, was induced to leave his important sphere there, and with his devoted wife to remove to the comparatively unimportant and lonely island of Rotuma. Mr. and Mrs. Fletcher remained six years on the island. He translated the entire New Testament. The Gospel of Matthew indeed, as already mentioned, was in print before his arrival, but from the circumstances under which it was made, so many alterations and amendments would be required as would be almost equivalent to a fresh translation. In 1870 Mr. Fletcher came to Sydney, and carried his translation through the press at the expense of the British and Foreign Bible

Society. It was printed in a clear, good type, and well bound. The number printed was 2500, and it was sold to the natives at four shillings per copy, the proceeds of sales no doubt being remitted to the Bible Society.

Mr. and Mrs. Fletcher returned to the island in 1873, and remained for two years and a half, when failing health again compelled them to visit Sydney. Mr. Fletcher's health did not allow of his returning to the mission field. As long as he was able he laboured in different parts of Australia, but ultimately he succumbed to the disease from which he had long suffered. He died on the 30th of June 1881, in the fifty-second year of his age. His end was in perfect keeping with his character and life. He suffered much towards the close. "It was a long and weary time," an eye-witness testifies, "but he rejoiced in the hope set before him, and passed away in great peace."

In the Report of the British and Foreign Bible Society for 1886, it is stated that the Rev. James Calvert had revised and carried through the press a second edition of the Rotuman New Testament, which is now, I suppose, on sale in the island.

The above is all the information I am able to give relative to Bible translation on Rotuma. Something may have been done of late years towards giving the people some portions of the Old Testament in their own tongue, but that I can only conjecture. It is matter for thankfulness that they have the New Testament complete; and it is satisfactory to learn, from the Report of the Australian Wesleyan Missionary Society for the year ending March 1887, that the mission appears to be in a satisfactory state.

The Rev. W. Allen, the missionary now in charge of the mission, concludes his report for that year as follows:—"We believe we are correct in stating that in spiritual matters never were the prospects of the circuit brighter, never were the teachers and leaders more alive to their individual responsibility. As we take a retrospective view of the past, and think of God's dealings with us as a Church here, we would praise Him for past mercies, and look forward hopefully for greater blessings in the future."

CHAPTER VIII.

NEW ZEALAND.

The New Zealand mission is one of the oldest of our South Sea missions. It was only a few years after the *Duff* bore the pioneer band to Tahiti and Tonga (in 1797) that the Rev. Samuel Marsden conceived the idea of introducing Christianity among the savage cannibals of New Zealand. Mr. Marsden was singularly adapted for carrying into effect the great undertaking, and from his position as chaplain to the convict settlement of New South Wales he had peculiar facilities at his command. He was animated by a noble missionary zeal which nothing could damp, and a faith in God which nothing could shake. He had only to be satisfied that God was calling him to a particular course, and he was prepared to follow that course, whatever self-denial it might involve, and whatever danger he might have to encounter. Well indeed is he entitled to the honourable designation which by common consent has been accorded to him, the "Apostle of New Zealand."

In the month of August 1793, Mr. and Mrs. Marsden sailed from England in a ship carrying convicts to New South Wales, and on the 1st of January 1794 they reached their destination. In 1808 Mr. Marsden visited England on business connected with his official relation to the then young colony in which he occupied so important and responsible a position; and during his stay he conferred with the directors of the Church Missionary Society with reference to the question of making an attempt to introduce Christianity among the then little known aboriginal inhabitants of New Zealand, and he succeeded in inducing them to unite with him in making the attempt; and in August 1810 he sailed from England on his return voyage to Australia, accompanied by two artisans, William Hall and John King. They were followed soon after by Mr. Thomas Kendall, a schoolmaster, and he and Messrs. Hall and King became the pioneers of the New Zealand mission. Clergymen could not be obtained at that time, and perhaps Mr. Marsden may have regretted this the less as he had an idea that savages must be civilised in a measure before they can be Christianised. This notion was entertained by many in those early days, but it has been proved to be utterly erroneous by the experience of nearly a century, and Mr. Marsden himself held a different opinion in later years. To a gentleman who was advocating the view he originally held, he replied:—"Civilisation is not necessary before Christianity, sir; do both together if you will, but you will find civilisation follow Christianity easier than Christianity follow civilisation. Tell a poor heathen of his true God and Saviour, point him to the works he can see with his own eyes, for these heathen are no fools, sir—great mistake to send illiterate men to them. They don't want men learned after the fashion of this world, but men taught in the spirit and letter of the Scripture. I shan't live to see it, sir, but I may hear of it in heaven, that New Zealand, with all its cannibalism and idolatry, will yet set an example of Christianity to some of the nations before her in civilisation." *

It was not till the year 1814 that Mr. Marsden succeeded

---

* It was to Bishop Broughton that these sentiments were uttered by Mr. Marsden a short time before his death.

in overcoming the difficulties he had to encounter in carrying out his great undertaking. It was regarded by the Governor of the colony and all the Government officials as rash and hazardous in the highest degree, indeed as little short of madness. Mr. Marsden's intention was to accompany the missionaries himself, and share with them the first dangers, and lay as it were the first stone. But this the Governor absolutely forbade; and being an agent of the Government, he could not leave the colony without the Governor's permission. "Nor indeed," remarks the author of Mr. Marsden's life, " were the Governor's objections altogether without foundation. The last news from New Zealand was that an English ship, the *Boyd*, had been seized and burned by the cannibals in the Bay of Islands, and every soul on board, seventy in all, killed and eaten. The report was true, save only that out of the whole ship's company two women and a boy had been spared to live in slavery among the savages." It was afterwards ascertained that a New Zealand chief had sailed on board the ship, and had been treated with brutal indignities, and on her return to the Bay of Islands he took his revenge in the above dreadful fashion.

All the concession that Mr. Marsden could obtain from the Governor at that time was permission to charter a vessel, if a captain could be found sufficiently courageous to risk his life and his ship in such an enterprise, and to send out the three missionaries as pioneers; with a reluctant promise that if on the ship's return all had turned out well, he should not be hindered from following. For some time no such adventurous captain could be found. At length, for the sum of £600 for a single voyage, an offer was made, but Mr. Marsden looked upon the sum as far too much; and this, with other considerations, induced him to purchase his own missionary brig the *Active*, in which Messrs. Hall and Kendall finally set sail for the Bay of Islands.* They carried a message to a native of New Zealand named Duatera, a friend of Mr. Marsden, of whom we shall hear more as we proceed. He had been for some time with Mr. Marsden in New South Wales, and had been treated by him with great kindness after having suffered great indignities and hardship on board English ships in which he had sailed. On the arrival of the *Active* with the missionaries—the first messengers of Christ who landed on the shores of New Zealand—Duatera was there to welcome them, and to repay to the utmost of his power the kindness he had received from Mr. Marsden. Having by his help, and under the favouring providence of God, succeeded in making a favourable impression on the chiefs and people with whom they met, in obedience to their instructions, they returned to New South Wales accompanied by Duatera, and six other chiefs, among whom was Hongi, Duatera's uncle, who was said to be the most powerful chief in New Zealand. They reached New South Wales on the 22nd of August 1814.

The successful termination of the voyage filled Mr. Marsden with joy and thankfulness; and as he could now claim the Governor's permission, he determined to accompany the missionaries on their return to the Bay of Islands, and no time was lost in making arrangements for the voyage. "On the 19th of November 1814," says his biographer, "he embarked on his great mission with a motley crew, such as, except perhaps on some other missionary ship, has seldom sailed in one small vessel—savages, and Christian teachers, and enterprising mechanics, their wives and children, besides cattle and horses." Here is Mr. Marsden's own description:—"The number of persons on board the *Active*, including women and children, was thirty-five; the master, his wife and son, Messrs. Kendall, Hall,

---

* For fuller particulars see the Life of Mr. Marsden, p. 90, &c., by the Rev. J. B. Marsden, published by the London Tract Society.

and King, with their wives and children, eight New Zealanders (including Duatera, and his uncle, the great warrior Hongi), two Tahitians, and four Europeans belonging to the vessel, besides Mr. John Lydiard Nicholas and myself. There were also two sawyers, one smith, and a runaway convict whom we afterwards found on board, a horse and two mares, one bull and two cows, with a few sheep and poultry, the bull and cows having been presented by Governor Macquarie from His Majesty's herd."

On the 18th of December land was sighted; and on the following day the New Zealanders on board were sent on shore, and communications were opened with the natives. Mr. Marsden's fame as the friend of New Zealand had preceded him, so his name had only to be mentioned to secure confidence. The *Active* anchored in Wangaroa, near the Bay of Islands, where the massacre of the crew of the *Boyd* occurred; and there, among the very cannibals by whom their countrymen had so recently been murdered, the first Christian mission to New Zealand was established. A terrible revenge had been taken by the crew of an English ship, and an important chief and his family had been killed, who had not been in any way implicated in the affair of the *Boyd*, and this gave rise to a fierce war among the natives, which was raging at the very time when Mr. Marsden and his party arrived upon the scene.

Mr. Marsden determined to attempt to mediate between the hostile parties, and if possible to effect a reconciliation; and with this view he and his friend Mr. Nicholas visited both camps, giving them to understand that they went amongst them as the friends of both parties. The first night Mr. Marsden and his friend spent in New Zealand was passed in a war camp. We give his own account of that night's experience slightly abbreviated:—" About eleven o'clock at night Mr. Nicholas and I wrapped ourselves in our overcoats, and prepared for rest. George, a New Zealand interpreter, directed me to lie by his side. His wife and child lay on my right, and Mr. Nicholas close by. The night was clear, the stars shone bright, and the sea was smooth in our front; around us were innumerable spears stuck upright in the ground, and groups of natives lying in all directions, like a flock of sheep upon the grass, as there were neither tents nor huts to cover them. I viewed our present situation with sensations and feelings that I cannot express, surrounded as we were by cannibals who had massacred and devoured our countrymen. I did not sleep much during that night. About three o'clock in the morning I arose and walked about the camp surveying the different groups of natives. When the morning light returned we beheld men, women, and children asleep in all directions like the beasts of the field."

Mr. Marsden had ordered the boat to be sent on shore at daylight, and in the morning he invited the chiefs of both parties to breakfast on board the *Active*. The invitation was accepted, and an interview took place which has had far-reaching and most blessed results. He managed to effect a reconciliation between the chiefs of the hostile parties, thereby putting an end to the bloody war then raging, and inaugurating an era of comparative peace, which, though often disturbed in subsequent times, was yet the beginning of the end of native wars in New Zealand; and from that interview the New Zealand mission took definite shape. The members of the mission were introduced to the chiefs, the object of their settling among them and their people was explained, presents were given and accepted, and the chiefs were virtually pledged to befriend and protect the missionaries.

The Sabbath following these important proceedings was a day to be remembered in New Zealand history. No such day had dawned on that dark and savage shore since it became the abode of man. It was the 25th of December

1815. The best arrangements of which the circumstances allowed had been made for the celebration of divine service under the direction of Duatera, who having made several voyages to foreign lands—England among the rest—was able to turn the resources at his command to the best possible account. Among other arrangements he had a flagstaff erected on the highest hill in the neighbourhood; and when Mr. Marsden went on deck on the Sabbath morning, his patriotic feelings were aroused, and his mind filled with joyous anticipations of a grand future opening upon the then dark shores of New Zealand, as he saw the grand old British flag floating in the breeze. "I considered it," he says, "as the signal and the dawn of civilisation, liberty, and religion in this dark and benighted land. I never viewed the British colours with more gratification, and flattered myself they would never be removed till the natives of these islands enjoyed all the happiness of British subjects."

Such was Mr. Marsden's confidence in the natives that he left the vessel with only the master and one man on board while divine service was being conducted on shore. There was a great gathering; chiefs and common people—women and children—all ages and all ranks clustered around the rude pulpit and reading-desk which Duatera had managed to extemporise.

"A very solemn silence prevailed," says Mr. Marsden; "the sight was truly impressive. I rose and began the service with singing the Old Hundredth Psalm, and felt my very soul melted within me when I viewed my congregation and considered the state they were in." Mr. Marsden preached from the appropriate words, "Behold I bring you glad tidings of great joy." The natives complained to Duatera that they could not understand what was meant. He told them not to mind that now, as he would explain all to them afterwards to the best of his ability. "In this manner," Mr. Marsden adds, "the Gospel has been introduced to New Zealand, and I fervently pray that the glory of it may never depart from its inhabitants till time shall be no more."

Confidence was now completely established between Mr. Marsden and the natives, and the great object of his voyage was accomplished; his leave of absence was drawing to a close, so he must soon quit New Zealand for the present. Before doing so, however, he determined to make a short coasting voyage to explore different harbours, increase his knowledge of the country, and making arrangements for the future extension of the mission. Many of the chiefs wished to accompany him, and he consented to allow twenty-eight of these cannibal savages, fully armed according to their custom, to sail with him in his little vessel, on board of which there were only seven Europeans. Whether he acted wisely or not it is hard to say. However, all ended well. Mr. Marsden's trust in the natives was reciprocated by them, and his influence was increased in no small degree.

Before leaving he secured by purchase from the chiefs about two hundred acres of land on behalf of the Church Missionary Society on which to erect buildings, and for purposes of cultivation, &c., that the missionaries might not be liable to be driven off the place where they had settled. The land was secured by a deed properly executed in legal form, and attested by witnesses.

All the necessary arrangements were now completed for the commencement of the practical work of the mission, and Mr. Marsden took leave of the missionaries and their families and his native friends, and started on his return voyage accompanied by no less than ten chiefs. Sydney was reached in safety on the 23rd of March 1815. Mr. Marsden and his friend Mr. Nicholas lost no time in presenting themselves to the Governor, who congratulated them on their safe return from what, in common with the whole colony, he had regarded as a most perilous and rash adventure.

And now having seen the great undertaking inaugurated, the foundation of the mission laid, we must confine ourselves to a very brief and general view of its subsequent history. Mr. Marsden continued to watch over it with intense solicitude to the very close of his life. He made no less than seven visits at longer or shorter intervals, and during some of these he remained for months labouring in season and out of season for its consolidation and extension.

Mr. Kendall commenced a school as soon as his knowledge of the language allowed, and got a number of children under instruction. He prepared a spelling-book, which was printed in Sydney, the first thing no doubt ever printed in the New Zealand dialect, which belongs to the same root as all the languages spoken throughout Eastern and Central Polynesia. Mr. Kendall also collected materials for a grammar and vocabulary, which were afterwards arranged with the assistance of Professor Lee of Cambridge, and printed in England.*

In 1819 the Rev. John Butler, and Messrs. Francis Hall and James Kemp, joined the mission. Mr. Hall was a schoolmaster, and Mr. Kemp a blacksmith. I cannot find any notice to that effect in Mr. Marsden's Life, but, according to Dr. Brown, this reinforcement accompanied Mr. Marsden to New Zealand on his second voyage. The date of Mr. Marsden's sailing from New South Wales on that voyage is not given in his Memoir, but we find him in New Zealand in the month of August 1819, and on that occasion he remained three months, and during that time he travelled over seven hundred miles exploring the country, and mingling with the people, with the view of more extended operations among them.

* See Dr. Brown's History of Missions, vol. ii. p. 271.

Referring to this journey, Mr. Hall writes:—"There is not one in ten thousand I think who could or would have borne the privations, difficulties, and dangers which he underwent. I pray that he may reap the fruits of his labours by the New Zealanders turning from their degraded state to serve the only living and true God." Mr. Marsden did endure hardness and brave dangers of no ordinary kind during his journeyings among the fierce savages of New Zealand on this occasion. He went among them with no human protection or means of defence, sleeping in their huts, and sometimes not having even a hut to shelter him. In one of his journeys he and his party were travelling over an open plain, far from human habitations: night was coming on, and a storm was threatening. Before them at a long distance was the bush, a thick dense forest. They pushed on with all their might to reach that if possible before the storm should burst, and obtain such shelter as it might afford. About nine o'clock at night they got to the wood; the natives cut branches of ferns and boughs of trees, and made a little shelter from the wind, and from the rain, which had now begun to fall heavily, and under these circumstances they passed the night. The remarks and musings of Mr. Marsden on the occasion are touching and interesting. "The blackness of the heavens," he remarks, "the gloomy darkness of the wood, the roaring of the wind among the trees, the sound of the rain falling on the thick foliage, united with the idea that we were literally at the ends of the earth with relation to our native land, surrounded with cannibals whom we knew to have fed on human flesh, and wholly in their power, and yet our minds free from fear of danger—all this excited in my breast such new, pleasing, and, at the same time, opposite sensations as I cannot describe.

"While I sat musing under the shelter of a lofty pine, my thoughts were lost in wonder and surprise in taking a view of the wisdom and goodness of God's providential care which had attended all my steps to that very hour. If busy imagination inquired what I did there, I had no answer to seek in wild conjecture. I felt with gratitude that I had not come by chance, but had been sent to labour in preparing the way of the Lord in this dreary wilderness, where the voice of joy and gladness had never been heard; and I could not but anticipate with joyful hope the period when the 'Day-star from on high' would dawn and shine on this dark and heathen land, and cause the very earth on which we then reposed to bring forth its increase, when God Himself would give the poor inhabitants His blessing. After reflecting on the different ideas which crowded themselves upon my mind, I wrapped myself up in my great-coat, and lay down to sleep."

Mr. Marsden had many very singular and curious experiences during his journeyings on this occasion which we must pass over. They are recorded in full in his Life. (See p. 132 and onwards.)

Many and great were the vicissitudes through which the mission passed in subsequent years. It was reinforced from time to time from England, and the missionaries continued their labours amid all the changes that occurred. They passed through dreadfully trying scenes, and encountered appalling dangers, yet they plodded on, their greatest trial being that for a long time they seemed to labour and suffer in vain in as far as the main end of their mission was concerned. At length, however, after weary years of suffering and toil, the reaping time came.

At a very early period in the history of the mission the Wesleyan Church took up a position in New Zealand. "The Rev. Samuel Leigh, a man whose history and natural character bore a marked resemblance to those of Mr. Marsden, was the pioneer of Methodism, and proved himself a worthy herald of the cross amongst the New

Zealanders. A warm friendship existed between the two. On his passage homewards he was a guest at Parramatta; and no tinge of jealousy ever appears to have shaded their intercourse, each rejoicing in the triumphs of the other."*

Like the respective pioneers of the two churches, those who from time to time were their associates or successors seem to have worked harmoniously together during all the early years of the mission's history, the representatives of each church aiming to advance the one common object of their mission.

In connection with Mr. Marsden's fifth visit to New Zealand in 1827, we find the first notice of Bible translation in the mission. Whether the notion that civilisation must precede conversion had any influence in inducing the missionaries to delay the translation of the Scriptures into the vernacular I am unable to say, but as a matter of fact I find no record of anything having been accomplished in that direction till the above-named date (1827). The following extract from the Life of Mr. Marsden shows the state in which he found the mission at that time, and informs us of what his biographer calls the "small beginnings" in the way of giving to the New Zealanders the Word of Life in their own tongue. He writes as follows:—
"He found the missionaries living together in unity and love, and devoting themselves to their work. 'I trust,' he says, 'that the Great Head of the Church will bless their labours.'

"In consequence of his co-operation with the missionaries, the beneficial labours of the press now for the first time reached the Maori tribes. During a visit to Sydney, Mr. Davis carried through the press a translation of the first three chapters of Genesis, the twentieth of Exodus, part of the fifth of Matthew, the first of John, and some hymns. These were small beginnings, but not to be

* See Life of Mr. Marsden, p. 54.

despised; they prepared the way for the translation of the New Testament, which was printed a few years afterwards at the expense of the British and Foreign Bible Society. The importance of this work can scarcely be estimated, and it affords a striking example of the way in which that noble institution becomes the silent handmaid, preparing the rich repast which our various missionary societies are evermore distributing abroad with bounteous hand to feed the starving myriads of the heathen world."

The New Testament was printed in 1837. The first edition, Dr. Brown tells us, consisted of 5000 copies, but such was the eagerness of the natives to possess the Book that it was soon exhausted, and in response to an application to the Bible Society a second edition was printed of no fewer than 20,000, which were equally divided between the missionaries of the Church Missionary Society and those of the Wesleyan Church; but even this large supply proved quite unequal to the demand, and in the course of a few years other two editions of 20,000 each were printed and sent out to New Zealand. The desire for copies was not confined to such of the natives as were able to read. Many who could not read were no less anxious to obtain them, either that they might have them read to them, or that they themselves might learn to read. Many copies were distributed gratuitously, others were paid for by the natives, who in many cases brought contributions of food and other produce in return. A translation of the Old Testament into the language of New Zealand was also carrying on at this time by the Rev. R. Maunsell, and part of it was printed.*

As regards the translation of the New Testament, the authorities to which I have access simply state that it was effected by the missionaries. The Report of the Bible Society for 1857 states that the Rev. R. Maunsell took

* See Dr. Brown's History of Missions, pp. 382-3.

part in the revision of the New Testament, and that he translated the entire Old Testament. Mr. Maunsell seems to have felt specially drawn towards this department of missionary work, and to have possessed special qualifications for it.

On the completion of his great undertaking, he wrote as follows to the Committee of the British and Foreign Bible Society:—

"The whole Word of God is now in Maori, and you, I dare say, can imagine the feelings with which I regard the completion, so far, of my labours. I have through God's great goodness been now spared to assist in the revision of the New Testament and Prayer-book, and to finish an original translation of the Old Testament. . . . The feeling has always been strong on my mind that God has called me to be useful in this particular service. Even when in England I longed, from reading Martyn's life, to render some service in the translation of God's Word, and commenced studying Hebrew, and laying in a stock of books on criticism. Whatever portion of my life may now remain, it is my earnest desire and prayer that I may have grace to give it entirely to Him."

In compliance with suggestions from the Committee of the Auckland Auxiliary Bible Society, "That a Committee of final revision be appointed by the recognised local authorities of the Church and Wesleyan Missionary Societies," the following missionaries were chosen for the important work, viz., on behalf of the Church Mission, the Rev. R. Maunsell, translator; Archdeacon Williams; and the Rev. G. A. Kipling. On behalf of the Wesleyan Mission, the Rev. T. Buddle, Rev. John Hobbs, and the Rev. Alexander Reid.

In the meanwhile the Old Testament had been printed in separate parts, and these were in circulation among the natives; and in due time the Revision Committee completed their work, and the way was clear for the printing and publishing of the entire Bible in one volume. The Committee state that they "had been blessed throughout their deliberations with a rich measure of harmony and concord. The Committee find much pleasure in stating that the translation is clear, concise, and faithful, even to admiration, while the translator himself has risen in their esteem by the impartial and noble spirit in which he has met their suggestions, and consented to what were thought improvements.

"The Committee cannot conclude their Report without their heartfelt thanks to Him who hath given us His Holy Word, who has enabled His servant to render it so faithfully and clearly into the Maori tongue, and who has been present with His blessing during the long sitting of this Committee, who have now finished their work. His holy name be praised."

The Committee began their work on the 17th of June 1857, and sat for about three months, five hours daily, except Saturdays.

The translation must have been subjected to further revision, as we find it stated in the Bible Society's Report for 1860 that the whole Bible in the New Zealand language had been printed, that the revision of certain books had not been completed at that date, and that on that account the printing of an entire and uniform edition of the Scriptures was being deferred, but that such an edition would be printed at no distant date. Accordingly we find in the Report for 1863 that the "Committee had cordially consented to prepare a complete Maori Bible in a single volume. Hitherto portions of the Old Testament have been printed as they were translated; but now that the whole is finished, the desire is strongly felt that both Testaments should be blended in one book. The text of a considerable part has undergone a careful revision at the hands of the most competent Maori scholars, and is being printed under the editorial care of Mr. Maunsell, son of the venerable Archdeacon Maunsell, assisted by the Rev. T. W. Meller. The work will occupy much time, as parts of the text are still being critically examined, with a view to improvement; but the supply of Scriptures in the country is adequate to meet all immediate wants."

In the Report for 1864 I find a very valuable letter from the Rev. C. S. Volckner, an extract from which will be read with interest. After speaking strongly as to the great desire of the people among whom he was labouring to possess the Scriptures, and of the difficulty they had in procuring them, he proceeds as follows:—

"A great many of these people are constantly exposed to the attacks of Papists; and the Scriptures are their strong weapon against them. The other day some natives expressed themselves thus to me—'When the Roman Catholic priests come, they say a great many things to us we do not know how to reply to, but they always are silenced and baffled when we use the Word of God in replying to them.' At another place I had a long conversation with a man who had lately been baptized by the Popish priest. I asked him why he had joined the Papists? 'Because I am an ignorant man, and do not know the Scriptures, as I cannot read. My friend at Maringa, Pohata, is a wise man; he knows how to read, and knows the Scriptures; the priests have tried again and again, much harder than with me, to make him a Papist, but in vain. In his place in the mountains he sometimes does not see the missionary the whole year, but he will never become a Papist, because he has the Scriptures, and knows how to read them. If I had not been foolish I would not have allowed the priest to baptize me.' A number of the people expressed their approbation, saying, 'You have just hit it: if any one has the Scriptures, and can read them, he will not become a Papist.'"

"I give," continues Mr. Volckner, "one more extract from my journal. Raniera, the teacher in a settlement in which the majority are Papists, was told by the Vicar-Apostolic when last there to become a Papist. Raniera answered, 'And are you a god to tell me what I ought to believe?' The Vicar replied, 'But there are so few, you are almost alone in this place.' Raniera said, 'If I were quite alone, and if all the people of this settlement became Papists, and if all the people of this island to the north and to the south, to the east and to the west, became Papists, and if there were not a Protestant missionary, minister, or bishop left in this land, I would not become a Papist, because I have the Word of God,' showing him the New Testament; 'this is my guide and my teacher, from it I know that you are wrong and I am right. It is the infallible Word of God. You may cut off my head, and strew my brains along the beach, but I will not become a Papist. I am a Protestant, be it known to you, and I shall remain one.'" A noble confession surely! The baffled priest shook his head and turned away from the obstinate heretic.

In the Bible Society's Report for 1869 we find the following announcement:—"It was stated in the last Report that the printing of the Maori Bible was advancing towards completion. The work had been suspended in consequence of the unavoidable delay in transmitting to this country the revised text of the New Testament. The volume is now issued from the press, and supplies have been forwarded to New Zealand. Great critical care and patient labour have been exercised in rendering this edition of the Scriptures in Maori as perfect as possible, and the most competent judges agree in the favourable verdict pronounced upon its idiomatic accuracy and fidelity to the sacred originals."

The Committee express their gratitude for valuable service rendered by the late Bishop Selwyn in correcting the proof sheets of the work when passing through the press; and add a prayer in which all lovers of the Bible will heartily join, "That the sacred volume might be received by the Maori race with docility and faith, and that, under the illuminating grace of the Holy Spirit, they might renounce the savage and idolatrous habits of their heathen state for the love, meekness, and purity of the Gospel of Christ."

With reference to the reception of this edition of the Scriptures by the New Zealanders, we find the following gratifying information in the Report of the Society for 1871. A communication had been received from the Committee of the New Zealand Auxiliary, in which special reference was made to the rapid sale of the Maori Bible. As soon as it was known that large supplies had arrived from England, the purchasers at the depôt became eager and numerous, showing great preference for the volumes in more costly bindings. It is thought more prudent to disseminate the copies by sale exclusively, and the circumstances of the people generally will enable them to comply with the condition, the price demanded being very moderate.

In the Report of the Bible Society for 1872 we find the following information:—"The enlarged facilities for the circulation of the Scriptures naturally leads the Committee to look forward to the time when a new edition of the Maori Bible will be needed, and as there are few men so well acquainted with the language as Archdeacon Maunsell, they have requested him both to undertake the task of revision and to prepare chapter headings in anticipation of that event. As some of those who were on the previous Revision Committee still survive, it is very desirable that this should be done whilst their critical knowledge and long study of the language under circumstances of greater advantages for its acquisition than young men now possess can be turned to good account.

And in the Report for 1879 the following important facts are recorded:—" During the twenty-one years following the formation of the colony in New Zealand, *i.e.*, between 1840 and 1861, the British and Foreign Bible Society printed no less than 120,000 copies of portions of the Holy Scriptures in the Maori language for circulation in New Zealand, at a cost of over £6000. A very large proportion of these were circulated by free gift. Subsequently an edition of 5000 copies of the entire Bible in Maori was published. A consignment was forwarded to the Local Auxiliary, and its Committee resolved to bring it into circulation by sale exclusively. As a result, 1538 copies of the complete Maori Bible, besides large numbers of Maori New Testaments, and other portions, have been purchased from the depôt by a people who previously protested that the Scriptures must be supplied to them, and the Gospel preached without money and without price."

The revision was undertaken by Archdeacons Maunsell and W. L. Williams as requested, and in 1866 we are informed that the printing of the Maori Bible as revised by Archdeacons Maunsell and Williams was progressing; and that is the last item of intelligence we are able to give relative to the translation and circulation of the sacred Scriptures in connection with the New Zealand mission.

We are sorry to be unable to speak so strongly with reference to the success of mission work and Bible circulation among the Maoris as we have felt warranted in doing with reference to other missions among kindred races in Eastern and Central Polynesia. As we have seen, men of apostolic zeal and martyr spirit have laboured for long years among the Maoris, and have given them, at the cost of a vast amount of toil, a complete version of the Holy Scriptures in their own tongue, yet, so far as we can gather from all available sources of information, the results are comparatively disappointing. There is enough to show that what the Gospel has done for cannibal Fiji and other savage tribes it has done in a measure for the Maoris; but it does not appear that Christianity has laid hold of them as a whole and effected such a general revolution as it has done among the Fijians, Sandwich Islanders, and others. We know that there have been great difficulties to contend with in New Zealand, but such, in a measure, has been the case also in other groups.

It seems a very desirable thing that some one of the venerable fathers of the mission who still remain in the field should favour the Church with a history of the mission down to the present time, that those who are interested in the welfare of the native races might be in a position to form a judgment as to their state now, and their prospects for the future.

In the meanwhile may God bless them, and those who are labouring amongst them; and may the churches of New Zealand yet take their place among the foremost of the sister churches in the other islands and groups of the Pacific, to the glory of their Head, and the extension of His cause and kingdom among the native races of that great land.

WESTERN POLYNESIA—THE NEW HEBRIDES.

CHAPTER IX.

FOTUNA AND NIUA.

We come now to the great division of the islands of the Pacific known as Western Polynesia, of which the New Hebrides group is the most easterly. That group is now so well known that little need be said of it by way of general description. It is about 400 miles in length, extending in a north-westerly direction from about 20° to 15° south latitude, and it lies between 171° and 166° east longitude, about 1000 miles nearly due north of New Zealand, 400 miles west of Fiji, 200 miles east of New Caledonia, and about 1400 miles north-east of Sydney. There are about thirty islands in the group, nearly twenty of them being inhabited, and several of them are large and populous. The island of Fotuna is the most easterly of the group, and so comes first in geographical order; and the island of Niua, though considerably distant, has some things in common which makes it convenient to embrace the two in one chapter.

Fotuna lies in 19° 13′ south latitude, and 170° 13′ east longitude. It consists of one high bluff mountain which seems to rise abruptly out of the ocean, and from a distance it looks like a great barren rock. There are, however, narrow valleys and ravines in which are found fertile and habitable spots.

Captain Cook estimated the circumference of the island at fifteen miles, and when teachers were placed upon it in 1841 the population was about 900. Probably it does not much exceed half that number at the present time. The inhabitants are a mixed race, evidently sprung from two distinct stocks—the Papuan and the Malayan. This is clearly indicated by the language, and by the fact that the island has two names—the one, Eranan, connecting it with Western Polynesia; the other, Fotuna, as distinctly pointing to the eastern division of the great Polynesian family. We cannot tell particularly where the name Eranan comes from, but there is no difficulty with reference to the other. Fotuna is the name of Horne's Island, and there can be no reasonable doubt that one branch of the ancestors of the present inhabitants came from that island, and gave to their new home the name of the old one. Savage races as well as civilised in most parts of the world form strong attachments to the places and scenes where and amid which they have spent the morning of life; and in this respect they give expression to their attachments in the same way.

When Christianity was introduced to the island we were favourably impressed with the appearance of the people, and did not imagine that they were the fierce and cruel savages which they afterwards proved themselves to be. After their own teachers were landed, Samuela and Apela, from Samoa, one of the chiefs went with us to the neighbouring island of Aneiteum, and it seemed very much owing to his help that we succeeded in getting teachers received at that island. The affinity of the language to the Samoan enabled us to make some use of him as an interpreter, and he evidently used his influence to induce the chiefs and people of Aneiteum to receive the teachers, yet, sad to say, that though he lived many years he died a heathen; and about eighteen or twenty months after the teachers were left on the island, the infatuated people murdered the whole party, two men and one woman, and a little girl, the daughter of one of the teachers.

After this barbarous deed the dark night of heathenism again closed over Fotuna, and long years passed before the darkness was again broken. Not till 1853 did "the dayspring from on high" again visit the bloodstained shore. During the course of that year two natives of Aneiteum, who, with others of their countrymen, had in the meanwhile become decided followers of Christ, were conveyed to it in the *John Williams*, and met with a cordial welcome from part of the people. The two men, Waihit and Josefa, who undertook the self-denying, if not hazardous service, of making known the Gospel on the dark spot, deserve to have their names had in remembrance, as they were the first natives of Western Polynesia who went forth as pioneer Christian teachers to make known the Gospel to their countrymen.

A third teacher from Aneiteum, and one from the Hervey Islands, were added in 1859, and in 1866 the Rev. Joseph Copeland settled on the island. At that time the language had not been reduced to writing. This was accomplished in due time by Mr. Copeland; and a Primer, a Catechism, and a few Hymns were prepared by him, and printed on Aneiteum by the Rev. John Geddie. The first portion of Scripture which Mr. Copeland translated was the Gospel of Mark. This was printed in Sydney in 1869. The translating of the remaining Gospels followed, and the whole four were printed in Sydney, and bound in a volume together with a new edition of the Primer, Catechism, and Hymn-book, extending to 174 pages.

In January of 1876, Mrs. Copeland, a most estimable woman, was removed from the toils and trials of earth to the rest of heaven, and after a brief interval Mr. Copeland was compelled, owing to failure of health, to quit the mission field, and retire for rest and change to the more genial climate of Australia.

After an interval of a few years, Dr. Gunn and Mrs. Gunn, from the Free Church of Scotland, settled on the island, and the book of Genesis and the Acts of the Apostles, which had been translated by Mr. Copeland, have been retranslated by him, and partly revised by Mr. Copeland, who has recently made a visit to the island. "These," Mr. Copeland remarks, "will appear in whole or in part in the two volumes in which Dr. Gunn hopes to complete the Bible for the Fotunese. Owing to the smallness of the population, he thinks a selection of books the wisest course." That is all the information we have at present relative to Bible translation on this island. It has been a hard field to cultivate, and so far the returns have been small, considering the amount of labour expended upon it. Perhaps no island in the New Hebrides has suffered more cruel wrongs at the hands of masters and crews of the so-called labour vessels. It is in a great measure owing to the infamous conduct of these men in carrying off from time to time young men of fairest promise to virtual slavery, and not seldom to death, that the population has been so much reduced, and that the results of mission work on the island are so small. Now we may hope that the accursed traffic has received an effectual check, and that there will be little or no further molestation from that quarter.

Mr. Copeland speaks hopefully of what he witnessed during his late visit. He says, referring to the New Hebrides mission generally, it was a pleasure to him to mark the manifest progress of the work, and to ascertain the trend of public opinion; and no man is better qualified to form a judgment as to mission work in the New Hebrides than Mr. Copeland. Before settling on Fotuna he was stationed for longer or shorter periods on Tanna, and Eramanga, and Aneiteum, and did valuable work on all these, especially on Aneiteum.

NIUA.*

This island lies about fifteen miles to the north of Tanna. It is a low uninteresting looking spot, probably not more than ten miles in circumference, and at the time from which its missionary history dates its population was estimated at from 400 to 500. The natives are a mixed race like those of Fotuna. Like that island it has two names, Immer and Niua, the one connecting it with the Papuan races, the other with the Malayan.

Though so small and comparatively unimportant it has rather an eventful history. Two Samoan teachers were placed upon it by the Rev. Thomas Heath of the Samoan mission in 1840. These, and others who followed them, remained on the island for a number of years, but no visible impression was made upon the people, and troubles arose which led to the suspension of the mission. After a long interval it was resumed. Two teachers from Aneiteum were introduced to the island, and had an encouraging reception. Circumstances which we must not stop to particularise led to the murder of one of these, but the other held on bravely, and the place of him who had fallen was soon filled by another courageous man, also from Aneiteum, and the island was in a measure won to Christianity.

* Spelt Aniwa by the Presbyterian missionaries who now occupy the New Hebrides group.

About the year 1866 the Rev. J. G. Paton settled upon it, and the labours of himself and his devoted wife, aided by Aneiteum teachers, have been crowned with a large measure of success. This will amply appear from the following information which Mr. Paton has kindly furnished:—

"In the language of Aniwa I have translated and printed the following books of Scripture—Matthew and Mark. These were printed in Melbourne, and carried through the press by myself in 1877. The Acts of the Apostles were printed in Melbourne, and carried through the press by my two sons, who were at school there in 1880.

"The Gospel of John, First and Second Timothy, Titus, Philemon, James, the three Epistles of John, and Jude, were printed and carried through the press by myself in Melbourne in 1882. An edition of 300 copies of each of these books was printed and bound, and given to the natives as they were able to read and value them.

"The Scriptures are not sold to the natives in our group, for the good reason that by planting and preparing arrowroot which has been sold by Christian friends, as a labour of love to Jesus, in the churches supporting our mission, our New Hebrides Christian converts have paid for the printing of all the books of Scripture translated and printed in their languages. The Aneiteumese paid £1200 for printing the complete Bible in their language to the noble British and Foreign Bible Society, which well deserves the sympathy and prayers and liberal support of all Christians in its grand work of giving the world the Bible with its heavenly light and enriching blessings.

"Following the example of the Aneiteumese, all our island Christians repay the British and Foreign Bible Society for the books of Scripture printed by it for them.

They continue this work in a praiseworthy manner. Money is not much in circulation among our islanders yet; but they so value the Word of God that they do everything possible to provide it for themselves, and to extend it to others.

"My Aniwans value the Scriptures very highly; indeed all our converted islanders do. They read and study them carefully, especially the Gospel of John, where they see Jesus in love and mercy bending over them, teaching and pleading with them. They carry the book with them on their journeys, on their fishing expeditions, and often to their work; and when wearied feel refreshed by reading a few verses, and by prayer. The love of God as displayed in Jesus, and recorded in the blessed book, they never tire meditating upon, and speaking about; and since they got the Gospel of John, they say it has made them so thirsty and hungry for the rest of the Bible, that in preparing arrowroot they are doing all possible to be able to pay for its being printed in their language.

"The book of Jonah is the only other book of Scripture I have translated into their language, but I have translated and printed on the island the first part of the book of Genesis, and other selections of Scripture peculiarly adapted to the circumstances of the natives. These, along with a Hymn-book and a Church Catechism or Confession of Faith, are bound up with initiatory educational books chiefly composed from Scripture."

Mr. Paton adds—"I could have been much further on in translating the Bible had I not been so much occupied pleading the cause of the mission, working and organising for its support and extension, and the keeping of our mission vessel the *Dayspring*.

"For the time we have been at work, the means at our disposal, and the missionaries engaged in our mission, God has given us wonderful success, and now our whole group is white to the harvest, which we hope will soon be reaped in the real conversion of thousands to love and serve the Lord."

God grant that so it may be to the praise of the glory of His grace!

THE NEW HEBRIDES.

CHAPTER X.

THE ANEITEUM VERSION.

Few of the many islands which have been brought under Christian culture in the South Pacific have a more eventful and instructive history than Aneiteum.* It bears a relation to Western Polynesia somewhat similar to that which Tahiti bears to the eastern division of the " Island World." As regards extent and population they are widely different, but in a missionary point of view they have much in common. Tahiti is the parent mission in the east; and to a considerable extent Aneiteum sustains the same relation to the now numerous missions in the west. Especially is this the case with reference to the New Hebrides group.

Aneiteum is the most southerly island of that group, and lies in south latitude 20°, and in east longitude 170°. It was discovered by Captain Cook in 1774, and by him named Anattom, and by this name, somewhat altered, it was known till Christian teachers were placed upon it. It is about forty miles in circumference, and at the time when our acquaintance with it began the population was estimated at 3600. It is lofty, some of its mountains rising to the height of 3000 feet. It is pleasingly

* The missionaries of the Presbyterian Church who now occupy the New Hebrides group spell the name Aneityum.

diversified by mountains of various shapes and sizes, hills and valleys, deep ravines, barren tracts and cultivated spots; and on the whole it presents a striking and picturesque aspect.

Its missionary history dates from the month of March 1841. On the thirtieth day of that month the writer visited the island in the London Missionary Society's brig *Camden*, and succeeded in introducing two Samoan teachers, Tavita and Fuataiese, amongst its then deeply degraded people; and thus, on that memorable day, the first step was taken in the train of events which led to the subversion of idolatry, and the establishment of Christianity throughout the island; and which was fraught with momentous consequences to the whole group to which it belongs.

A glance at the state in which we found the Aneitenmese will prepare the reader to form an estimate of the mighty change which, as we shall presently see, was effected among them by the introduction of the Gospel of the grace of God. We may just remark that they belong to the Papuan stock, and that they are an inferior race compared with the Asiatic races found throughout Eastern and Central Polynesia. Their moral and social state was very low. War, murder, cannibalism, the strangling of widows, infanticide, polygamy, and the consequent degradation and oppression of the female sex—these and kindred cruelties and abominations were the characteristics of the Aneiteumese when the dayspring from on high opened upon their dark and cheerless shores. And when we add that in addition to wars and feuds, which were of common occurrence, they lived under the most abject bondage to their natmasses—a sort of inferior deities—of which they were in constant dread, it will be seen that their condition must have been wretched in the extreme. They were accustomed to sleep with their clubs and spears by their pillows, to be in readiness to defend themselves against the midnight assassin, so that between the dread of spiritual wickedness and human enemies, they were all their life under deplorable bondage through fear of death.

For seven years the mission was in the hands of Samoan teachers, occasional visits being made by missionaries from Samoa and the Hervey Islands. The trials which the teachers had to endure were many and great; their lives were often in danger. On two occasions especially they had a very narrow escape from being murdered. Armed men came upon them headed by a savage chief who thought very little of human life; but though the strangers were entirely defenceless, the natives were not suffered to carry their diabolical purpose into effect. The All-seeing eye was over them, and an unseen arm was their defence. Amid all their privations and perils they were enabled to hold on, and in due time labourers better able to cope with the difficulties came to their aid.

In the month of May 1848, the Rev. John Geddie from Prince Edward Island, Nova Scotia, and the Rev. Thomas Powell of the Samoan mission, were conveyed to the island in the *John Williams*. They were coldly received by the natives—just tolerated. Only one decided case of conversion had occurred during the seven dreary years that preceded their arrival, but there was substantial encouragement even in that solitary case. As the faintest ray in the eastern sky heralds the advent of day, so did the conversion of Umra herald the bright day which, after a few more years of suffering and toil, filled Aneiteum with light from on high.

At the close of twelve months, Mr. and Mrs. Powell returned to Samoa, and Mr. and Mrs. Geddie were left with only the Samoan teachers to assist them in carrying on their work. As soon as Mr. Geddie's knowledge of the language allowed, he reduced it to a written form, and prepared a Primer, a Catechism, a few Hymns, and a small selection of Scripture extracts. Before leaving home he had acquired some knowledge of the art of printing, and he brought with him a small second-hand printing press, and a small fount of half-worn types; and thus imperfectly equipped, he did the first printing I suppose that was ever done in the Western Pacific. It was emphatically printing done under difficulties, but Mr. Geddie was not the man to be daunted or discouraged where success was at all practicable. The little book did good service during this twilight time, and more adventurous work was soon attempted and accomplished. The first portion of Scripture translated was the Gospel of Matthew; the Gospel of Mark followed; and unmistakable signs had now appeared that God was working with His servants, and crowning their labours with marked success. Light and life were marvellously spreading throughout the island—all the more marvellous that the instrumentality was so inadequate—one solitary missionary, and a few native helpers who but a few years before were themselves in a state of heathen darkness.

And at this juncture, when the growing needs of the mission were such as to demand additional help, help was provided in a very remarkable manner. The Rev. John Inglis and Mrs. Inglis, at that time connected with the Reformed Presbyterian Church of Scotland, and afterwards with the Free Church of Scotland, joined the mission.* Mr. Inglis had had about seven years experience of missionary and ministerial work in New Zealand, so that he and Mrs. Inglis entered upon their work in Aneiteum

---

* The circumstances under which Mr. and Mrs. Inglis were led to connect themselves with the New Hebrides mission are fully stated in a work entitled "In the New Hebrides," by Mr. (now Dr.) Inglis, lately published by Nelson & Sons, London, chap. v., p. 45.

with qualifications such as experience alone can give. They arrived in the month of July 1852.

So far no complete portion of the Word of God had been printed in the native language. Mr. Geddie, as already mentioned, had translated the Gospels of Matthew and Mark, and about twelve months after the arrival of Mr. Inglis, he and Mr. Geddie resolved to get one of the Gospels printed, and to appeal to their friends to help them to meet the expense. The Gospel of Mark was chosen, as being the shorter of the two, and the manuscript was sent to Sydney by the *John Williams*, in charge of the Rev. J. P. Sunderland, who was on board, and an arrangement was made with him to get it printed in Sydney, and this was carried into effect, to the satisfaction of all concerned. "Considering the circumstances," Mr. Inglis remarks, "it was, though not perfect, a highly creditable production, and it gave an immense stimulus to education all over the island."

It was printed during the stay of the *John Williams* in Sydney, and on her return voyage to Aneiteum, which she reached in October 1853, she bore the precious treasure to the grateful islanders, who rejoiced over it as one who findeth great spoil. The edition consisted of 3000 copies, and its printing and publishing is worthy of special note as being the first portion of the sacred Scriptures printed in any language of Western Polynesia.

The next portion printed was the Gospel of Matthew. This was done on the island by Mr. Geddie. A new printing press and a new fount of type had been obtained; hence his ability to accomplish so important a work. As many months had passed since the translation was made, he felt that it might now be greatly improved, so he made a new translation, and Mr. Inglis was now able to assist him in revising it. And so retranslated and carefully revised it was printed on the island of Aneiteum.

The next portion printed was the Gospel of Luke. The manuscript was sent to London, and it was printed by the British and Foreign Bible Society. The Gospel of John, and the Acts of the Apostles, and the Epistles of Paul, from Galatians to Philemon inclusive, were printed on the island.

And now the brethren began to make preparations for the printing in London of the complete New Testament. It was arranged that Mr. and Mrs. Geddie should go home on furlough by the *John Williams*, which was to leave the islands for England towards the close of 1859, and apply to the Bible Society to undertake the work. Owing to family circumstances, however, in the case of Mr. and Mrs. Geddie this arrangement could not be carried out, and it was finally decided that Mr. and Mrs. Inglis should go instead.

The New Testament was all translated when this arrangement was made, but the departure of the *John Williams* was too near to allow of the translation undergoing a thorough revision by the brethren on the island, and to meet this in the best available manner it was arranged that Mr. and Mrs. Inglis should take with them one of the most competent native pundits to assist in preparing the work for the press, and accordingly Williamu, an intelligent man, and a man of tried Christian character, accompanied them to England.

The *John Williams* had to visit all the principal stations of the London Missionary Society between the New Hebrides and Tahiti, and this occupied three months and a half, and after finishing her work among the islands she was three months and a half on her way to England, so that the whole voyage occupied seven months, and when Mr. and Mrs. Inglis and their pundit reached their destination they had read and corrected about half the manuscript. The Committee of the Bible Society readily undertook to do their part; and in due time the revision was completed, important help being rendered by the Rev. T. W. Meller, M.A., the Editorial Superintendent of the Society's translations. Mr. Meller had an extraordinary aptitude for the acquisition of languages. He had carried through the press the Gospel of Luke in the Aneiteumese language some time before, and he had so analysed that Gospel as to form a lexicon of the language so far as a single Gospel supplied material for so doing. Hence he was able to form a judgment as to the accuracy of the translation of other books of the New Testament, and to assist Mr. Inglis materially in the work of revision.

Mr. Inglis does not mention how much time was occupied in completing the revision and carrying the work through the press, nor does he mention the number printed; but we find that in 1863 the natives had the book in their hands, and no doubt it was a day of great rejoicing on Aneiteum when the complete New Testament was borne to their shores. This is clearly deducible from the following remarks of Mr. Inglis in a letter to the Bible Society written in 1865:—"The natives are for the most part reading the New Testament with great diligence, and are advancing steadily both in scriptural knowledge and Christian character. One-fourth of the entire population have been admitted to Church fellowship, and I have at present on my side of the island a candidates' class of 127. Some may think that our admissions must be very loose when we receive so many, but that is not the case. We rarely admit any one till after a year's instruction and probation. It must also be remembered that every person on the island above children is reading the Scriptures and hearing them expounded every Sabbath. The Bible is their only book, and Scripture truth is thus kept more constantly before their minds than it ordinarily can be before the minds of most communities."

The following extracts from Mr. Inglis' work, already referred to, show very strikingly the extreme care which was exercised in translating, revising, and editing the Aneiteumese Bible.*

"The process by which we produced the Aneityumese Bible was this. Saturday was the day which I generally appropriated to translating, and if I could not say *Nulla dies sina versu* ('No day without a verse'), I could say to a large extent, 'No week without a chapter.' After I had been six months on the island, I began to translate Genesis. At first I got only a few verses done, and in a very imperfect manner. But week by week, and month by month, the work became easier. After I had finished Genesis, I translated Luke. Our mode of proceeding was this. The first duty of a translator is to ascertain and fix upon the meaning of the author. For this end I read the original text, versions, and commentaries, and all helps that I could lay my hands upon. Then I translated the original into the Aneityumese as best I could. Then I brought into my study one or two of the most intelligent of the natives, and read the passage to them, verse by verse, asking them if this word or that sentence was correct Aneityumese; and, such and such being the meaning, was that the best word, or the most suitable expression? or what changes would they suggest? and making every correction that could be thought of.

"On the Sabbath morning before church-time, when the people began to assemble, I brought in ten or a dozen of the most intelligent of the natives, and read the portion translated over to them verse by verse, and embodied whatever suggestions they might suggest. This was to the natives a kind of Bible lesson, as they necessarily heard a good deal of exposition under circumstances very favourable for being remembered. Subsequently I read it

* See chap. v., p. 103.

in the church to the whole congregation, following it up with a running commentary—a kind of lecture after the manner of a Scotch forenoon service in the olden time. I had previously instructed the congregation that if any of them observed any words incorrectly used, they were to come to me and tell me after the service. And though they were anything but forward to display their critical acumen, yet now and again one and another would come to me and say, 'Misi,' would you read over that verse near the beginning, or the middle, or the end, as the case might be, where such and such a word occurs; 'I was not sure about it.' The verse was read, and the remark would be made, 'Oh! it is quite correct—I had not heard it right;' or, 'I think such and such a word would be better there.' When I had embodied the results of all available criticism, I wrote out a clean copy of the translation, and when the book was finished I sent it over to Mr. Geddie, and he went over it all carefully with his pundits, bringing a fresh eye and a new critical apparatus to eliminate remaining errors, and secure further improvements. If there were any doubtful passages left, these were marked, and we examined them together when we met. Mr. Geddie did the same with his translations, and finally we read them over together in the hearing of two or three of our best pundits before we said *Imprimatur*.

"In the case of the New Testament Mr. Meller read over the translation, book by book, and sent them back to me. He wrote no fewer than nine hundred pages of notepaper filled with criticisms, which I stitched up into a volume. Williamu and I examined all his suggestions, and approved or rejected as the case required. Finally, besides daily consultations during the whole time, Mrs. Inglis and I went over the entire translation, verse by verse, as it was printed. She read the English and marked every stop. I followed her in the translation, and watched most carefully that nothing was omitted, and that nothing was added. We then reversed the process. I read the translation, and she checked me with the English. To make so many corrections, to revise and revise again, to read the Greek, or the Hebrew, the English, and the Aneityumese may appear like a work of supererogation. But those who know anything of the work either of translating or editing the Bible will feel no surprise. I once heard the late Dr. Mitchell, Professor of Biblical Criticism in the United Secession Church, say to his class in the Hall, that not one person in a thousand who reads the English Bible has the slightest conception of the labour that has been bestowed on that book, which they can now buy for a shilling. When I came home in 1860 to carry the New Testament through the press, Mr. Meller gave me a copy of the Greek New Testament of the received text, published by the Bible Society, that I might have an authorised standard to guide me. This Greek Testament had been printed at Cologne in Germany, and the proof-sheets had been read over in succession by four German professors, so that perfection might be secured. And yet when Mr. Meller read the book after it was printed he found that half a verse had been omitted, viz., the first half of 1 Cor. x. 23. Instead of 'all things are lawful for me, but all things are not expedient: all things are lawful for me, but all things edify not,' the first half was left out.

"In the Aneityumese New Testament there are about a quarter of a million of words, and in the whole Bible more than a million. To read over a million of words in a foreign language, and see that not one of them is misspelled, that not a capital is misplaced, and that not a point is omitted, is no easy task. To revise, correct, and edit the whole Bible under the very exact conditions imposed by the Bible Society is a very laborious work. Dr. Chalmers, however, says that the most imperfect translation of the Bible that ever was made, if honestly done, will not fail to convey to the reader a knowledge of the way of salvation. We can safely say of ours, that it was honestly made, and executed to the very best of our ability, and that we called to our aid every available help, whether the works of Biblical critics, or the living voices of intelligent natives.

"The translation of the New Testament was prepared wholly by Mr. Geddie and myself. I translated Luke, 1st and 2nd Corinthians, Hebrews, and the Revelation. Mr. Geddie translated all the rest. I revised, corrected, and edited the whole with the assistance of Williamu. Of the Old Testament, Mr. Geddie translated the last four books of the Pentateuch, Joshua, Judges, 1st and 2nd Kings, and 2nd Chronicles, Ezra, Nehemiah, the Psalms, the historical portion of Daniel, and Jonah. Mr. Copeland translated Ruth, Esther, the prophetical chapters of Daniel, and all the twelve minor prophets except Jonah. I translated Genesis, 1st and 2nd Samuel, Job, Proverbs, Ecclesiastes, Song of Solomon, Isaiah, Jeremiah, Lamentations, and Ezekiel. Mr. Geddie by mistake translated Job after I had finished it, and I by a mistake also translated Judges; and as the latter half of Mr. Geddie's translation of Leviticus was lost after his death in some printing office in Melbourne, I had also to translate that. But in revising I compared both these translations, and they were improved thereby. Mr. Geddie hastily revised the first half of the Old Testament. Mr. Copeland revised the whole. I had to revise, correct, and edit the whole of the Old Testament as well as the New. Mr. Geddie brought out an edition of the book of Psalms printed in Nova Scotia. This edition was used up before the Old Testament was printed. He also edited the first half of the Pentateuch in Melbourne before his death, which was put in circulation some years before the Old Testament was published."

We add two or three more extracts from Mr. Inglis' book, which will give the reader a pretty complete history of Bible translation and Bible circulation on Aneiteum. "When I came home," he remarks, "in 1877, to carry the Old Testament through the press, Mr. Meller had gone to his rest and reward, after eighteen years of valuable labour for the Society. Another Editorial Superintendent was occupying his place, viz., the Rev. W. Wright, M.A. (now also D.D.), who had been for ten years a missionary to the Jews in Damascus from the Presbyterian Church in Ireland. Dr. Wright is an eminent Hebrew scholar, and has greatly distinguished himself by his researches and discoveries in connection with the Hittite inscriptions. My relations with him were in every way as satisfactory as they had been with Mr. Meller. We printed the last volume of the Old Testament first, and sent it out to Aneityum, because they had less knowledge of the prophetical books than of the historical. They got the second volume in 1879, and the first volume in 1881. I was not on the island when the Old Testament was received, nor have I been there since, but I know that its reception must have been much the same as that accorded to the New Testament in 1863."

With reference to the influence that is being exerted on the people of Aneiteum, Mr. Inglis writes as follows:— "As soon as they know their letters, they commence reading some portion of the Scriptures. Our education therefore is thoroughly scriptural; and the results may be seen in the striking contrast between this and the adjoining islands which are still in heathen darkness. All here is peace and quietness; life and property are secure. We may say that we have no crime."

Again Mr. Inglis remarks:—"The same process is going

on, and the same results are being brought about in all the islands occupied by the mission. The leaven of God's Word is beginning, it may be slowly, but still steadily and surely, to leaven the whole mass of heathenism."

It is highly gratifying to be able to add that the people of Aneiteum, poor as they are, and comparatively few in number, are likely to refund to the Bible Society the entire amount incurred in the printing and binding of the Scriptures in their language. With reference to this matter, Mr. Inglis wrote as follows in 1876:—"The natives paid the full price, about four shillings a copy, for 2000 copies of the New Testament, and about one shilling and sixpence a copy for 2000 copies of the Psalms; and there is every probability of their being able to pay for 1250 copies of the Old Testament as soon as they are printed." The complete Bible, as we have seen, has been printed and is now in the course of sale on the island, and I have no doubt whatever that the debt which the people owe the Society will in due time be paid to the full, if indeed this has not been already done.

It is a touching consideration that one of the two principal workers did not live to see the completion of the great undertaking. Dr. Geddie was called to his home and his rest on the 15th of December 1872. In his late work Dr. Inglis, who happily is still spared to bring forth fruit in old age, bears the following graceful testimony to the character and worth of his departed fellow-labourer:— "He will be remembered as the father and founder of the Presbyterian mission on that group; as one who has left his mark broad and deep on the New Hebrides, but especially on the island of Aneityum, and whose memory will be long and gratefully cherished by the natives; as one also who has increased the usefulness, extended the boundaries, elevated the character, and heightened the reputation of the Presbyterian Church of Nova Scotia; and as one whose example will fan the flame of missionary zeal in that and other churches for many years to come. Oh that many such as he may respond to the divine call, and say, 'Lord, here am I; send me.'"

We trust Dr. Inglis will be spared yet for a few years to serve by tongue and pen the cause he loves so well, and has served so faithfully throughout a long life; and that when the time comes for him to rejoin the loved ones who have gone before, he will have an entrance ministered to him abundantly into the everlasting kingdom of our Lord and Saviour Jesus Christ.

CHAPTER XI.

TANNA.

CHRISTIAN teachers from Samoa were placed on the island of Tanna by John Williams on the 18th of November 1839, the day before he fell on the neighbouring island of Eramanga. It was the first island of the New Hebrides group on which missionary operations were commenced. A vast amount of labour has been expended upon it, and very much suffering and self-denial have been braved by the faithful men and women who have toiled to bring its benighted tribes out of darkness into light, not counting their lives dear unto them if by any means by God's help they might succeed in their grand object. Yet the results, so far, have been disappointing. Instead of being in the van of progress, as might have been expected, it is far in the rear of other islands of the same group on which missions were commenced at a much later date.

We need not say much with reference to the island and its people. These are largely described in works which have long been before the public, such as Dr. Turner's "Nineteen Years in Polynesia," Dr. Steel's "New Hebrides and Christian Missions," and "Missions in Western Polynesia." The island is about forty miles to the north-west of Aneiteum, and about eighteen or twenty to the east of Eramanga. It is a fine island, one of the most beautiful and fertile of the New Hebrides group, and as regards extent and population one of the most important. It is about eighty miles in circumference, and the population is estimated at from 6000 to 8000. The natives have much in common with their neighbours on other islands already described. They are perhaps a shade or two more fierce and savage than the worst of these.

The mission has a sadly chequered history. We must confine ourselves to a very brief outline. As already stated it was commenced in November 1839.* After a few months the island was visited by the Rev. Thomas Heath of the Samoan mission. All was found going on fairly well, and the mission was reinforced by the addition of two more Samoan teachers, Pomare and Vaiofanga. The next visit was made by the writer in April 1841, when a very sad state of things was found. The teachers had suffered much from illness and neglect, and two of their number, Pomare and Salaméa, had died. The survivors had recovered their health: a few of the natives had attached themselves to them, and they were willing to remain, so we were able to keep the door open.

In June 1842 the Rev. George Turner and the Rev. Henry Nisbet, recently from England, were, with their heroic wives, settled on the island. They entered upon their work with fair prospects, and high hopes were entertained that the time to favour Tanna had come, and that a bright future was in store for its benighted people. Alas! for our short-sighted forecast. Only a few months had passed when the infatuated people drove the messengers of peace from their shores. They had to flee for their lives, and they were saved by one of the most remarkable interpositions of Divine providence on record.

In 1845 the island was again occupied by eastern teachers, and from that time till 1858 it was one continuous struggle to retain a hold upon the island. There

* The names of the teachers placed on the island by Mr. Williams were Lalolangi, Salaméa, and Mose.

was disaster upon disaster. Twice the mission was suspended for a short time, and one of the Samoan teachers, Vasa, was murdered, and another, Ioane, was barbarously beaten and apparently left for dead, and a house in which were a number of teachers was set on fire, evidently with the design of compassing the destruction of all; all, however, were mercifully preserved. Thus the infatuated people resisted, desperately resisted, all our efforts to confer upon them the highest boon which Heaven has to bestow, but they knew not what they did.

In 1858 European missionaries were again settled on the island. The Rev. Joseph Copeland and the Rev. J. G. Paton from Scotland, and the Rev. J. W. Matheson from Nova Scotia, took up their abode on the island; and in 1859 the Rev. S. F. Johnston and Mrs. Johnson, also from Nova Scotia, joined the mission. Messrs. Paton and Matheson were also married, and accompanied by their wives. After a time Mr. Copeland was removed to Aneiteum to take temporary charge of Mr. Inglis' station, while he was absent in England superintending the printing of the Aneiteumese New Testament. Still with such a force of consecrated men and women progress might naturally have been expected, but the reaping time was still distant. Within the space of three short years the mission was again broken up. Messrs. Johnston and Matheson were dead. Mrs. Paton and her child were also dead, and Mr. Paton and Mrs. Johnston alone remained. Mrs. Johnston, after the death of her husband, withdrew from the island and became an inmate in the family of Mr. Geddie, and but one solitary representative of the mission remained, and he a sorely stricken man. In addition to the terrible trial of losing his wife and child, Mr. Paton had suffered much from frequent and severe attacks of fever and ague, and again and again he had been in imminent peril of his life, still he was slow to quit his post. At length matters came to extremities, and he was obliged to flee to escape being murdered; and Tanna was again left in heathen darkness.

In 1868 mission work was resumed on the island. The Rev. Thomas Neilson from Scotland, with his wife, a daughter of the late Dr. Geddie, settled at Port Resolution, which had become a sort of hallowed spot, consecrated in a manner by the sufferings and deaths of so many of Christ's witnesses. Mr. and Mrs. Neilson entered upon their work with a measure of encouragement and pursued it with all diligence. Early in 1870 Mr. Neilson began regular preaching to the natives in their own tongue, and was soon able to report a little progress. "We have worship," he said, "in six different villages every Sabbath day; in the first, in the little church, then I send two teachers to conduct worship on one Sabbath in two villages at a distance, and I myself with two other teachers go to those near at hand. In each of these villages there is an average attendance of from twenty to thirty persons every Sabbath day, so that the Gospel is preached to from one hundred and twenty to one hundred and eighty persons in and around Port Resolution every Sabbath." Mrs. Neilson was also working among the women, and had taught several of them to read and sing hymns; and Mr. Neilson applied himself to the work of Scripture translation as soon as his knowledge of the language allowed, and according to Dr. Steel he prepared a version of the Gospels.*

In 1869 the Rev. William Watt and Mrs. Watt from the Presbyterian Church of New Zealand settled at another part of the island, named Kwamera, and took up the work which had been begun by Mr. and Mrs. Matheson, and with the exception of an interval during which they were absent on furlough, they have laboured on to the present

* See Dr. Steel's work, p. 180.

time, happily with a measure of encouragement. Patiently and zealously they have plodded on amid difficulties and trials such as fall to the lot of comparatively few missionaries in the islands of the Pacific in these days. They soon gained a good knowledge of the language, and they appeared to get a firmer footing among the people than any of their predecessors.

With reference to the translating and printing of the sacred Scriptures, Mr. Watt has furnished the following information:—"It was not till 1869 that any portion of God's Word appears to have been printed in Tannese. In 1869 Mr. Paton, who had been driven from Tanna in 1862, got a portion of the Gospel according to Mark printed in Auckland. The portion consisted of the first three and part of the fourth chapters. In the same year Mr. Neilson got a small book printed at Aneityum containing the Lord's Prayer and the Ten Commandments. The following year I got a small book of Scripture extracts printed.

"In 1873 the Glasgow Foundry Boys Religious Society provided me with a printing press, and since that date all books printed in Tannese have been printed by me with that press, and have been my own translations. In 1875 I printed two books, the one in small pica type, containing the parables of our Lord, and the other in double pica type, containing the miracles. In 1878 the Gospel of Matthew was printed, followed in 1881 by the Acts of the Apostles; in 1883 by the book of Genesis; and in 1884 by the first nineteen chapters and part of the twentieth chapter of Exodus. In each case the edition consisted of 200 copies.

"Arrangements are now being made with the National Bible Society of Scotland, with the consent of the British and Foreign Bible Society, to get the whole of the New Testament printed in this dialect of the Tannese language, and nearly all has been translated. In many cases Mr.

Neilson and I have translations of the same books. In addition to those translated by me, Mr. Neilson has left translations of the Epistles of Paul to the Thessalonians, Timothy, the Epistle to the Hebrews, the Epistles of John and Jude, and the book of Revelation. He has also left translations of the books of Joshua, Judges, and Jonah. These are all, however, first translations, and will require much revision before they will be ready for the press.

"On Tanna no charge has ever been made for books. We have not even adopted the custom introduced on Aneityum of getting the natives to make arrowroot in payment of them. We have been in the habit of asking for a contribution of arrowroot, but it has been applied to other purposes. As soon as a new book is printed and bound copies are distributed to all who can use them. Our people have had a great dread of books,* and our desire has been to put no obstacle in the way of any one's obtaining them.

"On Tanna, as elsewhere, the entrance of God's Word gives light. One of our young men gave as a reason for urging his neighbours to learn to read that if they read the book they could not but believe it."

In the month of October 1881 a noteworthy event occurred at Mr. Watt's station—a church was formed. Of this important fact I find only the following brief notice in the Annual Report of the mission:—"On the 6th of October I baptized six adults and three children, and on Sabbath, the 9th of October, the sacrament of the Lord's Supper was dispensed by Mr. Neilson, who had kindly

---

* This arises from a fear lest by receiving books they should bring upon themselves disease or some other calamity; and the same reason has all along influenced them in their treatment of missionaries and teachers, so that superstitious fears have been the chief cause of their long continued opposition to Christianity.

come round to assist at the formation of the first Christian church on Tanna."

In December 1882 Mr. Neilson withdrew from the mission, and retired to Australia, so Port Resolution was again left without a missionary. A few of the natives kept up a sort of service, conducting it as best they could, and in June 1883 an Aneiteum teacher was placed in charge of the station, Mr. Watt making periodical visits and taking the general oversight.

In October 1882 a new station was opened at a place called Weasisi, and the Rev. W. Gray and Mrs. Gray from South Australia commenced work under circumstances remarkably encouraging for Tanna. A number of the natives gathered round them at once, and they were soon able to commence teaching, and conducting services which were fairly well attended, and there seems to have been steady progress. In 1885 Mr. Gray was able to report as follows:—"We hold two services every Sunday, when we have a good and steady attendance. At the morning services I read a portion of Scripture from Mr. Watt's translation, and the translation of Scripture which I have prepared during the previous week. Afterwards I give an address explaining my translation. This I have done since the beginning of this year. One of the native teachers gives an address at the afternoon service. The attendance at the service on Wednesday afternoons is good, sometimes large. We have school every night. We have forty-eight names on the school roll for this year. We have grey-headed men and women and toddling children among our scholars. Some of the boys and girls make progress in reading. Three days of the week we hold an advanced class for our teachers and servants."

The above extract indicates progress and encourages hope, and the Report for 1886 from Kwamera and Port Resolution was also of an encouraging character. Of these

Mr. Watt writes as follows:—" At both places the work has been carried on uninterruptedly during the past year, and in some respects steady progress at both places may be reported. We have celebrated in all four Christian marriages during the year. We have added one member to the church. When visiting Port Resolution in the month of August, the people turned out much better to the service than they usually do. The last evening about forty were present at worship. Our annual contribution of arrowroot amounted to 265 lbs."

And now we must take our leave of Tanna. As the reader has seen it is still the day of small things there. "The missionary work on Tanna," Dr. Steel remarks in his book, "yet awaits its harvest after a long and trying spring-time. Many would have abandoned the island long ere this; but as so much influence for good has been gained, the reaping time will come."

So we believe. Mr. and Mrs. Watt have stuck to their work right nobly, and though the results, so far, are comparatively small, yet there are substantial results. The first fruits have been gathered, and the harvest will surely follow. God is faithful who hath promised, "In due season we shall reap if we faint not." And these faithful labourers have not fainted, nor are their younger fellow-labourers likely to faint either. So far there are pleasing indications that God is working with them, and if their lives are spared and their health continued, we may reasonably hope that their labours will be crowned with growing success. God grant that so it may be. Soon may the long-looked-for blessing descend in its fulness, and the little one become a thousand, and the small one a strong nation.

CHAPTER XII.

ERAMANGA.

The early history of this island is a mournful one. It was discovered by Captain Cook in 1774, and his intercourse with the natives was inauspicious. A serious quarrel took place between a watering party and the natives. Two of Captain Cook's people were wounded, not seriously, and "four of the natives," he states, "lay, to all appearance, dead on the shore; but two of them afterwards crawled in among the bushes. It was a fortunate circumstance for our assailants that more than half our muskets missed fire, otherwise we should have done much more execution among them." Captain Cook was a cautious and humane man, but in this case he felt himself compelled to adopt severe measures for the protection of his own people. Such was the unfortunate commencement of intercourse between the Eramangans and foreigners, and probably it had something to do in giving a character to that intercourse in subsequent years. For a length of time voyagers and traders seem to have shunned the island in consequence of the fierce and savage character of the natives as disclosed by Cook's narrative of his visit. He named the cape near which the affray took place Traitor's Head, a name which it still bears.

Eramanga is about seventy-five miles in circumference. It is, as already remarked, distant from Tanna about eighteen or twenty miles. It is not equal to Tanna in fertility and beauty, still it is a fine island. It is mountainous; some of the mountains are so lofty as to be visible at the distance of forty miles. A large part of the coast looks rugged and barren, and though there are several bays, there is no really good harbours. Dillon's Bay is the best, but it is open to the sea, and is not safe in all weathers. In the interior there are large tracks of rich cultivatable land, but not much round the coast. The population is small for the extent of the island. What it was at the time of its discovery we have no means of knowing, but the Rev. G. N. Gordon, the first white missionary who settled upon it, thought it did not exceed 5000 in his time.

The natives of Eramanga are the lowest of all the tribes inhabiting the New Hebrides. They are inferior in their physical development, darker in colour, and rather more than less savage and barbarous in their character, customs, and usages. They may be classed somewhere between their neighbour islanders and the aborigines of Australia, who are the lowest of all the races of the human family with whom it has been my lot to come in contact.

It was not till about 1820 or later that Eramanga began to be resorted to by white men. Sandal-wood of very superior quality, and in great abundance, was discovered, and a rush of adventurers followed somewhat similar to what takes place when a new gold field is reported. Sad outrages were committed by men who resorted to the island in search of the coveted treasure; and it is not surprising that the natives retaliated, and committed atrocities upon the white men, and coloured men too, for they were not all white men who engaged in the sandal-wood trade. White men were generally the leaders, but they often had in their employ natives of other islands, who assisted them in their outrageous conduct, and were involved in the reprisals of the often most cruelly treated

Eramangans. Sometimes, I suppose, the natives were the aggressors, but it may be safely affirmed that in the great majority of cases it was the other way. The traders, as a general rule, go to the islands determined to obtain what they are in search of, whether it be sandal-wood or anything else, and they are not scrupulous as to the means they employ to accomplish their object; the claims of the natives, and even their lives, are not of much account. Fearful confirmation of these statements have again and again been supplied during the last fifty years by sandal-wood traders, and men-stealers, and other traders throughout the New Hebrides and other islands. When the sandal-wood was exhausted in Eramanga and elsewhere, the natives themselves were decoyed away, or seized and carried off by force into virtual slavery by men from Christian lands, and alas! the infamous traffic is not yet at an end.

It was owing to one of the sandal-wood outrages that the first martyrs of Eramanga, John Williams and James Harris, lost their lives; and the labour traffic led also to the murder of Bishop Patteson and his fellow-martyrs. When on a visit to Eramanga some years after the death of Messrs. Williams and Harris, the actual murderer was found. The poor man expressed sorrow, pleading that he did not know that they were missionaries, and mentioning, as an extenuation of his deed, that a short time before a son of his own had been shot dead by a white man.

Two Christian teachers were placed on Eramanga by the Rev. Thomas Heath of the Samoan mission in 1840, but when the island was again visited in April 1841 it was found necessary to remove them. The natives had failed to fulfil their promises to protect them and provide for them, and it was little short of a miracle that we found them alive.

Eight years passed away before we were able to regain

our hold upon the island, and then it was rather a negative than a positive hold. In September 1849 the Rev. Charles Hardie of the Samoan mission and the writer visited the island. The way was not yet clear to place teachers upon it, but we succeeded in inducing four natives to go with us to Samoa, and this proved to be the first link in the chain of events that have issued in Christianity being firmly planted on Eramanga. Alas! the interval is deeply shaded; the end has been gained, but at a heavy expenditure of suffering and precious life!

The four youths remained in Samoa about three years, and three of them appeared to become sincere disciples of Christ. They left Samoa in the *John Williams*, in charge of the Rev. J. P. Sunderland and the writer, who were the deputation on that occasion. What appeared to us a very sad calamity occurred during the voyage. Nivave, one of the most hopeful of our Eramangan youths, died when we were almost within sight of his native land. We were greatly grieved, and somewhat apprehensive as to what effect the news of his death would have upon his countrymen. However, we had done what we could, and we had hope that poor Nivave had been taken to a better home than he could have found on Eramanga; and having the full confidence of those that remained, we went forward in hope, and succeeded by the help of God in gaining our object. Two Rarotongan teachers, Va'a and Akatangi, were placed on the island, and had an encouraging reception. We owed our success, no doubt, under God, to the natives who had been to Samoa. Their testimony produced an effect such as nothing else could have produced on the minds of their countrymen. One of them was a mere youth. He got away among his relatives, and we lost sight of him, but two, Joe and Mana, kept by the teachers, and lent invaluable help to the mission. The teachers were landed on the 25th of April 1852, and from that time the history of the Eramangan mission really dates.

As soon as the teachers had got a sufficient hold of the language, they prepared a spelling-book, which was printed by Mr. Geddie, so they were able to commence teaching the wild Eramangans to read, and in this way to get a little light into their dark minds.

The teachers had a rough and trying time, but they plodded on, and did something towards preparing the way for workers better able to grapple with the difficulties of the situation than they were. In the month of June 1857, the Rev. G. N. Gordon from Nova Scotia, and Mrs. Gordon, a native of London, settled on the island. They took up their abode in Dillon's Bay, and entered upon their work and prosecuted it with untiring zeal, and with some encouragement during their short term of service. Their trials were many and great. Mrs. Gordon suffered much from fever and ague, and their lives were in constant peril. A few young men, however, headed by Joe and Mana, the two lads who had been to Samoa, gathered around them and stood by them amid all their dangers and trials, never flinching even when danger was most imminent. Mr. Gordon soon so far acquired the language as to be able to do some literary work. He prepared school books and a catechism, and translated the Gospel of Luke, the Acts of the Apostles, and the book of Jonah. Some of these were in use before they were printed, and corrections were made as the language was better known—indeed nothing seems to have been printed till after Mr. Gordon's death.

The particulars of the sad tragedy which terminated the lives and labours of these devoted and heroic witnesses for Christ have long been before the public. Full particulars were obtained by the writer from Joe on the spot, soon after the event occurred, and may be found in

"Missions in Western Polynesia," p. 417, and in "The Martyrs of Polynesia," chap. vi. p. 91.

The following interesting and touching information, connected with the translation and printing of the Gospel of Luke in the Eramangan language, has been communicated to me by the Rev. Samuel Ella. In the course of the year 1864 Mr. Ella was obliged to remain about five months on the island of Aneiteum, through the high-handed action of the French authorities on New Caledonia, in refusing to allow him to land on the island of Uvea, on which he had been appointed to labour as a missionary of the London Missionary Society. During his detention on Aneiteum, he and Mrs. Ella were the guests of Mr. and Mrs. Inglis (now Dr. Inglis); and Mr. Ella having a knowledge of printing, and having a printing-press with him, he set it up, and turned his stay on Aneiteum to good account. With reference to his detention Dr. Inglis remarked in the Annual Report of the mission for that year:—"Satan overreached himself when he shut out the Rev. Mr. Ella from Uvea, for during his enforced stay on Aneiteum he rendered valuable aid to our mission by printing the Eramangan Gospel of Luke and other useful works."

"The Gospel of Luke," Mr. Ella remarks, "was translated by the Rev. G. N. Gordon into the principal dialect of Eramanga a short time before his martyrdom on that bloodstained shore, and the manuscript was copied by his devoted wife in a *bold text hand* on demy folio paper in order that the whole class sitting around this heroic lady might read while she retained the valuable treasure in her own hands. This work must have been one of great labour, and have occupied considerable time, not much less than the work of translating entailed. The Rev. Joseph Copeland, with the assistance of an intelligent native of Eramanga, revised the translation as the printing progressed." Such were the circumstances under which the first portion of the sacred Scriptures was given to the Eramangans in their own tongue, and through it the translator and the transcriber, though silent in their martyr graves, will speak to successive generations through God's imperishable truth.

Eramanga was not left without a missionary for a great while. At the time of Mr. Gordon's death, a younger brother, James D. Gordon, was studying for the ministry at their home in Nova Scotia, and when the sad news reached him that his brother had been murdered, he at once determined to take up the fallen standard. He reached the island in 1864, and took up the work where his brother had laid it down. A church had been formed by the deceased brother, consisting of three members. After a time sixteen more were baptized and added to the little company. Over these Mr. Gordon watched while he laboured to lead others to the Saviour, and went forward with the work of Scripture translation as his knowledge of the language and other engagements allowed. He translated the book of Genesis, and got it printed in Sydney, and the Gospel of Matthew, which was printed in London, the expense in both cases being borne by the British and Foreign Bible Society. The translation of these books was begun by the elder brother. Genesis must have been printed in the course of the year 1868, and Matthew in 1869. Of Genesis only 500 copies were printed, the number of readers on Eramanga in those early days being very small, and, I suppose, the same number of the Gospel. "Besides these," Dr. Steel remarks, "a primer, two catechisms, and a Psalter were prepared and printed;" and the next notice we have of translation work by Mr. Gordon is in connection with the sad close of his life and labours, for he too fell a victim to the ferocity of the deluded people whom he sought to bless and save.

He had great longings to carry the Gospel to other and larger islands than Eramanga, and moved by what he seems to have regarded as a providential call, he went to the great island of Espiritu Santo early in 1869, and remained there to the close of that year. Two natives of that island had been with him for some time on Eramanga, and from them he had acquired a knowledge of one of the dialects spoken on the island, in which he prepared a primer which he got printed in Sydney. He was well received by the natives, and did some valuable pioneer work.

Eramanga was not left without missionary superintendence during his absence. In 1866 the Rev. James M'Nair, a man of great promise, joined the mission. He possessed in a high degree the qualities needful for effective service in the mission field, and had his life been spared, he would doubtless have done valuable work. Alas! however, his course was cut short soon after his work was begun. He died on the 16th of July 1870, leaving a widow equally devoted to mission work as himself. She with her child returned to Scotland, her native land, and became the second wife of the Rev. Dr. Turner of the Samoan mission; and she is still spared to share with her husband the important literary labours by which he is rendering invaluable service to the cause to which he has devoted a long life with singular fidelity and a measure of success such as falls to the lot of few even of the most favoured workers in the great mission field. May they still be spared for years to come to bring forth fruit in growing measure, to the praise and glory of God!

A fellow-labourer of Mr. M'Nair, the Rev. T. Neilson of Tanna, speaks of him in the following terms:—"James M'Nair, as devoted a missionary, as prayerful, as sincere a man as the church has ever sent to these Southern Seas."

We think with sadness that a man of so much promise should have been so early taken to his rest, but we fall back on the assurance that He with whom we have to do does all things well.

On his return from Espiritu Santo, Mr. Gordon commenced a new station at a place called Portinia Bay, on the opposite side of the island to Dillon's Bay, and entered upon work there, and prosecuted it with his usual energy and diligence. A stone church was built, and the services he conducted were well attended, and a number of people gathered around him, and a bright future seemed opening before him. Alas! his work was well nigh done. It was at the close of 1869 that he returned from Espiritu Santo, and in March 1872 the end came. The summer had been unusually wet and unhealthy, and there had been much sickness among the people, and for this Mr. Gordon was blamed by the heathen. A man named Nerimpow had lost two children, to both of whom, it is said, Mr. Gordon had given medicine, and the father determined to avenge their death on the unoffending missionary. He, with another man, came to Mr. Gordon's house. They found him at home. He had just, with the assistance of a native named Soso, finished the revision of the seventh chapter of the Acts of the Apostles, in which the martyrdom of Stephen is recorded. He gave the manuscript to Soso to read, while he went into the storeroom to get some rice to give to the cook to prepare for dinner. Having done this he went into the front verandah where Nerimpow and his companion were standing. Mr. Gordon gave them two empty bottles (these they valued much in their heathen state), whether at their request or not does not appear. They received the bottles with apparent satisfaction, but murder was in their hearts. Mr. Gordon sat down and began to talk with them. Nerimpow was evidently watching his opportunity, and when that was presented he struck Mr. Gordon a blow with a tomahawk on the right side of his head. There was no need for a second blow. The tomahawk stuck in the skull. The murdered man staggered through a French window into his room, and fell, dying almost instantaneously. The sound of his fall drew Soso, the native pundit, to the spot. He found him lying with his face on the floor. He heard him breathe twice, observed his mouth fill with blood, and he was gone. The murderer and his companion had fled.

As if Mr. Gordon had thought that a sudden termination to his life was not improbable, he had marked out a spot where he wished to be laid when such an event might occur. He had pointed out the selected spot to the natives, and charged them as follows:—"If I die, bury me here; afterwards send word to the missionaries." So the faithful natives made a rude coffin and buried him in the evening of the day of the murder, "according," as they said, "to the word which he had spoken."* The little Christian party, numbering in all, men, women, and children, forty-three, seemed to have no heart to remain at the place where their teacher, to whom they were evidently warmly attached, had been murdered. After three days they gathered together their little movable property, Soso taking charge of manuscripts and some things of value that had belonged to Mr. Gordon, and crossed the island to Dillon's Bay and joined their brethren there, who, no doubt, were of one mind with them in deploring the death of their teacher and guide.

One cannot think of the brief life and the cruel death of this lone man without a feeling of sadness. He was a brave heroic spirit, eminently devoted to his work, ready to do or dare anything for the sake of the Saviour, under the constraining power of whose love he seemed habitually

* See the " New Hebrides and Christian Missions," p. 202.

to live. But we must be still. Has He not a right to do what He will with His own?

It is a comfort to think that his labours and sufferings were not in vain. How clearly does this appear from what took place at his death. Who were they who tenderly and lovingly committed his mangled remains to the grave, and made great lamentation over him? Were they not Eramangans, countrymen of his murderers, and but lately as blind and savage as they? And what a tale does this fact tell of the power of those blessed truths which he had taught them to raise the lowest, and subdue the fiercest, and renovate the vilest of the children of Adam!

It would have been no matter of surprise if after the murder of five missionaries on Eramanga, difficulty had been found in obtaining another to venture among so treacherous and savage a people. It was not so, however. Towards the close of the year of Mr. Gordon's death, the Rev. H. A. Robertson and his wife arrived from Nova Scotia, and with the heroism of martyrs chose Eramanga as their sphere of labour, thereby evincing in as far as the spirit went their fitness for the position, and their subsequent history has proved their fitness for the practical work. They took up their abode in Dillon's Bay at the close of 1872, and with the exception of a short furlough spent in their native land, they have toiled on till the present time, and a remarkable blessing has crowned their labours, so that of the Eramanga of to-day compared with the Eramanga of fifteen years ago we may say without much exaggeration, "Old things have passed away, and all things have become new."

As soon as his knowledge of the language allowed, Mr. Robertson took up the work of Scripture translation where his predecessor left off on the day of his death. He completed the Acts of the Apostles, and in 1879 one thousand copies were printed in Sydney at the expense of the British and Foreign Bible Society.

The following extract from a letter of Mr. Robertson to the Society is especially noteworthy, as showing what a wonderful change had come over the Eramangans:—Mr. Robertson had said to the native converts that he thought they ought to pay for the printing of the book. There was no lack of willingness, but how was the thing to be done? Well, where there is a will, a way will generally be found.

"They consulted among themselves, entered heartily into the thing, and any who had money brought it. Others brought weapons of war—clubs, spears, bows and arrows, &c., and sandal-wood—indeed anything they could give to be sold, and the price used to pay for the printing of the book. Thus they contributed over £23 in money and value in a few days, which, we think, was very good for bloodstained Eramanga, where five missionaries have fallen by the savages."

From this time onwards there has been steady progress. The "night of toil" had been long and dreary, but morning had come at length.

In the Report of the Bible Society for 1882 we find the Rev. D. Macdonald of Fate writing as follows:—"Very cheering reports continue to come from Eramanga. A large portion of the people are under instruction. A handsome Martyrs' Memorial Church has been built: a son of the murderer of John Williams laid the corner stone. Mr. Robertson says—'The Christian people of this island are beginning to realise the blessing of giving. A few years ago they raised £24 towards the cost of printing the Acts of the Apostles. This year they prepared 2000 lbs. of arrowroot of the finest quality to pay for Scriptures and in part to defray the expense of a mission cottage at Traitor's Head. The most gratifying circumstance is the way in which they value God's Word, and their desire to read and know it for themselves.'"

In the same Report the Rev. Dr. Steel writes:—"I have the pleasure to enclose £32, 13s. 4d., proceeds of sale of arrowroot from Eramanga. I have been requested to convey the thanks of the missionaries and converts for the prompt consent of the Committee to pay for the printing of the Acts of the Apostles in the language of that blood-stained shore. The Gospel of Christ is now taking hold of the islanders, and all the native teachers employed, over twenty in number, are Christian natives of the island."

In the Bible Society's Report for 1885 we find the following most gratifying intelligence:—"Two thousand copies of the Gospels of Matthew and Mark, prepared by the Rev. H. A. Robertson, and carried through the press at Toronto, have been sent out to Eramanga;" and in the Report for 1886 Dr. Steel writes:—"I have pleasure in forwarding £25 for Eramanga; and, what you will be pleased to receive, a free contribution of £10 to the funds of the Bible Society from the native Christian teachers of Eramanga, as a mark of their gratitude to the Society for its kindness in printing portions of the Holy Scriptures in their language. When you know that these teachers do not receive more than £6 a year in money, the contribution will appear in its liberality. There are now thirty-two Christian natives of Eramanga who are employed in teaching their fellow-islanders, and in conducting religious services in different parts of the island, which they cover as by a network of hallowed influence. Since the Rev. H. A. Robertson returned (last April) he has been much encouraged by the state in which he found the island and the mission, which has been entirely in the hands of the Christian chiefs and teachers. At the Holy Communion 179 partook of the memorials of the Redeemer's body and blood. The whole congregation contained about 600 persons. Mr. Robertson baptized thirty-seven adults and twenty-four children. He also married eight couples. These services were held in the Martyrs' Church, which is erected near the spot, just across the river, where John Williams and his fellow-martyr fell.. The river is now called the Williams River, and the overhanging hill where the Rev. G. N. Gordon and his wife were killed, Mount Gordon."

And now we must close our notice of Eramanga. As we have seen, the Gospel has fairly taken root. God has unmistakably put His hand to the work. Mission stations occupied by native Eramangan teachers encircle the island; a considerable part of the Bible is already in the hands of the people in their own tongue; and if life and health are continued to the missionary, other portions will soon follow. It is only a question of a few years, and, unless unforeseen hindrances arise, this land of mournful memories will be the abode of a Christianised community living in peace and harmony, and showing forth the praises of Him who shall have called them out of darkness into His marvellous light. We have the earnest now, the sun is above the horizon, and, as he ascends, the remaining darkness will be scattered, and Eramanga will be "filled with the knowledge of the glory of the Lord as the waters cover the sea." "The Lord hasten it in His time!"

CHAPTER XIII.

FATE OR SANDWICH ISLAND.

THIS island, the native name of which is Fate or Vate,* was discovered by Captain Cook in 1774, and by him named Sandwich Island, in honour of his patron, the Earl of Sandwich, at that time First Lord of the Admiralty. It is about sixty miles north-west of Eramanga, and lies in east longitude about 168°, and in south latitude between 17° 29' and 17° 43'. According to Captain Cook it is seventy-five miles in circumference. The present population is estimated at 3000. It is a beautiful island, unsurpassed by any island of the New Hebrides, but it has been so fully described of late years in missionary work that not much need be said here on that head; nor need we say much with reference to the natives and the state in which they were found when the steps were taken which have resulted in bringing them into the comparatively prominent position they now occupy.†

All that seems required in this work is to give the reader a few hints as to the state in which the Gospel found the natives, such as will prepare him to appreciate the results which have been realised by the labours of missionaries, and the circulation of the Scriptures among

---

* Pronounced Fātè—the *a*, as *a* in father; the *e*, as *a* in fate.

† Ample information may be found in the works already referred to, viz., Dr. Turner's "Nineteen Years," Dr. Steel's "New Hebrides and Christian Missions," and "Western Polynesia."

them of late years. The island, we may remark, is likely to become an important centre of influence in the group. Its position between the southern and northern divisions of the group, its large tracts of low land fertile in the highest degree, and its bays and harbours—especially its one grand harbour (Havannah), one of the finest and most spacious in Polynesia—will certainly attract to it visitors and settlers in large numbers, and make it a commercial centre of no small importance in future years. Planters and traders are already settled in different parts, chiefly in Havannah harbour, and others will follow.

The natives in some respects are superior to those of the southern islands. They exhibit a finer physique, and seem altogether a more capable race. They had much superior houses, made finer mats, and more beautiful ornaments, &c.; but while in these respects they were in advance of their neighbours, they were not a whit better as regards matters of higher moment.

With the exception of the Fijians, so far as my knowledge extends, there have never been found more revolting and inveterate cannibals in any country in the world. And they practised infanticide to a frightful extent; and the sick, and the aged, and the insane, were treated with the most revolting cruelty. The aged were buried alive, generally, perhaps, at their own request, such is the force of custom; but it was otherwise with the insane—no mercy was shown to them; they were compelled to submit to their cruel fate; and this was also the mode in which infants were put to death. Polygamy was extensively practised, and women were degraded and debased as they invariably are among savages such as the Fatese were. We must not stop to speak of their wars. What we have said will convey a correct idea, so far as it goes, of the state in which the people were when the dayspring from on high opened upon their beautiful island.

The introduction of Christianity was in this wise. In the month of April 1845, two members of the Samoan mission, the Rev. Dr. Turner and the writer, were on a missionary voyage in the first *John Williams* among the New Hebrides and other islands of the Western Pacific. We had visited several islands, and had got as far as Eramanga, a spot in which an intense interest was felt at that time, as only a few years had passed since the massacre of Williams and Harris. We had reserved four teachers whom we fondly hoped we should succeed in introducing to the island. After ascertaining, as fully as we were able, the state of things at Dillon's Bay, the only place where there seemed any likelihood of success, we were constrained to conclude that the time had not come to resume the mission. Our brave teachers offered to land and remain at all risks, but we could not see our way to take the responsibility of leaving them under the circumstances. We were sorely perplexed as to what course we should adopt. The programme of our voyage did not embrace any other island of the New Hebrides—indeed we knew little or nothing beyond the bare names of the northern division of the group in those days. Of course we looked earnestly for help and guidance to Him whose cause we were seeking to advance, and we did not look in vain; nor had we long to wait. Light arose in the darkness, and from about the last quarter to which we should have thought of looking.

A small vessel engaged in the sandal-wood trade lay at anchor alongside of us, and from that most unlikely quarter a call came to us which we could not but regard as the voice of Providence. The captain of the said vessel came on board the *John Williams* and informed us that he had just been to Fate, and that he had found there the remnant of a large party of Samoans and Tongans who many years before (probably not less than twenty) had lost their way at sea, and had been carried by winds and currents to the New Hebrides. They made Tongoa, a small island of that group, remained there about two years, and then left with the intention of trying to find their way back to Tonga or Samoa. In that they failed, making Fate instead; and landing there, they took up their abode at the part of the island where we found them. Out of a party of about fifty only a few individuals remained at the time of our visit; but among them was a Samoan named Sualo, who had formed relations with the natives, and had acquired great influence. He was a daring energetic fellow, had for one of his wives a daughter of the principal chief of the district where he lived, and had made himself famous and formidable by the part he had taken in native wars. He appeared as complete a savage as those among whom he dwelt, but he professed now to be desirous of leading a different life. He had heard of the introduction of Christianity to Samoa and Tonga, and had earnestly begged Captain L——, our informant, to try and get teachers sent to Fate. And to make our way still more plain Captain L—— furnished us with a guide, a young man from New Zealand, who had lived some time with the Samoans and Tongans, and was able to lead us to the very spot where we should find them. The young man was willing to go with us, so with grateful hearts we accepted the Captain's offer, and were soon off to Fate. We found everything as it had been represented, and succeeded, under deeply interesting circumstances, in accomplishing the object of our visit. Our four teachers, Mose, Sipi, Taavili, and Setefana, were placed, two and two, at Pango, a village near the place at which we anchored, and at Erakor, where Sualo and his friends lived. Many interesting incidents occurred which we must not stop to particularise. They may be found in Dr. Turner's "Nineteen Years," and in "Western Polynesia."

The pioneer teachers were brave courageous men. They stuck to their work nobly, though they had to endure trials and encounter dangers great and long continued. One of them, Setefana, after a number of years of faithful toil, died of disease; another, Sipi, died by the hand of violence; and more than once during the early years of the mission it was on the eve of extinction. Repeated visits of missionaries, and reinforcements of teachers from Rarotonga and Samoa, with God's help, enabled us to retain our hold upon it, but at one stage of the mission's history the island was without foreign teachers for between three and four years, and but for a little band of native converts the darkness of heathenism must again have closed over it; but God had put His hand to the work, and the little company had been enabled to hold fast their integrity and witness for Him till a brighter day dawned. From 1854 till July 1858 the little flock was left, owing to circumstances which we could not control, as sheep without a shepherd.

It was in July 1858 that the Rev. George Stallworthy from Samoa, and the Rev. George Gill from Rarotonga, visited the island and reoccupied it with Eastern teachers. They found a state of things which greatly surprised and delighted them. At Erakor the faithful few were found to whom we have referred. The following extract from the report of the deputation will tell its own marvellous tale, and convey a more definite idea than any mere general description. "After leaving an open bay," the deputation writes, "we passed an island, and pulled a mile and a half up a beautiful lagoon to Erakor, which is on the right hand side, and beyond which village it extends at least a mile and a half. We were at once conducted to the chapel, a wattled and plastered building, with a pulpit and seats, which had been built by the natives in the place of one erected by the former teachers which had been blown down.

"A short time after we landed, the hollow trunks of two decayed trees, standing near the chapel, were beaten as a substitute for the church-going bell, and 130 persons, including a large number of children, assembled for worship. We requested the teachers to conduct the service in the usual way. One of them, Petela, entered the pulpit, and gave out a hymn from a small manuscript book which he held in his hand, and a person in the centre of the chapel started the singing, when men, women, and children joined the song, the language and tune of which were alike unknown to us, except that we recognised in it the name that is above every name, which it was music indeed to find cherished and adored in so dark a land as Fate, by a handful of people surrounded by cruel heathen, and with the smallest possible aid from the churches of the Saviour. Petela then requested Pomare (the chief, father-in-law to Sualo) to pray, gave out another hymn, made a short address, and concluded with prayer." The teachers spoken of must have been natives of Fate who had learned more than others from the Samoan and Rarotongan teachers, and had probably been appointed teachers by them, and so naturally took the lead when they were gone.

The above extract gives a deeply interesting glimpse of the "little spot enclosed by grace" out of the surrounding darkness, and furnishes a striking illustration of the vitality of Christianity. Delightful indeed must it have been to hear the praises of Jesus sung by Fatean lips in such circumstances. Speedily may the day dawn when His dear name shall be as ointment poured forth throughout the length and breadth of that beautiful island!

On this occasion three Rarotongan teachers, Teamarn, Teautoa, and Toma, were left on the island, and a fresh start was made, and no serious interruption in the work of the mission again occurred.

The next visit of the mission ship to the island was in October 1859, and Dr. Turner, who was the visitor on that occasion, found on the whole much for which to be thankful. There was one drawback—one of the teachers, Teautoa, and his wife, had died; the remaining two were well, and some progress was being made. The whole population of the village of Erakor (250) were nominally Christian. The Eastern teachers were being kindly treated—the natives supplying them with food without stint and without price. Eight of the natives were employed by the teachers as helpers in Christian work, and these, with six others, the Eastern teachers thought, might be admitted to church fellowship were a church constituted. The Christian party had not been molested by the heathen, but, owing to a superstitious belief that unusual sickness and death followed wherever the new religion was received, they would not allow them to go amongst them to preach.

The next visit was in 1861, the visiting missionaries being Mr. Geddie and the writer, and during that visit a step was taken which marks an era in the history of the mission. This was the formation of a Christian church. The teachers reported to us, as they had done to Dr. Turner, that they believed a number of the people were genuine converts. We conversed individually with those whom they regarded in this light, and were surprised and delighted with the clearness of their views on doctrinal subjects, and the apparent sincerity and earnestness of most of them. Ten were selected, and on the following day, Sabbath, September 13, 1861, a Christian church was constituted on Fate. Eight men and two women were baptized, and the ordinance of the Lord's Supper was observed under circumstances intensely interesting. The Lord's death was commemorated on Fate for the first time—a step was taken which will connect with all the subsequent history of the church on Fate till He come to claim the kingdoms of the earth for His own, and introduce the glorious millennial reign.

We wound up the interesting services of that memorable day by instructing and encouraging the little company of witnesses for Christ, and commending them to Him, and to the word of His grace, which is able to build them up, and to give them an inheritance among all them that are sanctified.

This was the second church that was formed on the New Hebrides; and it is worthy of special note that it was not on Tanna or Eramanga, on which white missionaries had laboured, but on Fate, where no European missionary had yet been stationed.

The time, however, had now come when it was very desirable that the work should be taken up by men of greater culture and capacity than were possessed by the brave pioneers who had laid the foundation and prepared the way. Work must now be taken up to which they were unequal, and, as in the case of Aneiteum, this want was soon to be met in a way very similar to that of the older mission. The Rev. Donald Morrison, who, like Mr. Geddie, had been for some time a settled minister on Prince Edward Island, Nova Scotia, was moved to offer himself for missionary service in the New Hebrides. He was eminently fitted for the position; his offer was gladly accepted by the Mission Board, and in 1864 he and his wife were passengers by the mission schooner *Dayspring*, on her first voyage from Nova Scotia, where she was built. They reached their destination in safety, and were settled at Erakor, the first white missionaries to Fate. They were warmly welcomed by the Eastern teachers and the native Christians, and entered upon their work with great heartiness, and with prospects which seemed to promise a long and useful career. The most pressing need of the mission was books, especially *the* Book, of which all they knew had been learned from the lips of their teachers.

Mr. Morrison must have applied himself with great diligence to the study of the language, seeing that about the space of two years from the time of his arrival he had translated the Gospel of Mark, which was printed in Sydney in 1866. He prepared a Hymn-book also, which was printed in Melbourne in 1867; and this is all the literary work he was permitted to accomplish of which we have any record. His health failed during the course of 1867, and he was obliged to leave the islands. He spent some time in Queensland and New South Wales, and in 1869 he returned to the New Hebrides, but, as it proved, only to take a last look at the place where he had hoped to live and labour for years in the work on which his heart was set, and to bid a final farewell to the poor people for whose salvation he longed with fond desire.

Symptoms of pulmonary consumption had developed themselves, and he went on to New Zealand, to which the *Dayspring* was bound, still cherishing a lingering hope of being able to return at a future time, but it was not to be; the disease developed rapidly, and his promising career was cut short on the 21st of October 1869. His death, like his life, was beautiful. Near the close he remarked to a minister who was visiting him, that now, as he was laid aside from the work to which he had given himself, he could hardly say that he was "in a strait," but was ready "to depart and to be with Christ." Beautiful resignation! And so he passed away to serve his beloved Lord in a higher sphere. He left a church of fifty-five members, and, as we have seen, a Gospel and a Hymn-book in print, and the example of a beautiful consecrated life, and by these his influence and usefulness will be perpetuated.

"Blessed are the dead who die in the Lord, for they rest from their labours, and their works do follow them."

Before Mr. Morrison's departure from Fate, the Rev. James Cosh, M.A., from Scotland, a man of his own stamp, and every way fitted to be his colleague and successor, was stationed with his wife at Pango. Mr. and Mrs. Cosh entered upon their work under encouraging circumstances, and pursued their labours with great zeal and earnestness while health permitted. The Gospel of John and the book of Genesis were translated, and a book of Scripture history was compiled. The Gospel was printed in New Zealand in 1871, at the expense of the British and Foreign Bible Society; the book of Genesis was printed in Sydney in 1874, also at the expense of the Bible Society.

In 1870 Mr. and Mrs. Cosh were obliged to sever their connection with the mission on account of the health of Mrs. Cosh, and the work of Scripture translation was again interrupted. Happily, after a short interval, they were succeeded by the Rev. J. W. and Mrs. Mackenzie from Nova Scotia. Like their predecessors they were warmly welcomed by the natives. They settled at Erakor, taking charge also of Pango, where Mr. and Mrs. Cosh resided. They began their work in 1872, and with a brief interval they have worked on during all the intervening years; and they have been permitted to render much valuable service in the way of Bible translation in addition to general missionary work.

In 1880 the Acts of the Apostles, which Mr. Mackenzie had translated, was printed, and with the Gospels of Mark and John, and the book of Genesis, was in the dialects spoken at Erakor and Pango and places adjacent. As Dr. Inglis remarks in his work recently published, "The curse of Babel has fallen heavily on the New Hebrides," and of this curse Fate has its full share.

In the same year in which Mr. Mackenzie was settled

at Erakor, the Rev. Daniel Macdonald, with Mrs. Macdonald, joined the mission, and were stationed in Havannah Harbour. They were sent by the Presbyterian Church of Victoria. Mrs. Macdonald is a daughter of the late Dr. Geddie. The station they occupy is a very important one, and perhaps it is the most difficult station in the New Hebrides group at the present time. But they seem peculiarly fitted for it, and, by the help of God, they have held on to the present time, and an encouraging measure of success has crowned their labours. To the work of Bible translation Mr. Macdonald has given much attention. In 1877 the Gospel of Luke, which he had translated into the dialect spoken in the district in which he labours, was printed in Sydney at the expense of the British and Foreign Bible Society. Only 300 copies were printed—the readers being few, I suppose, at that date.

In 1883 a revised edition of the same Gospel of 1500 copies was printed in Melbourne; and a translation of the Epistle to the Romans was also printed at the same time and place, and the two portions were bound in a volume. The cost was £60, which was borne by the Bible Society, and refunded by the proceeds of sales of arrowroot made by the natives.

The following extract from a paper full of valuable information, kindly furnished by Mr. Macdonald, shows how the difficulties arising from the variety of dialects is being got over, and what progress has been made up to the present date in making the sacred Scriptures accessible to the people. Mr. Macdonald writes as follows:—

"It will be noted in the foregoing that there are more dialects than one on Fate. In fact, as a rule, every village has some peculiarities of dialect, but all people speaking Fatese understand each other. Hence it soon became a question with Mr. Mackenzie and myself how to deal in the interests of the people, and so as to keep down expense, with this problem of dialects. Our general conclusion was that eventually when the whole New Testament came to be printed, it should be in a compromise dialect, but that meantime we should each print in his own particular dialect single books of Scripture, it being provided that we should not both print one and the same book. We have adhered to this throughout, and the time has now come for carrying part of our plan into execution, and printing the whole New Testament. We have it all translated, and more than two-thirds of it revised, and shall have it ready, D.V., for the press by the latter part of this year (1887).

"In 1885, it having become necessary to reprint the Gospel of John, it was revised and printed as a first attempt at a compromise dialect, which has been found to answer admirably, so that we have no doubt whatever of the wisdom and practicability of our method; indeed, any other method would simply be madness, considering all the circumstances of the case.

"This revision of John was also printed at the expense of the Bible Society, and Mr. Mackenzie's people and mine have jointly refunded the whole of the amount. In like manner we fully purpose, that the Society bearing in the first instance the expense of our New Testament, our natives will fully refund it. We do not sell the books singly to the natives, but all the natives join together at the proper season every year, and make arrowroot, which, being sold, provides for the printing and binding of our translations. Each native is thus entitled to a copy of any book free as soon as he can read it.

"The natives do appreciate the books of Scripture very highly. With them the Word of God as written is the bread of life and the water of life; and unquestionably final judge and settler of all strifes, controversies, and matters whatsoever. The introducing of such a literature among these people, from every point of view, is an incalculable blessing, and undoubtedly one of the noblest and most fruitful works in which any human being can engage is that of giving the Bible to those who have it not.

"How much we missionaries are aided in this work by the noble British and Foreign Bible Society I need not here say. The written Word gives in a peculiar manner also permanence to the work of the missionary, for missionaries and generations of the people pass away, but the Word of God remains for ever.

"Our books (Mr. Mackenzie's and mine) circulate throughout Fate, and in some parts to the north of Fate, as, for instance, on part of Mai, and also on part of Epi (or Api), where Fatese is spoken."

Towards the close of his paper Mr. Macdonald remarks:—"Our work continues to go forward hopefully. But now, in addition to French soldiers, we have two French Roman Catholic missionaries on the island. Should the French establish themselves permanently on the island troubles great and manifold will certainly arise, and Romish priests will add to the trouble. It is a great mercy, however, that the mission is so firmly established, and that so much of the Word of God will shortly be in the hands of the people. We do not fear the priests much when the people have the Bible in their hands; but the secular power of France in alliance with the emissaries of Rome is a thing to be dreaded, as the history of our South Sea missions during the past forty years mournfully proves. But the Lord reigneth, therefore will we not fear."

May He have His servants under His safe keeping continually, may their labours be more and more abundantly blessed, and may they be spared for many years to bring forth fruit to His glory, and to scatter blessings far and wide, not only on Fate, but elsewhere throughout the great New Hebrides group!

CHAPTER XIV.

NGUNA AND OTHER ISLANDS*

NGUNA is a small island to the north of Fate, only about six miles distant. It is about six miles in length by four in breadth, and it has a population of about 1000; but, though small, it is important as a basis of operation in relation to other islands in its neighbourhood. No less than fourteen islands are visible from it, and on thirteen of these the same language or dialect is spoken or understood—a remarkable thing for the New Hebrides—and on these thirteen islands there is a population estimated at 4500. These islands are separated from each other by short distances, Tongoa, the most distant, being only about twenty-five or thirty miles from Nguna; hence they are of easy access the one from the other. Some of the other islands are larger than Nguna, but it has the largest population, and for that and other reasons it is the most eligible for a principal mission station. Next to it in importance is Tongoa, which has a population estimated at 800. The islands are generally lofty. Nguna rises to the height of 1500 feet, and Tongoa to 1800, and the lowest is between 400 and 500 feet; and being all small, and the regular south-east trade winds blowing over them for about nine months out of the twelve, and there being no low marshy ground to generate malaria, they are much

---

* This is a very awkward name to pronounce. The two first letters are sounded like the terminal letters *ng* in English—a *nasal* sound.

more healthy than the larger islands of the group. Thus they furnish a fine field for missionary enterprise.

The natives are very similar to their neighbours on Fate, so we need not trouble the reader with any particular description of them. They were fierce savage cannibals in their heathen state. Some dreadful encounters have taken place between them and white men engaged in the labour traffic which brought the worst side of their character into sad prominence. Though it is difficult to determine which party were guilty of the greatest savageism, it is easy to see on which side the greatest blame rests. Sad facts illustrative of the character and doings of the men who engage in the labour traffic may be found in Dr. Steel's book (p. 242, &c.).

The missionary history of the island dates from 1870. In the course of that year the Rev. Peter Milne and his wife, from the Presbyterian Church of New Zealand, settled upon it. Little seems to have been done to prepare the way for their settlement, so they must have had rough work in the early years of their mission life, and must often have been in great peril. They had counted the cost, however, and were prepared to hazard their lives in order to make known to perishing men the Gospel of the grace of God. Two Rarotongan teachers, Ta and Iona, were associated with them; but whether these preceded them or accompanied them I am not aware. The greatest trials which they had to encounter arose from the quarter to which we have already referred—the vile labour traffic. Patient, persevering work, however, was in due time crowned with success. Mr. Milne's labours were extended to several other islands, and a good work is in progress on some of them, especially Pele and Mataso.

For seven years Mr. and Mrs. Milne laboured alone, but in 1878 they had the joy of welcoming a fellow-labourer, Mr. Oscar Michelsen, from the Presbyterian

Church of Otago, New Zealand. In the course of 1879 Mr. Michelsen removed to Tongoa, the largest island of a group of five islands named the Shepherd Isles. From that all the islands of the group can be easily reached, so from it on the north, and Nguna on the south, all the thirteen islands referred to above can be worked without much difficulty; and with the assistance of native teachers, we may hope that in a few years they will all be under Christian culture, and that a large harvest will be gathered in.

In a letter from Mr. Milne, dated June 30th, 1887, with especial reference to Bible translation, he gives much valuable information. He writes as follows:—" The complete books of Scripture translated by me and printed are not many, only the Gospels by Matthew and John bound together, and the First Epistle of John bound by itself. Besides these we have three small books of Scripture extracts, also translated by me, containing portions here and there throughout the Bible from Genesis to Revelation, the book of Jonah in full, with the exception of his prayer in the fish's belly, which is difficult. The books translated, but not yet printed, are the Gospel by Luke and the Acts of the Apostles, which I hope to get printed and bound together soon. The portion now on hand is the Gospel by Mark; it is almost finished, as I am now at the thirteenth chapter. When it is finished I intend to begin the Epistles, and hope to get the whole New Testament translated and printed before I die.

"I got Matthew and John printed at the expense of the British and Foreign Bible Society in 1882. Two thousand copies were printed, and we get them bound and sent out by instalments as we required them, and we pay for them as we get them. We have already paid the Society for 1100 copies from proceeds of sales of arrowroot, some of which we make every year, and send it either to Otago or Scotland to be sold.

"My translations are intelligible to about 7000 people, from Fate to the south-east end of Epi inclusive. A different language is spoken on some of the intervening islands, but the people generally understand both languages. The Nguna dialect is spoken by a large number of people on the north side of Fate: on other parts of Fate the dialect differs, but not so much as to make the Nguna books unintelligible. The Nguna books are used by Mr. Michelsen on Tongoa. The Nguna dialect is the one spoken by far the largest number of people, and is the purest; the others seem to be corruptions of it. Every syllable ends with a vowel, as in the Eastern languages.

"As to how the portions of Scripture are received. As soon as any one makes up his mind to be a Christian he is anxious to get the books even before he can read them, and there can be no doubt but that the influence for good exerted by them is very great. Some on applying to me for baptism have told me that they were afraid on account of such passages as this, 'Even now is the axe laid unto the roots of the trees,' &c. The heathen used to have a superstitious dread of the books, and would not let their children come to school, or even take a book to learn to read, lest they should die. That superstition is now breaking down, though it still prevails to a considerable extent. Very few of the heathen will let their children come to school till they make up their minds to come along with them.

"Our prospects now are brighter than they have ever been before. Since this time last year I have baptized 129 adults, and 20 children. Our church members are now 246. Of these 45 belong to Emae or Three Hills Island, where I have five schools. There are at present about 150 candidates for baptism. I have at present in the different islands under my care fifteen schools, with an aggregate attendance of more than 1000, and by the time you receive this letter I hope to have two more schools opened, the houses for which are in the course of erection. We have this year supplied Mr. Michelsen on Tongoa with three couples as teachers, for all which we have much reason to thank God and take courage."

THE ISLANDS OF EPI AND AMBRYM.

In 1882 the Rev. R. M. Fraser from Tasmania and his wife settled on Epi. They had a good reception, and entered upon their work with much to encourage. On no island of the New Hebrides, I think, has there been a more hopeful commencement, or rather I ought to say recommencement, for an attempt to introduce Christianity to the island was made many years ago. In 1861 two Rarotongan teachers, named Iro and Pipo, with their wives, were placed upon it; but after a short time both the teachers died, the mission was broken up, and the widows were taken to their homes in the *John Williams*. In 1886 Mr. Fraser was able to make the following encouraging report:—"The Gospel by Mark in the Baki language has been put into the hands of the people at Burumba, and there it has been my privilege to form a church of five members, first-fruits from Epi. A teacher was settled in Bieria in August, where a hopeful beginning has been made. In the Sakan district the interest in the Word is spreading. A good number have joined the worshipping people during the year. Three couples from this district are now under training with a view to be teachers."

These facts are highly encouraging. There is evidently a good beginning made on Epi. But while the missionary was able to give so cheering a report of his work and of the prospects of the mission, he had a very sad tale to tell with reference to himself. "The year now closing," he says, "has been one of sad loss to me personally as well as to the work on this island. My loved wife and two children have been called to their rest; still we have much to thank God for." This is all the good man says about his terrible trial. May the God of mercy sustain and cheer him.

The island of Ambrym lies about sixteen miles to the north of Epi. Missionary operations were commenced on it in 1883. In August of that year the Rev. W. B. Murray, M.A., and his wife settled on the island. Their reception, like that of Mr. and Mrs. Fraser, was all that could be expected under the circumstances, and they entered upon their work full of hope and zeal. Alas! however, their fair prospects were soon clouded. Mr. Murray's health failed. Symptoms of pulmonary disease appeared, and he was obliged to quit the field and come to Australia, as it proved, to die. He was a young man of great promise. He longed to return to his loved work in the islands as long as any ground for hope remained, but it pleased the Master to call him to other service. He translated a few brief Scripture extracts, and strove in every way open to him to serve the great cause during his brief term of service.

In 1884 he was succeeded by his brother, the Rev. Charles Murray, M.A., and he and his wife were soon at work on the island. Writing in November 1886, he reports that Mr. Watt had printed a primer for him, and that he had opened school, and that some were making fair progress in learning to read. He was able to address the people in their own language, and his congregation numbered as many as seventy-eight. "There is not the slightest breath of opposition," Mr. Murray remarks; "on the contrary, the people manifest the greatest goodwill and kindly feeling."

One very interesting fact Mr. Murray mentions, as follows:—"On the 2nd of September we stationed an

Eramangan teacher at a place about ten to eleven miles to the south. The dialect spoken here differs somewhat from the one spoken there. The teacher's reception was exceedingly favourable and encouraging. For about a year his example will be his most eloquent address." Here surely is something worthy of special note—a Christian teacher from Eramanga settled on Ambrym! Savage Eramanga sending forth her sons to teach and exemplify the Gospel of peace and love—what a marvel is this! Verily,

"Wonders of grace to God belong."

Mr. Murray closes his report as follows:—"This is our day of small things, and we have lots of little troubles and difficulties to cope with, but we trust that time and the diffusion of knowledge will ultimately clear these away." *

Epi and Ambrym are both large and important islands. Epi, as we have seen, is only about seventeen miles to the north of Tongoa, and it and Ambrym are about the same distance from each other. The two islands are about the same size, being estimated at sixty miles in circumference, and probably they are about equally populous. They are both lofty, the highest mountain on Epi being 2800 feet, and the highest elevation of the mountains of Ambrym being 3500 feet; and they are both fertile in the highest degree, and they are not excelled in beauty by any island of the New Hebrides group. For a most interesting description of both, see Dr. Steel's book, chaps. xiv. and xvi., pp. 273 and 297.

---

* Since the above was written I have learned, with deep regret, that Mr. Murray has been obliged for climatic reasons to leave the islands, and that he is not likely to return. Should this prove the case I trust a worthy successor will speedily be found to take up and carry forward the work so hopefully begun by his deceased brother and himself.

THE LOYALTY ISLANDS.

CHAPTER XV.

MARÉ.*

THE Loyalty Islands lie about 120 miles to the west of the New Hebrides, and about 60 miles to the north of New Caledonia. When Christianity was introduced to this group in 1841, it was very little known to the civilised world. Captain Erskine of H.B.M. ship *Havannah*, who visited it in 1849, says it was so little known at that time as "scarcely to have a place on our charts; and their western sides and the position of their different points had never been ascertained till our hurried visit in the *Havannah*."

Of the island of Mare, Captain Erskine writes as follows:—"The discovery of Mare has been claimed for a Captain Butler of the ship *Walpole* in 1800, and by others for the *Britannia* in 1803, which latter name appears first on any chart as attached to one of the larger islands of the group. M. d'Urville states that in 1827, although the uncertain group of the Loyalty Islands appeared on a chart of Arrowsmith's, M. Rossel, his hydrographer, doubted their existence; and their extent was certainly first ascertained by M. d'Urville." M. d'Urville gave the names of Chabrol and Haglan to Lifu

* Pronounced Mārē—the *a* as *a* in father, and the *e* as *a* in fate.

and Uvea, and retained Britannia as the name of Mare. The name by which the natives call the island is Nengone, but it is now known by the name of Mare.

Mare is a low flat island of coral formation about eighty miles in circumference, and having a population of about 4000. Clumps of pines appear on some parts near the coast, and at others there are immense blocks of coral, somewhat resembling artificial fortifications, which relieve the monotonous appearance of the island, and make it in some parts look quite picturesque. One of these is named Castle Point, from its resemblance to an old castle or fortification, and others, both on Mare and Lifu, might with equal propriety bear the same name. In some parts, instead of the bold and barren coast, there are tracts of lowland sloping down to the sea and terminating in a sandy beach.

The natives are a robust, brave, hardy race, of the Papuan stock, but superior to many of the tribes belonging to that division of the human family. In their heathen state they were fierce cannibal savages, addicted to all the vices and revolting practices usually found in savage life.

It was the writer's privilege to introduce Christian teachers to the island in April 1841. Very strikingly was the hand of God manifested in the manner in which this was accomplished. We made the island in the London Missionary Society's brig *Camden* on the morning of the 8th of April. All the forenoon we kept close in to the shore, looking anxiously for indications of the presence of human beings: nothing of this kind, however, appeared; huge coral barriers seemed to warn us off, and nothing to encourage could be discerned. After dinner a boat was lowered, and we pulled in as close to the land as we could with safety, and proceeded slowly along the coast till night was drawing on and hope was almost extinct, when to our great joy light appeared in the darkness—a canoe was descried in the distance; hope revived, and we made all haste to get within hail of the little craft, and what was our surprise when, as we drew near, a man stood up in the canoe and shouted to us in the Samoan language, "Ua ou iloa le Atua moni"—"I know the true God." It seemed like a voice from heaven. All that was needful to the accomplishment of our object was provided to our hand. Our most urgent need was an interpreter, and next to that a guide; and here were both in one. The man who hailed us proved to be a native of Niuataputapu, an island of the Tongan group, who with others of his countrymen had lost their way at sea many years before, and were now as familiar with the language and the island as the natives themselves. We resigned ourselves without misgivings to the guidance of our newly found friend, whose name was Taufa, and by his help, and under the guidance of Divine providence, we succeeded in accomplishing our object. Two Samoan teachers, Taniela and Tataio, were introduced to the island. They met with an encouraging reception, and we left rejoicing that God had so far prospered our way. We were very favourably impressed with the appearance of the natives, and everything seemed to encourage the hope of an easy conquest. In this expectation, however, we were sorely disappointed. The "night of toil" was long and deeply trying; eight weary years passed before the hearts of the toilers were gladdened by a single ray of light, and during these years they endured great privations, and their lives were often in imminent peril. They plodded on, however, and at length they had their reward. One of the two pioneers, indeed, rested from his labours long before the dawn appeared—entered, we trust, into the joy of his Lord; but after a time reinforcements came to the help of the survivor, and in due time success crowned their toil, and a precious and most abundant harvest was gathered in. In few parts of the mission field have more striking displays of the power and grace of God appeared than on the island of Mare.

In 1854, thirteen years after the introduction of the Samoan teachers, the Rev. S. M. Creagh and the Rev. J. Jones, with their wives, settled on the island. They were accompanied by the Rev. J. P. Sunderland and Mrs. Sunderland of the Samoan mission, who remained with them for ten months, and during that time rendered very valuable service. Their experience would have been valuable under any circumstances, but in the state in which the mission then was it was doubly so. About one-third of the population had renounced heathenism and embraced Christianity. Hundreds had learned to read, and services and schools were attended by crowds of eager worshippers and learners, and not a few gave evidence of having passed from death unto life; and these especially were hungering and thirsting to know more of the great truths which had so stirred their souls, and introduced them, as it were, into a new world. What they had learned had only whetted the appetite and made them long for more.

All they had in print when the missionaries settled among them were four chapters of the Gospel according to John, which had been translated by the Rev. William Nihil of the Melanesian mission, who resided a few months on the island, before the arrival of the missionaries of the London Missionary Society; about a dozen hymns, and a few pages of Scripture extracts which must have been translated by the teachers from the Rarotongan or Samoan. The four chapters of the Gospel were printed at New Zealand, and the hymns and Scripture extracts at Rarotonga. We need hardly remark that the missionaries applied themselves with all possible diligence to the study of the language. Mr. Sunderland had the advantage over the young brethren, as he could freely communicate with the Samoan teachers, and from them obtain invaluable help, of which he made the best use. During the few months of his residence on the island he so far mastered the language that with the assistance of the Samoan and Rarotongan teachers he translated the Gospel of Mark, and thus rendered a service of incalculable value.

Happily Mr. Creagh was acquainted with the art of printing, and he had a small folio printing press which he had obtained in Samoa on his way to Mare, so the precious treasure was soon in the hands of the natives. Mr. Creagh composed the type and set up the pages, and set the natives to work off the sheets. Two thousand copies were printed, and the hunger of the natives was so far met. They, we need hardly remark, received this first instalment of the Book of God with the greatest avidity. The number printed was such that I suppose every family got a copy, so there was doubtless universal rejoicing. Those who have been familiar with the Bible from infancy can form but a faint idea of the feelings with which those receive it who have grown up to manhood and womanhood in heathen darkness when they look upon it for the first time. It is something like passing from midnight darkness to the light of the noonday sun.

"In almost every hut," says Mr. Jones, "or seated on the grass outside, the natives might be seen trying to spell out and learn the 'Word,' as they called it. With such avidity did they study it that plantation and other work was much neglected for a time; and when the women would gently hint to their husbands that they might lend a hand in providing for the wants of the family, they would reply, 'How can I help you? Don't you see I am reading the Word?'"

Mr. Jones mentions the case of one young man who was living on the mission premises, who committed the entire book to memory in the short space of two weeks. He used to repeat a chapter to the missionary every night with scarcely a mistake till his task was completed.

The next portion printed was the Gospel according to Luke. It was translated in equal parts by Messrs. Creagh and Jones, and printed by Mr. Creagh at the Samoan mission press. Four thousand copies were printed, and were a great boon to the natives, thirsting as they were for more copious supplies of the Word of Life.

Towards the close of 1867 the translation of the New Testament was completed, the whole, with the exception of the Gospel of Mark, having been done in equal proportions by Messrs. Creagh and Jones. It had been printed and published in parts on the spot. The printing and binding was all done by Mr. Creagh, with the assistance of natives whom he instructed in both these arts.

At the close of 1867 Mr. Jones proceeded to England on a visit, and during his stay there he carried through the press a second edition of the New Testament, the whole having been thoroughly revised by himself and Mr. Creagh. The British and Foreign Bible Society, with their usual generosity, undertook the work of printing and binding. The edition consisted of 4000 copies. It was a handsome volume, demy 8vo, small pica type, in different styles of binding. The first instalment of 2000 reached the island in 1870, and their arrival was no doubt hailed with joy by the natives.

In 1858 Mr. Creagh was in Sydney, and in response to his appeals friends there presented him with a good demy albion press and longprimer type; and a gentleman in England, Richard Peek, Esq., of Hazlewood, Devonshire, sent Mr. Creagh, at his request, a quantity of pica type, so he was able to carry on the work of printing more satisfactorily than he had hitherto been.

During Mr. Jones' absence in England, Mr. Creagh translated the books of Genesis, Exodus, Leviticus, Isaiah, and Jeremiah; and he printed Genesis and Exodus at the mission press on Mare.

In 1871 Mr. Creagh removed to the neighbouring island of Lifu, and Mr. Jones was left alone on Mare, and had to carry on the translation of the Old Testament single-handed. He translated the book of Psalms, which was carried through the press by Mr. Creagh during a visit which he made to England in 1876. No other part of the Old Testament has yet been printed. Mr. Jones had well nigh, if not quite, completed the remaining portions when he was expelled by the French from the scene of his life-long labours on the 9th of December 1887; and for the present the work of revision is suspended on account of that high-handed proceeding.

On Mr. Jones' arrival in Sydney after his expulsion, he and Mr. Creagh commenced the revision of the entire Bible, and were proceeding with it when a telegram from the Directors of the London Missionary Society instructed Mr. Jones to proceed at once to England. If, however, life is spared, and health continued, the work will be resumed, and completed; and though those who rule the French nation may take from the defenceless people of Mare their liberties, appropriate their lands, and expel their missionaries, they will find it a difficult task to prevent them from obtaining possession of and reading God's own Book. Surely the home authorities of the great French nation will never sanction the proceedings of their representatives on New Caledonia when the state of the case between them and the missionaries is properly understood.

Mr. Jones remarks that "in every case the British and Foreign Bible Society has rendered very effective aid, being ever ready to print the translations, or supply paper for printing on the islands." Mr. Jones also bears testimony to the high estimation in which the Scriptures are held by the natives. "This," he remarks, "is shown by the efforts they make to purchase them.* Not having money at first, instructed by the missionary, they prepared cocoa-nut fibre, and afterwards the copra industry was started; and though the island is poor in cocoa-nuts, they were willing in most cases to part with these, to them so valuable, in order to obtain the Scriptures.

"They lose many of their books through fires, hurricanes, &c., and they consider the loss of their Bibles the greatest loss of all; and many are the applications made to the missionary to replace lost ones. The missionary generally refuses, however, on the ground that the books belong to the Bible Society, and recommends the plan of a subscription, heading the list with a franc from himself, and sending the applicant away to collect from his friends. This plan is always successful, as the natives generally are kind towards each other; and besides, no one knows how soon he may need to ask a similar favour."

The following remarks from Mr. Jones will not be out of place in a work on the translation and circulation of the Bible. They show that on Mare, as elsewhere throughout our Polynesian missions, the Bible has been the bulwark of Protestantism. It has under God kept the bulk of our people steadfast in their adherence to the doctrines which it teaches, and it has cheered and sustained them under the cruel persecution which, especially on the Loyalty Islands, they have had to endure. Mr. Jones writes as follows:—

"The people of Mare have of late suffered very much persecution from the French Government in consequence of their conscientious scruples about joining the French State Church. Their churches, which they built themselves, have been closed by the French authorities; and

---

* The island edition was not sold, but given gratuitously, on the ground that in early years the natives were too poor to purchase books.

they are not allowed to gather for worship on the Sabbath or any other days. But they have their Bibles; and with these they may be seen on Sundays, in almost every house on the island, with their families gathered around them, reading the Bible and explaining it as they are able. They have also family Sunday schools for teaching their children to read the Bible."

The remark as to teaching the children to *read* the Bible in Sunday schools has reference to the fact that the schools for teaching in the vernacular have been closed for some time past, and that the French language only is allowed to be taught in the schools.

It is deeply painful to think of the wrongs which the defenceless people have suffered at the hands of their French rulers. They began by seizing their country without the shadow of a claim, and subjecting them to their rule, entirely ignoring their right to have any voice in the matter, as though it were a thing that concerned them not. They placed them under laws in the making of which they had no voice. They divided out their lands in the most arbitrary manner, put down in some cases the rightful chiefs, and set up others as supposed interest or caprice inclined them; and not content with thus stripping them of their civil rights, and reducing them to a state of complete thraldom, they have taken from them that which to a Christian man is his dearest heritage—"freedom to worship God" according to the dictates of his own conscience. At this moment, February 1887, the Protestant pastors of Mare are in exile on New Caledonia, charged with no other crime than refusing obedience to the Government in matters of conscience.*

* Since the above was written the gratifying intelligence has been received from Mr. Jones that M. Nouet, the recently appointed Governor of New Caledonia, has released and returned to their homes all the Mare exiles; and that his excellency has determined that the persecutions

And the inflicter of these cruel wrongs on a defenceless people is the great French nation, which prides itself on its chivalry and boasts of its freedom, and professes to allow religious liberty to all its subjects. The pretext for seizing the Loyalty Islands was that they were dependencies of New Caledonia, which they were not. They were just as little dependencies of New Caledonia as France is of England; and even if they were, the French would have to show that they had a right to New Caledonia, which they cannot do. The truth is that they took possession of that island without the shadow of a claim. If any nation could lay a claim to New Caledonia that nation was England. It was hers by right of discovery, and it was hers on another ground, which France, in her own case, would not, when it suited her purpose, regard as of small importance—Captain Cook, England's great navigator, hoisted the British flag on New Caledonia, and took possession of it in the name of the King of England.

Alas! for the whole group! It was a dark day for it when the grand nation hoisted its flag on the shores of New Caledonia. God pity the remnant that is left on that great island, and help and succour the persecuted and downtrodden people of that and the Loyalty Islands!

carried on in the Loyalty Islands under the rule of his predecessors shall entirely cease.

CHAPTER XVI.

LIFU.

The island of Lifu is the largest and most populous of the Loyalty group. It is about thirty-five miles distant from Mare, and about sixty from New Caledonia. It is fifty miles in length, and twenty-five in breadth. It is a low coral island very similar in its general appearance to Mare. Its highest parts do not exceed 250 feet.

The natives are similar in every respect to their neighbours on Mare. In bodily appearance, in manners and customs, and in character they were almost identical in their heathen state, and the same influences have been operating on both islands since the introduction of Christianity, so the similarity between them continues to the present day. The number of the population a few years since was estimated at 7000, and probably it is rather under than over that now.

Christian teachers were introduced to the island in 1842. Two Rarotongan teachers, Paoo and Sakaria, were left on Mare by the Rev. Aaron Buzacott of Rarotonga and the Rev. Thomas Slatyer of Samoa, with instructions to proceed to Lifu as soon as that might be judged advisable by themselves and their brethren on Mare. During the course of the same year they carried out their instructions. The Mare teachers accompanied them, and introduced them to their sphere of labour, and they seemed to have entered upon their work under fairly promising circumstances.

In 1845 the first visit by white missionaries was made to the island in the first *John Williams*. At that time the mission was found in a most critical state. One of the teachers, Sakaria, had apostatised (a rare thing happily among our teachers), and Paoo had been left to labour and suffer alone; and most nobly had he held on in circumstances about as trying as can well be conceived. A few of the natives, about thirty or forty, had attached themselves to him, and among these was Bula, the most influential chief in the island; and to him no doubt, under God, Paoo was indebted for his safety and the success that had attended his efforts. The mission was reinforced by the addition of two teachers, and the brave pioneer and his little band of followers were greatly cheered and encouraged. A fresh start was made, and a little progress followed, and for twelve months or more the prospects continued to brighten. The time for continued advancement, however, had not yet arrived. Trials long and perilous began towards the close of 1846, and continued throughout a large part of 1847, which well nigh led to the extinction of the mission. The powerful chief Bula died, and inter-tribal wars broke out in consequence. The Christian party were scattered, and the teachers thought it advisable to retire for a time to Mare, and there wait the issue of the war. They had not long to wait. In a few months they returned and resumed their labours, and they were soon cheered by decided indications that the labours and sufferings of former years had not been in vain. The seed sown in tears, which had lain dormant for a season, had not lost its vitality; and now under favouring circumstances it sprang up suddenly and with marvellous fruitfulness. In the few months after the return of the teachers a wonderful change came over the island. A reaction indeed had begun before their return, and messengers had been sent to beg them to return. The reaping-time had come, and from that time onward there was rapid and uninterrupted progress for a number of years.

Of course the work had to be carried on under immense disadvantages. The teachers had not even elementary books in the native language, and it was not till 1855 that any attempt was made to translate any portion of the Word of God into the vernacular. During the course of that year the Rev. William Nihil, who has already been mentioned in connection with the Mare mission, translated, with the assistance of the teachers, the first chapter of the Gospel according to John. The translation of course must have been very imperfect, as Mr. Nihil knew only the Mare dialect, but under the circumstances the attempt was laudable as an effort to give a taste of the Bread of Life to the thousands of souls who were hungering for it. It was printed by Mr. Creagh at the mission press on Mare.

For the above interesting item of information, and for all that follows relative to the translation of the sacred Scriptures into the language of Lifu, I am entirely indebted to Mr. Creagh, who has spent thirty-three years of his life in the Loyalty Islands, and has taken a leading part in the translation work which he describes, and has superintended all the printing that has been done on the two islands of Mare and Lifu from the commencement of the mission to the present day.

The first Gospel printed in the language of Lifu was that of Mark, translated by the late lamented and much beloved Bishop Patteson of the Melanesian mission, who at the time was chaplain to the late Bishop Selwyn. Bishop Patteson had an extraordinary aptitude for the acquisition of languages, and having spent a few months on Lifu before the arrival of missionaries from the London Missionary Society, he rendered the above invaluable service to the mission. The printing was done in New Zealand in 1859, and the edition consisted of about 500 copies, and it was a priceless boon to the natives.

In October of the same year the Rev. Samuel M'Farlane and the Rev. William Baker, with their wives, arrived from the London Missionary Society, and settled on the island. Mr. Baker retired from the mission in 1862, and towards the close of that year Mr. M'Farlane had completed the translation of the Gospel according to Matthew, which was printed on Mare. The edition consisted of 4000 copies, and the pressing need of the mission was so far met.

From this time the translation of the other books of the New Testament by Mr. M'Farlane went on apace. The Gospel by John was completed, and an edition of 5000 copies was printed on Mare in 1866; the Acts of the Apostles, the Epistle to the Romans, and the First and Second Epistles to the Corinthians were printed in 1867, 5000 copies each; and Galatians to Revelations followed in 1868. Thus in a marvellously short time the translation and printing of the New Testament in the Lifu dialect was completed. I suppose the work was accomplished in a much shorter time than under ordinary circumstances would have been practicable owing to the calamities which came upon the island, and compelled Mr. M'Farlane to refrain in a great measure from the more active work of the mission. These calamities arose from the conduct of the French authorities on New Caledonia, referred to in the chapter on Mare. It would not comport with the design of this work to enter into details respecting the cruel outrages that were inflicted on the unoffending and defenceless natives and their teachers. A full account may be found in the "Story of the Lifu Mission," by Mr. M'Farlane, published by Messrs. Nisbet & Co., Berners Street, London, in 1873.

For a time the native schools were closed, and the Samoan and Rarotongan teachers were compelled to leave the island after having been treated in the most brutal manner, and the native teachers and even the English missionaries were not allowed either to preach or teach. What a mercy therefore was it that the people had in their hands so large a portion of the sacred Scriptures, and so were in possession of a treasure of which no tyranny of man could deprive them; and no doubt the cruel persecution they had to endure drove them to cleave more closely to Him who is a refuge in the time of trouble, and who knoweth them who trust in Him.

In 1869 the book of Psalms, which had been translated by the Rev. James Sleigh, who joined the mission in 1862, was printed, the edition consisting of 5000 copies. "All these books," Mr. Creagh remarks, "were printed in long-primer type, double column, in verses, without headings to chapters or pages, demy 12mo. The paper for all was furnished by the British and Foreign Bible Society. For the same reason that the island edition of the Mare version was given to the people, the Lifuans received their books which were printed on the islands gratis."

The whole of the New Testament in the two dialects of Mare and Lifu (except the Gospel of Luke in Mare, and Mark in Lifu), the Psalms in Lifu, and Genesis and Exodus in Mare, were printed on Mare between the years 1855 and 1869.

In anticipation of a visit to England by Mr. M'Farlane, he and Mr. Sleigh in 1870 revised the whole of the New Testament; the Psalms having been so recently printed did not receive so minute a revision. In 1873 these, the New Testament and Psalms, were printed in England by the British and Foreign Bible Society, under the editorship of Mr. M'Farlane, the edition consisting of 4000. The book was similar to the island edition, except that small pica type was used, and the size was demy 8vo. The first 2000, bound in dark sheepskin, gilt edged, and lettered sides, were soon disposed of; a third thousand, bound dark calf and gilt, are now in the course of sale. The price for those bound in sheep was four shillings, and for those in calf four shillings and fivepence.

The first books of the Old Testament translated and printed (except the book of Psalms already referred to) were the books of the Pentateuch—Genesis, Exodus, and Leviticus being the work of Mr. Sleigh; Numbers and Deuteronomy being done by Mr. Creagh. In 1874 and 1875 these were revised by Messrs. Creagh and Sleigh in committee, assisted by three native pundits, and they were printed in London, under the editorship of Mr. Creagh, by the British and Foreign Bible Society in 1877. The style and binding were uniform with the New Testament and Psalms. Four thousand copies were printed. One thousand were bound up with the New Testament and Psalms in dark roan. These sold rapidly at six francs (four shillings and tenpence) per copy. The Pentateuch by itself is sold at four francs (three shillings and twopence) per copy.

The translation of other books of the Old Testament was proceeded with in due course. The book of Job was done by Mr. Sleigh. All the other books, from Joshua to Malachi inclusive, except the Psalms, were translated by Mr. Creagh, the work being completed in 1884.

In 1881, Mr. Sleigh having returned from a visit to England, Mr. Creagh and he entered upon the work of giving a thorough revision to the whole Bible, with a view to its being printed in England in one volume. This great work was completed in August 1884, the revisers having sat 361 days of nine hours each.

The work was evidently gone about in the most careful manner; the best available aid was secured, and the brethren strove to the utmost to convey to the native mind the truth of God with the least possible alloy. "The committee meetings," Mr. Creagh remarks, "have been of the greatest service to ourselves in improving our knowledge of the language, and they have been seasons of enjoyment. In investigating texts so as to give the true idea in the native idiom new light has broken in on many portions of the Word of God, and our minds have thereby been much benefited."

The brethren had the assistance of six native pundits all through this final revision. These deserving men gave their services most willingly, though at some considerable sacrifice. They esteemed it an honour and a privilege to have a hand in so important a work. Beyond being supplied with provisions, partly furnished by the Christian community and partly by the missionaries, and having two suits of clothes each from the British and Foreign Bible Society, given at the suggestion of the missionaries, they received no remuneration from man.

This edition it is expected will be printed in London in 1888. It will be printed in paragraphs, with marginal references (which have been supplied by Mr. Creagh); bourgeois type, dark calf binding with red edges, and no headings to chapters nor pages. With reference to the carrying out of this revision Mr. Creagh has furnished the following interesting information:—"In our revision work, every verse was read over many times; every hemistich, every sentence, every word was fully discussed and criticised, the natives being required to look well after their own idioms; but much of the matter being entirely new to them, it involved no little trouble and explanation to enable them to obtain an intelligent idea of the meaning. I read the manuscript and made the corrections. In the Pentateuch alone we had 13,376 corrections; in the Gospels there were 17,490; in the Acts 4080; in the Epistles 13,312; and in the Psalms 6790 = 55,048. These corrections refer only to the previously printed portions; the corrections in the unprinted manuscripts would not be fewer in proportion. All these corrections in the printed portions had to be written twice; first the original sheets; then we made a copy for safety, so that in case the MS. should by any unforeseen accident be lost, we should be able to obtain another without having to go over all our work again. The written portion had to be copied; my wife and daughter rendered me good help in that way. I tried native copyists, but they were not sufficiently careful to be depended on.

"We used all available help, notwithstanding we are conscious that our translation is anything but perfect. The versions consulted were the Hebrew, Greek, Latin, French, English Authorised, and Revised versions; the Samoan, Rarotongan, Mare, and Aneiteumese. With my daughter's assistance I went over all the proper names in the Old Testament in order to have the orthography uniform. This we easily managed by the help of the Englishman's Concordance. I found I had to make a great number of corrections in the proper names."

These minute particulars have, I think, a special value. They show, as no mere general description could, the extreme care with which the work of Bible translation was gone about in the case of the Lifu version, and warrant a large measure of confidence in the accuracy of that version. Mr. Creagh modestly remarks that he and his fellow-labourer regard their version as anything but perfect. That remark indeed will apply to the best translation ever made. It is only an approximation to perfection that can be attained; but we may conclude with a comfortable assurance that the Lifu version is such that it will not mislead the natives on any point of vital moment, and that the errors and imperfections are of trivial importance; and I think from a considerable acquaintance with our South Sea versions that the reader may regard the Lifu version as a fairly representative one, and the promoters of Bible circulation may rest assured that those who are workers together with them are devoting themselves with conscientious fidelity to the great work to which God has called them. And it is matter for devout gratitude that hundreds of men of similar stamp are spending their lives in other parts of the great mission field in opening up the treasures of Divine truth to the nations of the earth.

Version after version, each representing a vast amount of consecrated toil, is being added to the hundreds already in circulation; and the work will doubtless advance with accelerated speed as the millennial age draws on when the mystery of God will be finished, and He who is the Alpha and the Omega—the beginning and the end of the Revelation of God—will sway His sceptre of peace and love over a ransomed and renovated world.

CHAPTER XVII.

UVEA.

UVEA is the name of a beautiful group of coral islands lying about sixty miles to the east of New Caledonia, and forming a portion of the Loyalty Islands. The principal island is a curved strip of land thirty miles in length, and about three miles in breadth, and about 150 feet in height. The island next in size is separated from its larger neighbour by a channel about a quarter of a mile in breadth, and is twenty miles in length. The other islands, numbering about twenty, are mere islets. The whole enclose a circular lagoon twenty miles in diameter, with soundings all over, and forming one of the finest and most spacious harbours in the Pacific Ocean.

The Rev. Samuel Ella, who laboured in the group for a number of years, has favoured me with a paper on Scripture translation in the Uvean language, of which what follows is largely a transcript. The population, which numbers about 2000, Mr. Ella tells us, consists of two distinct races, one of the Papuan stock, who were the original inhabitants, the other consisting of Eastern Polynesians from Tonga and Uvea (Wallis' Island). These had drifted away from their own lands at some remote period, and made the island of Lifu, where they were hospitably received and kindly treated. A famine arose on Lifu, and the castaways were advised to proceed to Iai * (the original name of the

* Pronounced Eai.

Uvean group), where there was good land, and but sparsely occupied. The refugees took the advice tendered, and proceeded in their large canoes to Iai, where they were also kindly received. The southern and northern portions of the inhabited islands were surrendered to them, and became their permanent homes. The Tongan refugees went to the south, and the Uveans to the north. The one party called their new home Tonga, and the other called theirs Uvea, and by this name the whole group is now called by foreigners, but Iai is the real native name. The two languages, Iaian and Uvean (a mixture of Tongan and Samoan), are spoken by the respective tribes, but Iaian is employed in their intercourse with each other.

Native teachers from the island of Mare were placed on Iai by Messrs. Creagh and Jones in 1856. Eight years later Mr. Ella was appointed to the charge of the mission, and with Mrs. Ella left Sydney in the Presbyterian mission schooner *Dayspring*, in May 1864, in order to fulfil his appointment. The French authorities on New Caledonia, however, would not allow him to land on the group; and he was compelled to go on to the New Hebrides, where he had to wait for six months before he could obtain permission to land on the islands on which he had been appointed to labour as an agent of the London Missionary Society. At length he was permitted to take up his abode on the islands simply as a foreign resident, and after a while he was allowed to engage in mission work.

As soon as he had gained a sufficient acquaintance with the language he reduced it to writing, formed an orthography of a purely phonetic character, and using the Roman letters, as has been done on all the islands we have occupied in the Pacific. He then prepared a primer and reading-book in the native language, which he printed and circulated among the natives. Unhappily Romish priests had obtained a footing on the group before Mr. Ella began his work, and upon the publication of the little book they assumed a hostile attitude, taking advantage of a Government edict which prohibited the use of the vernacular in the schools, and allowed only of the French language being taught. As the week-day schools were thus closed, the only opportunity for using the primer and reading-book was that afforded by the Sabbath schools, which were allowed by the Government on the ground that they were for the imparting of religious instruction.

The priests, however, set themselves in determined opposition, and through their tools, some native chiefs who had attached themselves to them, had recourse to violent measures. On a certain Sabbath they seized the church, on the ground that the school was held in it, while the service was being conducted, and the Lord's Supper was being observed, and forcibly ejected the worshippers in the most violent and outrageous manner. Mr. Ella and his adherents managed, however, to continue the Sabbath schools, and the Protestant part of the community, young and old, in these and in their own homes, learned to read in spite of the efforts of their persecutors to keep them in ignorance.

As soon as Mr. Ella had sufficiently mastered the language he set about the all-important work of Scripture translation. But before printing any complete portion of the Word of God he prepared a small book, consisting of selections from the Gospel according to Matthew, and a few Psalms. Mr. Ella had a knowledge of both printing and binding, so he was able to get his books and translations into the hands of the natives without the delay which would have been occasioned had it been needful to send his manuscripts to be printed elsewhere.

The book of Scripture extracts was printed in April 1867; and in August 1868 the Gospel of Luke was issued from the mission press—the first complete portion of the Word of God which saw the light in the language of Uvea. It was received with great delight by the teachers and people; it was indeed to them as cold water to a thirsty soul.

One of the girls of Mrs. Ella's school, on receiving her copy, sat down under the shade of a cocoa-nut tree, and did not move till she had read it through; and when she had finished it, she came to Mrs. Ella with tears in her eyes, exclaiming, "Oh, Mrs. Ella, how beautiful is the story of Jesus!" Similar indications of warm appreciation appeared on every hand, and encouraged the translator to proceed with the object on which he had set his heart, viz., to give the Uveans the complete New Testament in their native tongue.

The Editorial Secretary of the British and Foreign Bible Society wrote very cheeringly, encouraging him to go on with his translation, and supplying him with some useful books to aid him in his work. Many difficulties had to be encountered, and obstacles overcome, which were placed in his way by the French authorities and the Romish priests. On the threshold it seemed as if the way would be blocked altogether. The Governor of New Caledonia and the Loyalty Islands objected to books being printed in the vernacular, and directed that the people should be taught to read in French, and that they should read the Bible in that language; but when the impracticability of that was represented to him, he yielded, and gave permission to print the New Testament and Psalms in the native tongue.

The Acts of the Apostles followed the Gospel of Luke, and the other three Gospels were translated and printed in due course. They were issued book by book as they came from the press, and were joyfully received and highly appreciated by a grateful people.

The work had proceeded thus far when in 1872 Mr. and Mrs. Ella were compelled, on the ground of failure of health, to leave the mission field and proceed to England for change and rest. In the beginning of 1874 Mr. and Mrs. Ella returned from England, and resumed their work on Uvea; but about two years later they were obliged, on account of Mrs. Ella's health, to quit their loved work in the islands, and remove to Sydney. Here Mr. Ella went on with the translation of the New Testament, and in 1878 that was completed and printed.

As already stated the four Gospels and the Acts of the Apostles were translated and printed on Uvea, and some of the Epistles were also translated, but the printing had been deferred till now. A native chief came from Uvea to act as pundit in revising these and the books that were translated in Sydney. The Epistles and Revelation were bound in one volume, as the Gospels and Acts had previously been.

After the completion of the New Testament Mr. Ella translated the book of Psalms, and in order to avail himself of the best assistance to be obtained from native help in revising the manuscript, he took it to Uvea, and spent some months there in giving it a thorough revision; and on his return to Sydney it was printed in bold pica type, and bound in a separate volume. All the paper on which the Uvean Scriptures have been printed has been supplied by the British and Foreign Bible Society; and the printing that has been done in Sydney has also been borne by the Society. The books are being sold to the natives at a price which will refund the outlay.

To the above information referring more particularly to Scripture translation on Uvea, Mr. Ella adds the following painfully interesting information:—" At a period prior to the commencement of missionary operations on Iai, a large tribe, once the dominant party, was defeated in a war in which all the other tribes united against it. The tribe was nearly annihilated, and the survivors fled to New Caledonia, and from them have sprung two tribes on that land." Mr. Ella has had intercourse with some of these people, and they have asked for native teachers to instruct them. Every attempt, however, to convey to them the Gospel has been frustrated by the action of French officials, and teachers have been compelled to leave New Caledonia.

Mr. Ella mentions a question that was put to him by an old native of Uvea which Christians would do well to lay to heart. The same question has more than once been put to missionaries in other parts of the world. "Why," said the poor old man, "why were you so long in bringing the Gospel to us? You now find only a remnant of a nation." About a third part of the population was swept away by measles about the year 1862.

No mission in the South Seas has a more sad history than that of Uvea. This is not the place, however, to give even the briefest epitome of that history. In the "Story of the Lifu Mission," by the Rev. S. Macfarlane, and in a work entitled the "Martyrs of Polynesia," by the writer, pretty full accounts may be found.

And now we must close our notice of Bible translation in the Loyalty Islands. Thirty-three years have passed since European missionaries settled on the group, and during that comparatively short period an amount of work has been accomplished in the department of service, of which this work specially treats, which is highly satisfactory when all the cirumstances are taken into account, for it is to be borne in mind that Bible translation is only one among the many duties which devolve upon the missionary especially in our South Sea missions. Here then we have in the Lifu dialect the Bible complete, ready to go into the hands of the printer, and in the Mare dialect it is all translated and is undergoing a final revision, and in the Uvean the entire New Testament and the Psalms are in print; and all this work has been accomplished by five men—Messrs. Creagh, Jones, M'Farlane, Sleigh, and Ella. Let the friends of the Bible and the promoters of Christian missions "thank God and take courage." The cause in which they are embarked is without doubt the cause of God; and if God be for us, who can be against us?

CHAPTER XVIII.

NEW BRITAIN.

THE mission to the large island of New Britain and islands adjacent was commenced in the year 1875. The pioneer missionary, who was also the originator of the mission, was the Rev. George Brown of the Australian Wesleyan Missionary Society. Mr. Brown had had fourteen years experience of mission work in Samoa, and being an enterprising, energetic man, full of missionary zeal, and of dauntless courage, was possessed of exceptional qualifications for being the leader of the difficult and hazardous enterprise. To him and the Rev. Benjamin Danks, who became his coadjutor some time after the commencement of the mission, I am indebted for all the information that follows.

The principal islands of the group, generally designated New Britain, are—New Britain itself, Duke of York group, and New Ireland. New Britain is about 300 miles in length, in direct geographical position, but from its irregular shape the actual coast line must be very much longer. The breadth of the island is from seventy to fifteen miles, and there are many outlying small islands near the coast. The Duke of York group lies mid-way in St. George's Channel, between the north-east end of New Britain and New Ireland, and consists of about ten islands, most of which are small. New Ireland is about 200 miles in length, and from fifteen to twenty in breadth.

The earliest distinct notice of the discovery of the group is given in the account of Le Maire and Schouten's voyage in 1615. Tasman sighted St. John's Island in 1643. Dampier first ascertained that New Britain was a separate island from New Guinea in 1700, whilst to Cartaret belongs the honour of discovering St. George's Channel in 1767, and of naming New Ireland, which he had thus proved to be separate from New Britain by the channel through which he had sailed.

Several attempts had been made by traders to form settlements in the group before the commencement of the mission, but with very little success. No white man had ever been able to live safely on the mainland of New Britain, and when the pioneer band of missionaries arrived there was not a single white man in the group. Some eighteen months previously two traders had been landed on Matupit, in Blanche Bay, from a German barque, with the view of opening up trade with the people. They were well armed, and supplied with boats, houses, and goods for trade; but they were only able to remain a few weeks, during which they were in great danger from the natives, and at length their house was set on fire, and they were obliged to flee for their lives, and only succeeded in reaching their boat after they had shot down several of the natives.

Mr. Brown sailed from Sydney in the mission brig *John Wesley* in 1875, as already stated, and on his way to the then little known lands to which he was bound, he called at Fiji, visited the Native Training Institution there, and made known to the students the object of his visit, viz., to enlist volunteers to accompany him on his mission. The dangerous character of the expedition was fully explained to them. They were told that the people of the New Britain group bore a very bad character, that white men had been driven away by them, that the climate was known to be very unhealthy, that they would have to remain there for some time alone, and that if they decided to go in all probability some of them would never again see their own homes; and then they were told to go home and pray for Divine guidance, and only to come to a decision after calm and prayerful consideration. On the following day, when they assembled again in the College Hall, they were asked if any of them would volunteer for the difficult and dangerous work, when, to their honour be it said, they all stood up, and declared their willingness to go. Nine of them were chosen, and a few days afterwards they were summoned to attend a meeting of the Fijian Government, and the Acting Governor of the colony warned them of the great risk they were incurring, told them that they were British subjects, that no missionary had any right to appoint them to such a dangerous work, and assured them that if they now desired to withdraw, he would take care that none of them should be sent away from Fiji. They thanked the Governor for his kind advice, but assured him that they were already fully aware of all that he had told them, that no one had appointed them, but that they had freely volunteered to go, and in concluding his remarks, one of them said, "And as to our lives, that you, sir, have been speaking to us about, we have fully considered that matter also. We have decided, sir, to do God's work; and if we die, we die; if we live, we live; but we will do Christ's work." Noble men! and no less noble women, for they were all married, and the wives no doubt were consenting parties. Mr. Brown remarks:—"It was a noble resolution, and the subsequent history of these brave men and women abundantly proves the sincerity of their determination, and the value of their service."

At Samoa, where the party also called, two teachers and their wives also volunteered to join the mission; and after spending a few days at Rotuma, and passing by the northern islands of the New Hebrides, the Santa Cruz and

Solomon groups, the party landed on York Island on Sabbath, August 18th, 1875. A momentous landing to all concerned—reminding one of another landing, widely different indeed in many of its aspects, yet having something in common—the landing of the Pilgrim Fathers on Plymouth Rock. What sought this little band of Fijian and Samoan Christians, and their solitary leader?—what sought they thus afar in these regions of savageism? Jewels of the mine or pearls of the deep? Not they indeed. They did seek gems and pearls, but not the gems of the mine, or the pearls of the deep. They sought "Pearls of price by Jesus bought, To His glorious likeness wrought."

It would not comport with the design of this work to relate the story of the dangers to which the brave party of pioneers were exposed, or to tell of their sufferings and trials in the prosecution of their grand object, even were we in circumstances to do so. It devolves on us simply to chronicle, and that in the briefest manner, the results which have been accomplished, so far, by the blessing of God, on their labours.

They found the people to whom they went to be of the Papuan or Melanesian stock. They were living in small isolated districts, having little or no intercourse with each other, and speaking dialects differing so widely as practically to constitute different languages. There were no competent interpreters; the acquisition of the language was therefore intensely difficult at the outset. The people were in about the lowest state of barbarism. In one respect they could not get lower—no covering was worn by either sex. And they were cannibals, and no more need be said in proof of their extreme degradation. They were cruel, savage, and vile, as indeed the great bulk of them still are; but the day has dawned now, and the light will spread, and the darkness, with all its foul and hateful accompaniments, will in due time pass away.

During the first year Mr. Brown was able to reduce the language of the Duke of York group, and to acquire such a knowledge of that as to enable him to get printed in Sydney a small lesson book, with a few hymns, the Lord's Prayer, and some short Scripture lessons, and a Catechism. After this some portions of the Gospels were from time to time translated, but not printed till 1881, when Mr. Brown returned to Sydney. In 1882 the Gospel of Mark, which he had translated, was printed by the New South Wales Auxiliary to the British and Foreign Bible Society. This was the first complete portion of Scripture printed in any of the dialects of New Britain, and its publication marks an important epoch in the history of the mission.

As a striking proof of the progress that had been made, a brief extract may be given from a letter of the Rev. R. H. Rickard, who had joined the mission some time before Mr. Brown left. Mr. Rickard wrote to Mr. Brown as follows:—"The little book was read, and understood at once, by the scholars who had been attending the schools of the teachers. I have just examined the schools, and there are forty-five of the lads who can read the Gospel, some of them as fluently as we can read our own Bibles."

Mr. Brown may well comment on the above fact as follows: —"When it is remembered that only a short time previously these lads were little wild naked savages, and that the Gospel which they read was printed in a language which only six years before had not been reduced to a written form, it will be at once apparent that a great work had been accomplished in a very short time, and also that the people on whose behalf this work had been done are a fairly intelligent and teachable race."

In 1883 the Rev. Benjamin Danks, who joined the mission in 1878, while recruiting in Victoria, prepared a small book of thirty-three pages, containing the first catechism of the Wesleyan Church, the Decalogue, some

Scripture portions, and twenty-three hymns. These were a revision of previous translations by Mr. Brown. The next notable event in the history of this part of the mission was the translation of the Gospel by Matthew by the Rev. B. Danks. The translation was very carefully revised by the Rev. Isaac Rooney, who became connected with the mission in 1881, and it was also printed in Sydney by the Auxiliary to the British and Foreign Bible Society in 1885.

Mr. Danks had the privilege of being the first resident missionary on the mainland of New Britain, having resided there for a few months in 1880, and being again appointed to the island on his return from Australia in 1883. While in Victoria, in addition to the literary work already mentioned, he prepared a small lesson book in the New Britain language, but there was no connected portion of Scripture as yet translated into that language, it being very imperfectly known at that time. In 1884 Mr. Danks prepared a book containing 100 lessons from the Gospels, also the first catechism, and fourteen hymns. These were sent to Sydney to be printed; but as that would occupy at least six months, and the need of books was urgent, Mr. Danks having a small hand printing-press, translated into the New Britain dialect and printed the Ten Commandments, the first Psalm, and brief extracts from the Gospels of Matthew, Luke, and John. The printing part must have been a formidable undertaking, as Mr. Danks had never even seen printing done. The book was issued in June 1885, and Mr. Danks remarks—"It bore immediate fruit in producing a marked improvement in the character of the young people. This was the first Scripture distributed on the mainland of New Britain."

While waiting for the larger book from Sydney, Mr. Danks prepared and printed a short life of Christ, the book of Jonah, the parable of the Ten Virgins, and a few Scripture texts. These were issued in book form in

November 1885, and in March 1886 Mr. Danks published another small book, containing a history of David and Esther. In June 1886 a work was prepared by Mr. Danks, consisting of 118 lessons translated from the four Gospels, filling 116 pages. To this was added a translation of the Acts of the Apostles by Mr. Rickard. The lessons from the Gospels were arranged in chronological order according to the Tract Society's Gospel Harmony, thus forming in Scripture language a continuous life of Christ. Mr. Rickard carried the book through the press, and Mr. Danks closes the paper, with which he has kindly furnished me, in the following words:—"It," the book, "is now in the hands of a people who four years ago had not a single book in their language. To God, who has given His servants strength to accomplish this great work, be all the praise."

From the Annual Report of the mission for the year 1886, by the Rev. Issac Rooney, Chairman of the District, we add a few extracts, which will be read with interest, as showing the present state of the mission, and foreshadowing its future. As in the case of all our great missions, more labourers are urgently needed, and there is surely ample encouragement for the Wesleyan Church to prosecute to the full extent of its ability a mission in which the labours of its agent have been so greatly owned and blessed of God. When all the circumstances are taken into account, the progress that has been made is marvellous—not exceeded, I should think, in any of our modern missions; but the work is only begun. The first-fruits have been gathered in, and they constitute a blessed earnest of the harvest to be reaped in due time; but an immense amount of work has to be done in bringing under culture the vast field. The number of the population can only be conjectured at present, but there must be tens of thousands even on the two large islands alone, besides the multitudes who people the smaller islands, the very number of which is scarcely known as yet. There are only three European missionaries at present in the group, and what are they in so vast a field? What indeed! The wonder is that so great a work has been accomplished by so inadequate an instrumentality. "It is the Lord's doing, and it is marvellous in our eyes."

Referring to the Duke of York section of the mission, Mr. Rooney writes as follows:—

"Our returns for the year show an increase in every department of our work. The increase is not large, but considering the difficulties with which we have had to contend, the wonder is that it is so large as it is. On Duke of York we have been cheered by the growing influence of the *lotu* (the Christian religion). Our work on New Ireland will not be so effective and thorough till we have a missionary residing on the spot.

"Missionary meetings have been held this year for the first time in the history of this mission. The proceeds, about £50, is a good beginning, and we hope to do better next year.

"A new Hymn-book containing seventy-two hymns, a Revised Catechism, and translations from the Old Testament, embracing the principal narratives from the creation to the death of Moses, all in the Duke of York language, have been sent to the printer during the present year. When these books reach us, and are placed in the hands of our scholars and local preachers, we shall feel amply repaid for many a weary day and sleepless night entailed by their preparation. The impetus which the arrival of the new book—one hundred Gospel lessons in the New Britain language—has given to school work is surprising. Already there is a large increase in the number of scholars who can read, and the best results may be expected to follow the diffusion of Scripture knowledge among the people.

The Circuit Training Institution has been carried on during the year." (The number of students is not given.)

With reference to his station on New Britain, Mr. Danks writes:—

"Our school department is the most cheering part of our work. Last year we had six young men who could read—to-day we have fifty; and twenty more will be able to read by the end of the year. There is a great thirst for knowledge among the young people. With good capable teachers we have no fear for this branch of our work. Nor is reading all they have learned. Already letters written by natives pass from one end of the district to the other, which give pleasure and a sense of importance both to writer and receiver. The importance of this work cannot be overestimated. Give these young people the Word of God, and we have a mighty power for good in our midst."

The Report concludes as follows:—"The calls for help on every hand are loud and urgent. The people hold out their hands to us. How fearful, how dark, how repulsive, cruel, and wretched is heathenism, none can tell but those who have met and handled it, lived in its midst, and seen its working. Our prayer is that the Lord Jesus would come quickly, and save this people, and in this prayer we are sure every true Christian will join."

The following figures will enable the reader to form a definite idea as to the progress of the mission to the present date.

In addition to the three English missionaries there are three ordained Fijian ministers.

The number of stations at which regular services are held and schools are in operation is thirty-seven, and there are thirty-five preaching stations at which services are conducted by local preachers.

The number of Church members in full standing is 473, and the candidate classes number 202.

In the day and Sabbath schools there are 901 scholars; and the total attendants on public worship are 3938.

God bless the devoted men and women who are bearing the heat and burden of the day in this promising field. Soon may showers of blessing descend upon them in such abundance as that the solitary place shall be glad for them, and the desert rejoice and blossom as the rose.

CHAPTER XIX.

NEW GUINEA.

WE come now to the greatest of all our mission fields in the Pacific—New Guinea—the limit of our South Sea missions. When this limit was reached in 1871, the dream of well-nigh forty years was realised. From the earliest days of the Samoan mission we talked of the then far-off day when we should shake hands with our brethren in the east across the Indian archipelago, few of us seriously expecting, I suppose, that the thing would become a reality in our day. Such, however, is now actually the case. Missionary operations have been in progress on New Guinea for over sixteen years, and the history of these years amply proves that we did not run unsent when in the month of May 1871, Mr. M'Farlane and myself embarked on the voyage from which such great results have already sprung. Till the report of that voyage was published to the world, New Guinea was shunned by voyagers and traders, from an idea which had got abroad that its people were such inveterate savages that to venture among them would be to court certain destruction.

Any particular description of New Guinea and its people would be out of place in a work like the present. In books recently published by the Rev. W. W. Gill, B.A., and the Rev. James Chalmers, ample information may be found. All we shall attempt will be to furnish a very brief account of the mission from its commencement to the present time, with special reference to putting the tribes who people the great land in possession of the Bible in their many tongues.

It was in the year 1870 that a mission to New Guinea was projected by the Directors of the London Missionary Society; and towards the close of that year definite steps were taken by their agents in the Loyalty Islands towards the accomplishment of that object. At their request a vessel named the *Emma Paterson*, about 80 tons burden, was chartered in Sydney by the Rev. J. P. Sunderland, and furnished with every requisite for the great undertaking, and the Rev. Samuel M'Farlane and myself were entrusted with the carrying out of the expedition. All the needful preparations were made. Teachers were selected, farewell meetings were held, and everything was got in readiness for the start we intended to make in April or May of 1871, at the close of the stormy season. The time for our departure had come, and we were in daily expectation of the arrival of our vessel, when, to our dismay, news reached us that as she was leaving New Caledonia to cross over to Lifu, where we were waiting for her, she had been wrecked, and everything that had been put on board for our expedition was lost. We were in sore perplexity, but God appeared for us. A small trading schooner, the *Surprise*, from Sydney, came to anchor in the harbour at Lifu just as she was needed. An arrangement was made with the captain, and on the 31st of May we embarked, and stood away towards the great land which had become to us an object of absorbing interest, and which for months had seldom been absent from our thoughts during waking hours. We took with us eight teachers, with their wives, all of whom were natives of the Loyalty Islands. The captain had stipulated that he was to be at liberty to spend some time off the coast of New Caledonia on his own account, the charter to date from the time his business was finished. Hence we did not reach our destination till the close of June. On the 29th of that month we had the intense satisfaction of looking upon New Guinea, the great land of mystery of which so little was known at that time. We stood in close to the reef, saw numerous parties of natives, but did not attempt to communicate with them, as we were bound for Darnley Island in Torres Straits, where we expected to find greater facilities for the accomplishment of our object than we were likely to find on the mainland. We reached Darnley Island on the following day, and on the 3rd of July 1871 we succeeded in introducing to the island a teacher named Gucheng. Gucheng and his wife had not by any means an enthusiastic reception. The people consented to receive them on the understanding that when we should visit them about twelve months hence, we should remove them if they so wished. We felt satisfied that if we could only get them received they would make their way, and so it proved, and thus the first stone of the New Guinea mission was laid.

From Darnley Island we proceeded to another small island, named Warrior Island, where there was a pearl shell fishing station. Here we were told of a small island named Cornwallis or Dawan, close to the mainland; but our captain, on the plea that all about that neighbourhood was unsurveyed, refused to go beyond Warrior Island, which was some forty or more miles distant. A boat was kindly lent us by Captain Banner, the manager of the fishing station, and in that, with a crew of native eastern islanders only, we set out on our somewhat adventurous voyage. By the help of God we succeeded, and now we felt as if we had the key that would lay open to the world the great unknown country. At the hour of evening prayer we got a number of the natives together that they might witness an act of worship to the true God, the first act of the kind, no doubt, that had ever been performed on that dark shore. That service being over, we (Mr. M'Farlane and myself) withdrew from our native friends, and at a little distance from the house, under the canopy of heaven, and with the great dark land of New Guinea before us and close at hand, we sang, with feelings such as language cannot describe, "Jesus shall reign where'er the sun;" poured out our hearts in fervent prayer, and talked of the spread of His blessed reign, and the far-reaching consequences of the step we had been privileged to take on that ever-memorable evening.

We left four teachers on the island, two of whom were designed for another island named Saibai, about four miles distant, but it was thought advisable for all the four to remain together for a time. We called at the island and had intercourse with the people. They received us in a friendly manner, but they looked a fierce, savage people, and a fuller acquaintance with them proved them to be as savage as they looked. They were willing, however, to receive teachers. Arrangements were made for the settlement of the others on Bampton Island, at the mouth of the Fly River, and on Murray Island, which afterwards became the headquarters of the Western or Papuan branch of the mission.

The great object of our voyage was now secured. Arrangements were made for the location of all the teachers we had to dispose of, but we did not feel inclined to turn our faces homeward till we had set foot on the mainland, so on our way back to Warrior Island, where our ship was waiting for us, we called at a place named Kataw, about thirty miles from Dawan, and were well received. And then returning to the ship, we stood away on our return voyage, calling at Redscar Bay, and adding considerably to our knowledge of New Guinea and its people. We had a long, tedious, and trying voyage, not unattended with danger. We did not reach Lifu till the 2nd of November, over five months from the time of sailing.

Soon after our return, Mr. M'Farlane, with his family, proceeded to England on a visit; and after occupying a station on Mare for about two months, we (Mrs. Murray and myself), at the request of the Directors of the Society, removed to Cape York, to superintend for the time being the New Guinea mission. For this purpose we sailed from the Loyalty Islands in the *John Williams*, on the 14th of September 1872; and on the 17th of October we reached Somerset, Cape York, and that became temporarily the headquarters of the mission. We were accompanied by a strong force of teachers. We had eight from the Loyalty Islands, and six from the Hervey group, of which the well-known island Rarotonga is the principal. These were in charge of the Rev. W. W. Gill, B.A., who, with Mrs. Gill and family, was on his way to England on furlough after an absence of twenty-one years. Mrs. Gill and the family went on to Sydney in the *John Williams*, and Mr. Gill remained with us for a time at Cape York, rendering me very valuable help in the location of the teachers, after which he followed Mrs. Gill to Sydney, where he arrived on the 22nd of January 1873.

We had the satisfaction of finding the teachers and their families left by Mr. M'Farlane and myself alive, and in fairly good health, with one exception. Tepeso, the brave man who made the memorable speech in answer to parties who sought to frighten him by parading before him and his fellow teachers the dangers they would have to encounter, that "wherever there were men, missionaries were bound to go," had been taken away to the land of safety and repose, and his wife and child had followed. He was the last that we should have chosen to part with, but the Unerring One did it, and it was not for us to murmur.

We succeeded in locating all the teachers now brought. Those from the East were placed in Redscar Bay, and those from the Loyalty Islands on different islands in Torres Straits, and on Bampton Island, near the mouth of the Fly River. And now the mission was fairly launched, but trying and anxious months followed which must be passed over in silence. Particulars may be found in "Forty Years' Mission Work in Polynesia and New Guinea," chaps. li.–liv.

The most important step taken while we were alone was the introduction of teachers to Port Moresby. As soon as I could find the means of getting to that place, after its discovery by Captain Moresby of H.M.S. *Basilisk*, I made a visit to it, and succeeded in introducing four Rarotongan teachers, Piri, Rau, Ruatoka, and Anederea—men whose names deserve to be had in remembrance as the pioneers of the mission in that now famous locality. My first visit satisfied me that we were not likely to find a more eligible place for the headquarters of the eastern branch of the mission, and subsequent visits confirmed the first impression. Those who followed me adopted the same view, and now it is the headquarters of the civil authorities of British New Guinea as well as of our mission.

In the autumn of 1874 Mr. M'Farlane joined us at Cape York, and on the 20th of October following Mr. and Mrs. Lawes arrived, and in the meanwhile the mission steamer *Ellengowan* reached us from England, and on the 2nd of November the *John Williams* also arrived with Mrs. M'Farlane and other parties connected with the mission on board. And now we were in a position to get the mission into something like complete working order. There was a leader for each of the two divisions into which the mission naturally shaped itself—the Papuan and the Malayan—and there was a ship under the exclusive control of the missionaries, and thus a want which had been sorely felt while I was alone was met.

Mr. M'Farlane took charge of the Papuan branch, and Mr. Lawes of the Malayan. In 1877 Mr. Chalmers joined the mission, and was associated with Mr. Lawes at Port Moresby, and from that time to the present that part of the mission has been chiefly under their management. We can only glance at the progress that has been made during the intervening years.

We take first

THE EASTERN DIVISION,

that under the management of Messrs. Lawes and Chalmers. As soon as their knowledge of the languages permitted, school-books, consisting chiefly of Scripture extracts, were prepared. In the preparation of these the teachers must have largely assisted, as it was necessary to have them in five languages or dialects. Hymn-books were also prepared, and little elementary works in arithmetic and geography followed after a time, and the schoolmaster was soon abroad in that part of New Guinea. It was my high privilege to have a look at Port Moresby in April 1882, and I was astonished at what I witnessed there. I left the people at the close of 1874 wild savages, scarcely a remove from absolute barbarism. Now I found a school numbering 158 learning reading, writing, arithmetic, and geography, some having made amazing progress. A church had been formed some considerable time before, and at the Sabbath services there were large congregations of apparently devout and earnest worshippers numbering about 500. And such has been the rapid extension of the mission that there are now forty-seven stations extending along the south coast of the eastern peninsula, and also some distance inland, and at each of these there is a Port Moresby on a smaller scale. Regular service on Sabbaths and week-days, a school, and at some of the more advanced a church, has been formed, and so the good work is spreading. There are at this date (1887) 300 church members, and there are always a number of young men under training at Port Moresby for teachers. The brethren are anxious to be able to dispense with the services of teachers from other lands, as so many of these have died through the unhealthiness of the climate. A good many years must pass, however, before an adequate number of properly qualified native teachers can be procured, and the brave eastern teachers, men and women, press forward in the spirit of martyrs to fill up the ranks when their brethren and sisters fall.

The first connected portion of Scripture that was printed was the Gospel of Mark, translated by Mr. Lawes in the Motumotu language. It was printed in Sydney, New South Wales, under the superintendence of the Rev. J. P. Sunderland, and in 1884 all the four Gospels were printed also in Sydney under Mr. Lawes' own eye, and bound together in a volume. No other portion of Scripture has yet been printed in the Motumotu (or Port Moresby) dialect; but the Gospel of Mark, translated by one of the eastern teachers in the dialect spoken at South Cape, has been printed. The translation was revised of course by the missionaries, nevertheless it is a noteworthy fact that men so recently enveloped in heathen darkness should go forth to other heathen lands, not only to preach the Gospel, but to translate the Bible into the languages of these lands.

For some time past, while Mr. Chalmers has been on a visit to England, Mr. Lawes has had the entire care of the immense district on himself alone. It is no wonder therefore that translation work has not advanced rapidly. He has now the Acts of the Apostles in hand; and as Mr. Chalmers, and another esteemed brother, the Rev. A. Pearce, who has had many years experience of mission work on Raiatea of the Tahitian group, are now on their way to New Guinea, he will soon have help, and be able to give more time to the all important work. Hence we may hope that ere a great while the New Guineans will have the complete New Testament, at least, in their own tongue. The cost of all the portions that have been printed has been borne by the Sydney Auxiliary to the British and Foreign Bible Society. The New Guineans are not yet in circumstances to pay for their books. This is not likely to be the case long however. It will not be out of place to mention here, on account of its connection with Bible translation, and the general interests of the mission, that Mr. Lawes has prepared a dictionary and a grammar of the language of Port Moresby. These were printed in Sydney at the cost of the Government of New South Wales, in consideration of their ethnological and linguistic value.

THE WESTERN BRANCH.

I am sorry that I am not able to furnish much information with reference to the Western or Papuan branch of the mission. The headquarters of this, as already mentioned, is on Murray Island, in Torres Straits. This is a pretty little island. It is a garden for fertility, and it is equal in beauty to many of the gems of Eastern and Western Polynesia. It is only a few miles in circumference, but it rises to the height of 750 feet, and it has the great recommendation for a mission station of being healthy—the most healthy, perhaps, of all the islands of Torres Straits. Captain Flinders, of the British Navy, who visited it in 1802, estimated the population at 700. What it is at present I am unable to say. Captain Flinders wrote of the natives as follows:—" Some of these people are of a dark chocolate colour, others nearly black. The men are about the middle size, active and muscular, their countenances being expressive of quick apprehension. The numerous dwellings seen near the shore, and the plots of cultivated land in different parts of the island, had an appearance of comfort and civilisation totally unknown among the savages of the adjacent coast of Australia."

Mr. M'Farlane and I had arranged to take a teacher to the island during our first voyage, but he, the teacher we had selected for it, and the Darnley Island teacher, requested to be allowed to remain together for a time, with the understanding that after some three months or so, Mataika, the Murray Island teacher, should proceed thither in case an opportunity offered. We had some ground to expect that such an opportunity would occur, but it did not. Mataika, however, was not a man to be easily turned aside from an object on which he had set his mind. With assistance which he procured on Darnley Island, he built a canoe—a sorry enough craft it was in which, with a crew of five, including himself, to make a voyage to Murray Island, which is thirty miles distant from Darnley, and dead to windward. The voyage occupied two days and one night. He was well received, and finding a foreigner on the island, a coloured man, who owned a boat, he hired the said boat, returned in it to Darnley Island, where he had left his wife and property, and taking leave of the place of his temporary sojourn, he proceeded to what he now regarded as his fixed abode, and so began the mission to Murray Island.

Soon after Mr. M'Farlane's return from England in the autumn of 1874, he fixed upon this island as, according to his judgment, the most eligible place from which to operate on the adjacent coast, including the Great Gulf of Papua, and extending eastward to the Fly River. Of all the work that has been carried on throughout that part of the island during the intervening years he had the chief management till his departure for England in 1885. The

Rev. J. Tait Scott was first sent to his aid in 1880. After a short term of service he withdrew from the mission, and after an interval the Rev. Harry Scott succeeded him, but he also left after a short time. He left on account of the failure of health, and the Rev. E. B. Savage joined the mission in 1885, and is now in charge; and the latest intelligence announces the arrival of the Rev. A. E. Hunt, so Mr. Savage is no longer single-handed.

From an early period of the mission's history there has been a training institution for the education of a native agency, and in addition to his work in connection with that Mr. M'Farlane did a large amount of pioneering work on the banks of the Fly River and elsewhere, and placed a large number of teachers at different points, thus opening up the country for the spread of the Gospel, and preparing the way for a more effective agency when the way seems clear for foreign missionaries to settle among the numerous tribes who are found upon the banks of the great water-way into the interior, and other parts connected with that branch of the mission. It is a necessity that foreign missionaries live among the people and learn their languages if mission work is to be consolidated and extended. In no other way can the Bible be translated, and other essential work be efficiently accomplished. A church has been formed on Murray Island, and also on the island of Saibai, and large numbers have been baptized. I am unable to say how many, or to give the numbers who have been admitted to the churches.

With reference to the work of Scripture translation, Mr. M'Farlane, in a letter of late date, writes as follows:—" In New Guinea I have translated the Gospels of Mark and John into the Murray Island language, and assisted the Lifu teachers in translating the Gospel of Mark into the language of Saibai and Mabuiag, and another Lifu teacher in translating portions of Scripture into the language of China Straits, besides, of course, preparing hymn-books and school-books."

It will be remembered that Mr. M'Farlane, during his connection with the Loyalty Islands mission, translated the entire New Testament into the language of Lifu.

Such is a brief view of what has been attempted towards the evangelisation of New Guinea, and of the results so far as man can trace them; and when the circumstances under which the work has been carried on are considered, there is surely ample ground for encouragement. True, the results have cost us dear. A vast amount of toil, suffering, and self-denial have had to be endured—especially among our brave eastern pioneers, who have emphatically had to "endure hardness," and many of whom, alas! have fallen in the struggle, some by the hand of violence, and many more from the effects of the sickly climate. Over these we mourn, yet we glorify God in them, and do not regard their lives as wasted or thrown away. No! they have fallen in a noble cause, and to that cause they have rendered valuable service by the work they did, and by the examples of heroism and consecration they have left behind them, the influence of which we cannot measure. Two ladies, also of the noblest type of womanhood, have fallen —the one, the wife of the Rev. William Turner, M.D., just as she was about to enter upon her work; the other, Mrs. Chalmers, a woman who, like her well-known husband, seemed a stranger to fear; and a young missionary, the Rev. Watson Sharp, has lately been added to the list of the departed before he had commenced his labours.

May the Lord of the harvest raise up worthy successors to these departed ones, and may the present day of small things in due time expand to a day of great things. A glorious achievement will be the conquest of New Guinea! —a grand consummation to the struggle begun on Tahiti ninety years ago, and a magnificent illustration of the power of the Gospel!

> "Fly abroad, thou mighty Gospel,
> Win and conquer, never cease;
> May thy lasting, wide dominion,
> Multiply and still increase:
> Sway Thy sceptre,
> Saviour, all the world around."

THE NORTH PACIFIC.

CHAPTER XX.

THE SANDWICH ISLANDS.

So far our attention has been exclusively directed to fields of missionary labour lying south of the equator; now we cross over to the North Pacific, and turn with great pleasure to lands occupied by the American churches.

The chief of these is the now well-known group, the Sandwich Islands.

A special interest attaches to this group, arising from the fact that it was the last discovery of Captain Cook, and that on one of its islands his illustrious career was brought to a close. The discovery was made in 1778, while he was in search of a northern passage from the Pacific to the Atlantic, and he consoled himself, under the disappointment he felt at failing in the immediate object of his search, with the fact that it was in consequence of his having gone in quest of that object that his voyage was "enriched with a discovery which, though last, seemed in many respects to be the most important that had hitherto been made by Europeans throughout the extent of the Pacific Ocean." Such was the great navigator's estimate of the importance of this group, and a glance at the principal islands of which it is composed, with their subsequent history and development, will, I think, confirm the soundness of his judgment.

As in the case of Fate in the New Hebrides, Captain Cook gave to the group the name it now bears in honour of his patron the Earl of Sandwich. The native name of the group is Hawaii, and by that name it will no doubt always continue to be designated by the natives, for this, among other reasons, that no native could possibly pronounce the name given it by Cook.* The group is situated between 18° 50′ and 22° 20′ north latitude, and 154° 53′ and 160° 15′ west longitude. There are ten islands—eight only are however inhabited; the other two being barren rocks, of little account except as resorts for fishermen. Hawaii is the name of the principal island as well as the general name of the group; and the names of the others are Maui, Molokini, Kahulawe, Lanai, Molokai, Oahu, Kauai, Nii-hau, and Kaula. They stretch from south-east towards the north-west in the order in which I have named them.

The whole group contains about 6000 square miles; the island of Hawaii itself having an area of 4000, or two-thirds of the whole. Hawaii is nearly 300 miles in circumference. Maui is about 140. Oahu and Kauai are about the same size as Maui. The others are much smaller, but some of them are fine islands, and in early days they seem to have been as populous and important according to their size as the larger. They are all of volcanic origin; they are mountainous, and the valleys and low land are in the highest degree fertile. Oahu is said to be the most romantic and picturesque of the whole group, resembling in its natural scenery some of the finest islands of the

* In the language spoken in the Sandwich Islands there are no double consonants. It is radically the same language as that found throughout the whole of Eastern and Central Polynesia.

Tahitian group.* In some of the islands, notably Hawaii, the mountains rise to an elevation of 15,000 to 18,000 feet.

Sixty years ago the population of the group was estimated at from 130,000 to 150,000. Since that date it has very much decreased owing to causes which we must not stop to particularise. A census made in 1860 places the native population at 67,084; the foreign at 2716—in all, 69,800. The influx of Chinese and other nationalities must have largely swelled the population of late years, but on that point I have not reliable information.

Native traditions point to the Tahitian group as the place whence the first settlers came; and this is confirmed by the fact that the language, manners, and customs, and general appearance of the natives, are almost identical in the Tahitian and other groups, which have evidently a common origin.

The attention of the American churches was directed to the Sandwich Islands, and their sympathies aroused towards their benighted inhabitants, in a very remarkable manner. About the year 1808 two youths, natives of the islands, found their way to the United States in a vessel which touched at the group—a whale ship, I suppose. On reaching the States, the captain took the two lads to his own home at New Haven, treated them kindly, and introduced them to Christian friends, and much interest was awakened, and much kindness shown to the strangers. We are unable to give particulars as to how they fared for the next few years, but about the year 1815 an incident occurred which connects them distinctly with the origin of the mission to their native land.

On a certain day a young man, a student of Yale College, as he was walking through the college grounds, saw a lad about seventeen years of age sitting on the steps

---

* See Ellis' Polynesian Researches, vol. iv. p. 11.

of the college weeping. He was clad in sailor garb. The colour of his skin indicated his foreign origin, and his appearance altogether was the reverse of prepossessing; but his distress touched the heart of the student, and he stopped and asked the cause of his forlorn and distressed appearance. Though he had been in America for a number of years, he could speak or understand English very imperfectly; but he made his interrogator, whose name was Mr. Edwin W. Dwight, understand that he was one of two youths who had come to America from the Sandwich Islands. Mr. Dwight asked him if he would like to be taught to read. At this his face brightened, and he replied, "Yes." Mr. Dwight then proposed that he should come to his room in the college, and that same evening his education was begun, and went steadily on for several months.

The name of this young man was Obookia,* and the other to whom we have referred was named Hopu. He had begun to learn to read some time before, but no one seems to have offered to teach Obookia, and his object in going and seating himself on the college steps was to attract the attention of some one who might put him in the way of getting taught; and it appears that the result was that the last became first. Obookia attended the services in the church, and was soon able to understand what he heard, and the truth of God took hold of his heart, and he afforded satisfactory evidence that he had passed from death unto life.

In 1816 both he and Hopu were placed in a school which had been established by the American Board of Commissioners for Foreign Missions, for the education of young men from Indian tribes in America, or from other lands, as the case might be; and the first teacher of this school was Mr. Dwight, Obookia's kind friend, who found

* Most probably Obookaia.

him on the college steps. The common branches of education were taught, and the doctrines and principles of Christianity had no doubt a prominent place in the curriculum. Obookia was deeply grateful for the privileges he enjoyed at this school, and he seems to have striven to improve them; and no doubt he grew in grace and in the knowledge of his Lord and Saviour. This inference is clearly deducible from the fact that a strong desire took possession of his heart to return to his own dark land, to tell to his countrymen the glad tidings which had brought peace and joy to his own soul. "Poor people," he would say, "worship wood and stone; shark and almost everything their god. There is no Bible there; and heaven and hell they do not know about it, and here I have found the name of the Lord Jesus in the Holy Scriptures, and have read that His blood was shed for many. My poor countrymen, in the region and shadow of death, have no Bible to read—no Sabbath. I often feel for them in the night-season concerning their souls. May the Lord Jesus dwell in my heart, and prepare me to go and spend my life among them. But not my will, O Lord, but Thine be done."

No, dear young man, it was not His will that you should return to the dark land of your birth. It was well that it was in your heart, but He had something better in store for you, and He had His own plan for bringing to pass that on which your heart was set.

This interesting young man died at the age of twenty-six. An account of his life and death was published, and the hearts of American Christians were deeply stirred on behalf of his people, and an interest was aroused which soon led to definite steps being taken to respond to the Macedonian cry which had reached them in so affecting a manner from the far-off isles of the sea.

And to this voice to the churches was added another

which strikingly emphasised the first. Two young men, graduates of Yale College, offered themselves for personal service in the Sandwich Islands, and so the duty to send the Gospel to these lands was made about as plain as if an audible voice from heaven had spoken to the churches. The two young men who offered themselves for this service were Hiram Bingham and Asa Thurston, of whom we shall have much to tell presently.*

And while the hearts of Christians in America were thus being stirred, a movement of a very remarkable character was taking place in the far-off isles towards which their sympathies were being directed. The prophet Jeremiah speaks of it as an unheard of thing that a nation should change its gods; but the Hawaiians, moved by some impulse which man cannot trace, went beyond changing their gods—they renounced them altogether. Of this strange proceeding Mr. Ellis speaks as follows:—" The way was prepared for them (the missionaries) by one of those remarkable events which distinguish the eras in the history of nations, whether barbarous or civilised. This was the abolition of the national idolatry, which, though it was closely interwoven with all the domestic and civil institutions of every class of the inhabitants, upheld by the combined influence of a numerous body of priests, the arbitrary power of warlike chiefs, and the sanction of venerable antiquity, had been publicly and authoritatively prohibited by the king only a few months before their arrival."

This act of the king produced a great commotion. It led to a civil war. A principal chief, with a portion of the people, rose in rebellion. A battle was fought; the

* For the above facts which led the American Churches to undertake a mission to the Sandwich Islands, I am indebted to a small work by Mrs. Jane S. Warren, published by the American Tract Society, entitled "The Morning Star."

victory was on the side of the king and his adherents; the rebel chief was killed; and the whole mass of the people went on with renewed vigour destroying idols, sacred enclosures, &c., and, all unconsciously to themselves, preparing the way for the advent to their shores of the kingdom of God.

It was on the 23rd of October 1819 that the first band of missionaries to the Sandwich Islands sailed from the United States, and early in the following year they reached their destination. They were a goodly company, and as the pioneers of one of the most successful missions of modern times, they have a claim to be held in grateful remembrance. The party consisted of ten—viz., the Rev. Hiram Bingham, the Rev. Asa Thurston; Mr. Thomas Holmes, a physician; Samuel Whitney and Samuel Ruggles, teachers; Elisha Loomis, printer; and Daniel Chamberlain, a farmer, and their wives; and Thomas Hopu, William Kanui, and John Honuri, natives of the Sandwich Islands.

The missionaries did not meet with the warm welcome which might have been expected considering the state in which the islands were found, owing to the movement described above. Their object was misapprehended, and there was some opposition in consequence to their taking up their abode on the islands. This, however, was so far got over that the king and the leading chiefs consented to their landing and remaining for one year.

Having gained a footing, the missionaries set themselves at once to prosecute the object of their mission. As soon as their knowledge of the language allowed they applied themselves to the difficult task of settling the orthography and reducing it to writing. In this they had the help of elementary books in the kindred dialects of the Tahitian Islands and New Zealand, and in January 1822 they were able to put to press the first sheet of a Hawaiian spelling-book, and to present the natives with the elements of their own tongue in a printed form.* The plan of this work does not allow of our noticing the great and formidable difficulties with which the missionaries had to contend in those early days. They are graphically detailed in a work by the Rev. Sheldon Dibble, one of the early missionaries, published in 1839. The good men plodded on with a zeal and a courage which nothing could daunt, and God was with them, and in due time, as we shall see, they reaped a golden harvest.

Having mastered the language, schools were established, and preaching and other departments of missionary labour were vigorously pursued; and in due time the work of primary importance in all missionary effort, the rendering of the Holy Scriptures into the native language, was commenced. To the Rev. H. Bingham belongs the honour of having led the way in this work in the Sandwich Islands. He translated the first portion of the Word of God which appeared in the language of Hawaii. It consisted of twelve pages of the Gospel according to Luke. It was printed at Honolulu, on the island of Oahu, and published in November 1827. This was followed by the Sermon on the Mount, also translated by Mr. Bingham. It was printed in 1828, the number printed being 25,000. The first complete Gospel, that of Matthew, translated by Mr. Bingham and Mr. Thurston, was printed in 1828, at Rochester, in the United States. The Gospel of Mark, translated by the Rev. William Richards, was printed in 1829; and the Gospel of John, translated by Mr. Thurston, was also printed in 1829. All these three Gospels were printed in America, at Rochester, under the superintendence of Mr. Loomis, the printer of the mission, who seems to have retired from the foreign field about this time. Of each of these Gospels 10,000 were printed. Among rein-

* See Ellis' "Polynesian Researches," vol. iv. p. 31.

forcements to the mission which arrived in 1832 and 1833 we find the names of two printers, so that important department of work was kept in full efficiency. The Gospel of Luke, the translation of which was completed by Mr. Bingham, was printed at Honolulu in 1829, the number printed being 10,000; and the Acts of the Apostles, translated by Mr. Richards, followed in the same year, also printed at Honolulu.

Other books of the New Testament followed in rapid succession. During the course of 1831 the Epistles to the Romans, 1st and 2nd Corinthians, Galatians, Ephesians, Philippians, and Colossians were all printed at the mission press, Honolulu. The translators of these books were the brethren Bingham, Thurston, Bishop, and Richards. The number printed of each book was 10,000.

In 1832 the remaining books of the New Testament were completed, the Rev. Lorrin Andrews taking part in the translation. These were also printed at the mission press; and in the month of May of the same year (1832) the entire New Testament was completed. One-third of the work of translation was done by Mr. Bingham; one-third by Mr. Richards; one-fourth by Mr. Thurston; and one-twelfth by Messrs. Bishop and Andrews.

Parts of the Old Testament were translated and in print some time before the completion of the New Testament. Parts of the book of Genesis, Exodus, and Leviticus were printed in 1829, a portion of the book of Joshua in 1831; and after the New Testament was out of hand, the translating and printing of the Old Testament proceeded apace, and the great work was finished in 1839, the last sheet being struck off on the 10th of May, and thus the work was brought to a successful close. An idea of the amount of labour and pains which had been bestowed upon the work may be inferred from the fact that eight missionaries were engaged upon it for fifteen years. And besides the labour bestowed by each of the translators on his own particular part, much was expended in revising each other's portions.

The following are the names of the honoured men by whom this great work was accomplished, and the proportion of the work which fell to the lot of each. The Rev. William Richards translated about one-third of the entire Bible, the Rev. Asa Thurston nearly one-fourth, the Rev. Hiram Bingham one-fifth, the Rev. Artemus Bishop one-seventh, and the Rev. Jonathan S. Green, Lorrin Andrews, Ephraim W. Clark, and Sheldon Dibble the remaining one-ninth. The larger part of the proof-reading was done by Messrs. Bingham, Clark, and Bishop; and with the exception of three of the Gospels, the whole was printed on the islands.

For the above particulars I am indebted to my esteemed friend, the Rev. Hiram Bingham, jun. Mr. Bingham is the son of the Rev. Hiram Bingham, who occupies so conspicuous a place among the pioneers of the Sandwich Islands mission; and he is spending his own life in the same cause to which his father rendered such valuable service. With a kindness for which I cannot sufficiently thank him, he has, notwithstanding feeble health and pressing engagements, explored the early records of the Sandwich Islands mission, and with the assistance of his estimable wife and sister, furnished me with the facts which have been laid before the reader.

A second edition of the New Testament, consisting of 10,000 copies, was printed in 1838, and a third after the publication of the complete Bible, also of 10,000 copies, in 1842; and while the translation both of the Old and New Testaments was in progress, there were frequent reprints of portions of both the editions of the New Testament, generally consisting of 10,000 copies. Hence there must have been a brisk demand all along.

"The first edition of the entire Bible," Mr. Bingham, jun., remarks, "was published in the very midst of one of the most remarkable revivals of religion since the days of Pentecost, and at a time when, within one year, 10,725 converted heathen were received to the church, on profession of faith in Christ, making the whole number of church members in good standing 15,915. The publishing of the Bible at this time was most opportune, and soon there was scarcely a family in the kingdom where a copy was not to be found, and where it was not constantly read. The American Bible Society of New York furnished the means for the printing of tens of thousands of portions of Scripture, and also of the first three editions of the entire Bible, viz., 20,500 copies at an expense of at least two dollars (eight shillings) per copy, and with their approbation they were disposed of either by sale or gift, according to the ability of the applicant."

The second edition of the entire Bible, an octavo of 10,000 copies, was printed in 1843, and this was followed by a quarto edition of 500 copies in the course of the same year; and of the New Testament one edition after another followed till a sixth was reached in 1850. In 1857 a Hawaiian and English New Testament was printed, to facilitate the acquisition of the English language, I suppose, by those natives who were desirous of acquiring a knowledge of it. The Gospel of John had been printed in the same fashion three years before.

In 1867 a stereotyped edition of the whole Bible was printed in New York under the superintendence of the Rev. E. W. Clark. With reference to this issue Mr. Bingham remarks:—"The stereotyped octavo editions since 1867 have been purchased by the Hawaiian Board of Missions, and sold to the natives at about two dollars per copy." "In the early years," Mr. Bingham continues, "extracts from various portions of the Scripture were printed as tracts at the expense of the American Tract Society of New York.

"The Philadelphian Bible Society met the expense of publishing the first two editions of the New Testament by a grant of ten thousand dollars" (£2000).

"The following incident,"* Mr. Bingham remarks, "will illustrate the joy with which the first edition of the entire New Testament was received by the Hawaiian chiefs and people in 1832. Queen Kahumann, the favourite wife of Kamehameha the First, and Regent of the Hawaiian kingdom during the minority of Kamehameha the Third, was hopefully converted in 1825. She continued to exert a powerful influence on behalf of Christianity until the time of her death, June 5th, 1832. During her last illness the printing of the translation of the New Testament was completed for the benefit of thousands of the people. We quickly had a copy of it put into neat morocco binding, and presented to the queen in her feeble state. She took the sacred prize in her hands as she lay upon her lowly couch, glanced through it to assure herself of what books it was composed, and looking at it attentively again and again both inside and outside, emphatically pronounced it *maikai* ('excellent'), wrapped it in her handkerchief, laid it on her grateful bosom, gently clasped her hands over it, and placidly looked upwards towards its source, as though she seasonably received the precious boon, the last will and testament of her Saviour as a passport to glory. Even in the paroxysms of disease she would attend to the reading of the Scriptures, and the exercises of devotion. The consoling words of Christ to His sorrowing disciples were read to her—'In My Father's house are many mansions; I go to prepare a place for you, that where I am there ye may be also.'"

* The above incident is from a work on the Sandwich Islands, by the Rev. Hiram Bingham, sen., published in the United States in 1847.

In 1869 an edition of the New Testament and Psalms was printed in 18mo; and in 1886 the entire Bible was printed in the same size; and this is the last thing we have to note in connection with Bible translation and circulation in the Sandwich Islands.

I regret my inability to give incidents illustrative of the manner in which the Bible was received by the Hawaiian people as successive portions issued from the press, and especially when the New and the Old Testaments were completed and published in one volume. However, we have the most satisfactory proof as to the general result. Nowhere perhaps throughout the vast fields in which missionary operations are being carried on have grander results been realised. Of this the following extract from the jubilee memorial volume of the American Board of Commissioners for Foreign Missions, edited by the Rev. Dr. Rufus Anderson, Foreign Secretary of the Board, and published in Boston in 1862, furnishes ample evidence:—"Since the press first put forth its efforts in the language on the 7th of January 1822, there have been issued nearly two hundred millions of pages. Through the blessing of God on these instrumentalities, a beneficent change has occurred in all the departments of the government in the face of fierce outrages from seamen and traders, and deadly hostility from not a few foreign residents. The very first article in the constitution, promulgated by the king and chiefs in 1849, declares that no law shall be enacted which is at variance with the Word of the Lord Jehovah, or with the general spirit of His Word; and that all the laws of the islands shall be in consistency with God's law. What was this but a public, solemn, national profession of the Christian religion on the high Puritan basis? And the laws and administration of the government since that time have been as consistent with this profession, to say the least, as those of any other

Christian government in the world. The statute laws organising the general government and courts of justice, the criminal code, and reported trials in the courts, printed in the English language, make five octavo volumes in the library of the Board. Court-houses, prisons, roads, bridges, surveys of lands, and their distribution with secure titles among the people, are in constant progress.

"Here, then, let us as a Board of Foreign Missions, in the name of the community for which we act, proclaim with shoutings of grace! grace! that the people of the Sandwich Islands are a Christian nation, and may rightfully claim a place among the Protestant Christian nations of the earth!"

Before leaving the Sandwich Islands, let us pause for a moment over the contrast which the present condition of the people presents to that in which the missionaries found them when they began their labours among them in 1820. The national idolatry had indeed been abolished, the temples burned, and the priesthood, *tabus*, and human sacrifices were things of the past; but the moral, intellectual, and social desolation were not less profound. Society was in ruins, and had sunk to about the lowest possible point at which society can exist at all. The nation was composed of liars, thieves, drunkards, and sensualists of the vilest type. The land was owned by the king and his chiefs, and the people were slaves. Property, life, everything was in the hands of arbitrary chiefs, who filled the land with discord and oppression. Such the people of the fair and beautiful islands of Hawaii were; what they are now let the foregoing records testify. And what has produced the change? What could have produced it but the mighty power of God? No other adequate cause can even be conceived. No; God has done it. By bringing His own remedy to bear upon the Hawaiians He has lifted them from the depths into which they had sunk and raised them to the dignity of a Christian nation; and thus another illustrious proof is added to the many which other lands supply, that the religion of the Bible does meet the case of man however deeply sunk and degraded.

Let therefore the friends of the Bible take heart; the Bible is God's book, and no power of man or devils can withstand God. In promoting the circulation of the Bible we are certainly working together with God; and His faithfulness is pledged that His Word shall not return unto Him void, but shall accomplish that which He pleases, and prosper in the thing whereunto He has sent it.

SUPPLEMENTAL.

At an anniversary meeting of the American Bible Society in 1841, an address was made by the Rev. Hiram Bingham, sen., from which we give a brief extract, which cannot fail to interest the reader. "I bring," said Mr. Bingham, "testimony from far off lands—from the lands long eclipsed in dismal night—to encourage you in the work of distributing the Bible wherever it can be carried, or wherever it can make an impression. I hold in my hand a translation of the Bible in the Sandwich Islands language, the product of nineteen years of anxious and laborious toil. It was printed by native hands, and has already found its way to thousands who are able intelligently to read it.

"It is proper that I should say here publicly that it is by the aid of this Society that these labours have been made available. It has been a great and difficult work. Much care and thought have been exercised to render it a fair and unexceptional translation from the original languages; much care has also been taken to produce a version which all evangelical denominations can safely use, and conscientiously circulate.

"It may be satisfactory to apprise you of the sentiments of the islanders towards this volume. I have with me several of the productions of the pupils of our missionary schools, written in reference to the Bible. I will read one of them, though I cannot do justice to it in a translation, since I have only the original before me. It reads:—
'O Holy Bible! glorious and distinguished gift of heaven, which has been disseminated through our land. There is no gift so precious, no treasure to be compared with it. It is to be compared to rich fruit, to honey exuding from heaven. Its excellence has been known from the first. It was known on the hills, and the mountains, in the valleys and plains. It was known on Mount Zion, on the Lake of Tiberias, on Mount Gerizim. And at last its excellence is known by us. We have seen it with our two eyes; we have known it to be good. It is the true rule by which the crooked hearts of the Hawaiians must be made straight. It is to be compared also to the hammer which breaks the stony heart in pieces; to the sword which pierces to the dividing of soul and spirit, and which cuts off all excrescences. It is to be compared to a looking-glass in which our hearts are shown to ourselves; to the compass by which we can alone be guided to the haven of rest.'"

In the same Report of the American Bible Society, that for the year 1880, we find the following statement with reference to the assistance rendered by the Society in aiding the translation and circulation of the Bible in the Sandwich Islands and Micronesia. Its relations with the missions of the American Church seem precisely similar to those of the British and Foreign Bible Society with the missions of the churches of Great Britain.

"The work thus accomplished in translating and printing the Scriptures for the Sandwich Islands and Micronesia in sixty years has been done under the direction of the

American and Hawaiian Boards of Missions, with liberal aid from the American Bible Society, which has furnished funds for the purpose amounting to more than $58,600, besides what it has expended in this country on the manufacture of plates and printed volumes."

The following testimony from an article which appeared recently in the London *Times* newspaper seems worthy of preservation, considering the quarter from which it comes. It indicates a marvellous change in public feeling with reference to Christian missions compared with what obtained thirty or forty years ago. It appeared early in 1877, and the extract which follows is from the *Christian* for February of that year :—

"The *Times* of Thursday last contained an article of three columns concerning the Sandwich Islands, now called the Hawaiian Kingdom. The monarchy is constitutional, after the model of England. The Judicature approaches perfection, with an excellent civil code. The system of free public schools is of the same admirable nature. The Sabbath is strictly observed. The commerce, in proportion to the population, is without an equal in the world, and renders the kingdom, in resources and stability, the most important in the Pacific Ocean. All this is traced to the missionary enterprise of about seventy years. 'The missionaries,' says the writer, 'have bequeathed to posterity a noble monument of self-sacrifice and labour.'"

CHAPTER XXI.

MICRONESIA.

WE now come to Micronesia, the third of the three great divisions under which geographers have classed the islands of the Pacific. These divisions are named respectively Polynesia, Many Islands; Melanesia, or the Black Islands, so named from the colour of their inhabitants; and Micronesia, or Small Islands, because the islands comprised in that division are all comparatively small.

The islands of Micronesia, with a few exceptions, lie to the north of the equator. They extend in a north-westerly direction from about 175° to 134° east longitude, and from 2° or 3° south latitude to about 12° north. Within this range of over 40° of longitude a number of groups or clusters of islands embracing many single islands, and groups larger and smaller known by the general names of the Caroline Islands,* the Pelew Islands, the Gilbert Islands, the Marshall Islands, the Ladrone Islands, &c.; and though most of these islands do not, so far as our information extends, appear to be very populous, yet in the aggregate their inhabitants number many thousands. Some of them were visited by Commodore Wilkes in 1841, and long before that date trading vessels and whalers had visited them in considerable numbers; but it was not till about

---

* The Caroline Islands were discovered by a Spanish navigator in 1686, and received the name they bear in honour of Charles II. of Spain.

the year 1849 that any steps were taken towards commencing among them missionary operations.

About that time the churches of Hawaii were moved to embark in a foreign mission. A society was formed, called the Hawaiian Missionary Society, and the parent society in America determined to co-operate with the Hawaiian society; and the islands of Micronesia were chosen as their field of operation. Three missionaries, the Rev. Luther H. Gulich, M.D., and the Rev. Benjamin G. Snow, and the Rev. Albert A. Sturges, were appointed by the American Board to lead the way in the new enterprise. These brethren, with their wives, proceeded to the Sandwich Islands, where they were joined by three natives of that group who had been selected to aid them in carrying out the object of their mission.

At the Sandwich Islands a vessel named the *Caroline* was chartered, and about July 1852 the party sailed on their important errand. Before their departure they were organised into a Christian Church under the designation of the Micronesian Mission Church, and intensely interesting services were held on the occasion; and when the hour of departure came a great crowd of people assembled on the wharf, and sang the stirring strains of Heber's grand hymn, "Shall we whose souls are lighted."

The missionaries carried with them a very remarkable document, which on many accounts is deserving of a place in the annals of Christian missions. This was a letter of commendation from the King of the Sandwich Islands, Kamehameha III., addressed to the rulers of the Micronesian Islands.

The following is a copy of His Majesty's letter:—
"Kamehameha III., of the Hawaiian Islands, King, sends greetings to all chiefs of the islands in this great ocean to the westward, called Caroline Islands, Kingsmill group, &c. Peace and happiness to you all, now and for ever.

"Here is my friendly message to you. There are about to sail to your islands some teachers of the Most High God, Jehovah, to make known unto you His Word for your eternal salvation. A part of them are white men from the United States of America, and part belong to my islands. Their names are as follows:—B. G. Snow and wife; A. A. Sturges and wife; L. H. Gulich and wife; E. W. Clark and J. T. Gulich;* Opunui and wife; Kaaikaula and wife; and Kekela. H. Holsworth is captain of the vessel.

"I therefore take the liberty to commend those good teachers to your care and friendship, to exhort you to listen to their instructions, and to seek their acquaintance. I have seen the value of such teachers. We here on my islands once lived in ignorance and idolatry. We were given to war, and we were very poor. Now my people are enlightened. We live in peace, and some have acquired property. Our condition is greatly improved on what it once was, and the Word of God has been the great cause of our improvement. Many of my people regard the Word of God and pray to Him, and He has greatly blessed us. I advise you to throw away your idols, take the Lord Jehovah for your God, worship and love Him, and He will bless and save you. May He make these new teachers a great blessing to you and your people, and withhold from you no good thing. Kamehameha."

Nothing untoward occurred during the voyage, and by the help and blessing of God the missionaries succeeded in effecting a settlement on two islands of the Caroline group, Kusaie and Ponape, and a measure of success crowned their labours. The promoters of the mission were encouraged, and after a time they determined to send reinforcements, and to extend their operations to

* E. W. Clark and J. T. Gulich must have gone as a deputation from the Sandwich Islands mission to lend temporary help to the young missionaries.

other islands and groups as God in His providence might furnish the means and open the way. But in order to this, it was felt that a ship, to be at the service of the mission, was a necessity. In no other way could the missions already established be sustained and carried on efficiently; and nothing could be done to any considerable extent in the way of carrying the Gospel to new fields. But to purchase or build a ship would involve a large outlay, and how was that to be met? The thing was taken up with great spirit by the American churches, and following the lead of British Christians in the case of the *John Williams,* an appeal was made by the American Board to the children of the Sabbath schools throughout the States, and the response was of the most enthusiastic character. Two thousand pounds were asked, but such was the interest aroused, and the hearty manner in which the thing was taken up, and money flowed in so liberally, that in a short time the offerings amounted to £15,000, leaving a large surplus, which was reserved towards meeting the expenses of the vessel in future years.

The story of how the money was raised, and of the deep and joyous interest that was evoked, is a thrilling one, but we must not yield to the temptation to enter into particulars. All classes of people caught the enthusiasm, and manifested an amazing interest. "Even in the stately halls of Legislation," writes Mrs. Warren, "it was not thought unworthy of notice." The following extract from a speech delivered in the Massachusetts House of Representatives will be read with interest.

T. H. Russell, Esq., said—" Permit me, sir, to recall to the minds of the House a notable instance just transpired. A few days before we assembled here, there lay at one of the wharves of this city, a beautiful vessel called the *Morning Star.* Let me say a word of her history. In the far-distant Pacific, some 15,000 to 17,000 miles away by the usual sailing route, there is found a group of islands just coming into notice, and known as the Micronesian group. They are inhabited by a race of savages, perhaps not much above the Hawaiians fifty years ago. Now there were found in New England, men, and women too, who were willing to give their lives to the elevation, socially, civilly, and religiously, of these far-distant and poor people. But how to get there? Commerce does everything, dares everything, when gain allures. But these rude people had little about them to attract thither the ships of commerce. Some one suggested, 'Let us build a missionary ship.' But where are the means? The Board of gentlemen just below us in Pemberton Square preside over this magnificent charity, and who this year will disburse over one-third of a million of dollars of voluntary offerings, find already the field too great for their harvesters. They can spare nothing.

"'Let us,' says another, 'lay the burden on the shoulders of the little children.' The thought was the deed. The keel of the ship was laid on the shore of the Mystic, and while she was receiving form and symmetry, the word went out—'The children are to build a missionary ship, and every child who can contribute a single dime may feel that it has a proprietary in the noble undertaking.' At once the little rills began to flow from every hillside in New England; they came from the Middle, Southern, and Western States, the far distant Territories, a little from over the border of Queen Victoria's dominions, and even the Choctaw mission, and the poor remnant of Tuscarora Indians, did not fail in contributing their mites. It was supposed the ship would cost six, then ten, and finally twenty thousand dollars. How is it now in the treasury? All these little gatherings poured in, they began to swell up until there were eight, ten, twelve, eighteen, twenty thousand dollars; and though the good Secretaries held up their hands crying, 'Hold, enough!' no one could tell where it would end.

"The little ship was completed, her freight and all on board, and weeks ago she sailed away; and I doubt not that already the beams of the beautiful constellation, the Southern Cross, are mildly shed on her; and I know that the prayers and blessings of the little proprietors are following her, like thousands of unseen angels, on her journey of Christian love. Yes, sir, *Christian love;* no atheism about it. One such fact is worth more to a soul that has a single hope or aspiration for man, to a heart that has a single pulsation in unison with the golden rule, than all that atheism has ever accomplished, or will, or can in an eternity of ages."

Well said, Mr. Russell! Your words deserve to live!

The enthusiasm reached its zenith in connection with the launching of the little ship and her departure on her glorious errand. On the day of launching from 3000 to 4000 people assembled. A stage had been erected near the bows of the vessel, and from that one of the Secretaries of the Board addressed the multitude in language fitted to fan the flame of enthusiasm already kindled. At the close of the address the vast multitude sang "From Greenland's icy mountains." Prayer was then offered, and the service closed by the singing of "Praise God from whom all blessings flow;" and when the little craft moved from the stocks and glided gracefully into the water, such a hurrah burst forth from the multitude as made the heavens and the earth ring again. At her departure the scene was somewhat different. In the hearts of many there was a feeling of sadness arising from the fact that farewells were about to be exchanged—final farewells as regards this life in the case of many.

The time fixed for sailing was the 1st of December 1856. At ten o'clock in the morning all was ready. The passengers were all on board. These were the Rev. Hiram Bingham, jun., son of the Rev. Hiram Bingham who, the reader will remember, was one of the first missionaries to the Sandwich Islands thirty-seven years before. He was present on this to him intensely interesting occasion, and took part in the services. Mr. Bingham, jun., and his wife were the only missionary passengers. The service was begun by singing "Jesus shall reign where'er the sun." An address followed by one of the ministers present, and Mr. Bingham, sen., offered prayer. He had seen great things, and his prayer was that his son might " see greater things than these." When the service was over, the day was so far spent that it was deemed advisable to defer sailing till the following morning; and on that morning, December the 2nd, the beautiful little ship, in which such an intense interest was felt by tens of thousands of loving Christian hearts, started on her glorious errand of mercy— a veritable morning star,* heralding the rising of the Sun of Righteousness on the benighted inhabitants of the far off Isles of the Sea.

The Rev. H. Bingham, jun., of whom the reader has already heard so much, was, as we have seen, a passenger by the *Morning Star*. He had gone to the United States to complete his education, and was now returning to his native Hawaii, thence to proceed to Micronesia to enter upon his life work there; and now we turn to the record which he has so kindly furnished of his own work and that of others in opening up the treasures of Divine truth to the various tribes who people these islands. To him I am indebted for the information that follows relative to the translation and circulation of the Bible throughout these widely extended regions, as well as in the parent

---

* My information about the *Morning Star*, and much beside, has been derived from Mrs. Warren's deeply interesting volume already referred to, in the chapter on the Sandwich Islands.

mission of Hawaii. He has either supplied the information at first hand, or procured it from others at no small amount of trouble.

THE GILBERT ISLANDS,*

to which Mr. Bingham's labours have been chiefly directed, lie near the equator, in longitude about 173° east. They are seventeen in number. The population, when they were visited by the United States Exploring Expedition in 1841, was estimated at about 50,000. This estimate was probably too high, as the number does not now exceed 30,000. Missionary operations were commenced on the group in 1857. On the 10th of November of that year, Mr. and Mrs. Bingham, with J. W. Kanoa and J. H. Mahoe, Hawaiian assistants, and their wives, landed upon Apaiang, one of the islands of the group, and entered upon the great work to which they had devoted their lives. We need hardly remark that there was no written language. The strangers and the natives were therefore in the literal sense barbarians to each other. Words had to be picked up from the lips of the natives; an alphabet had to be adapted, and the language reduced to writing. This difficult work occupied of course a considerable time, and two years passed before much could be done in the work of translating the Scriptures.

Mr. Bingham in his notes mentions a personal reminiscence which forms an interesting link of connection

* Forty years ago these islands were included in what was then called the Kingsmill group. How the name has come to be changed I am not aware. The natives of this group, and of other islands and groups included in the general name of Micronesia, appear to be all of Malay origin. The tradition of the Gilbert Islanders is that their ancestors came in two canoes—the one from an island named Barness or Baneba, lying to the south-west; and the other from an island named Amoi, lying to the south-east, pointing respectively to the Malayan archipelago on the west, and Eastern or Central Polynesia in the east. See Wilkes' Narrative, vol. ii. p. 212.

between the mission to the Gilbert Islands and the parent mission. "In 1839," he tells us, "when he was a boy at Honolulu, he used to carry from his father's study to the mission printing-office corrected proof-sheets of the Hawaiian New Testament, nearly one-fifth of which he had translated. Twenty years after it was his own privilege to commence in February 1859 at Apaiang the translation of the New Testament for the Gilbert Islanders, living more than two thousand miles distant from the Hawaiian group."

"About five years after the commencement of the mission," Mr. Bingham writes, "we sent a copy of the Gospel of Matthew by the hands of Kanoa to be printed at Honolulu, as also a small hymn-book. Thirteen months after Kanoa returned in the *Morning Star* bringing an edition of the hymn-book, but no printed copy of the Matthew. We were very sorry, for we had often told our people that they would soon have an entire Gospel. The first eleven chapters of Matthew to the thirtieth verse of the twelfth chapter had been printed some time before at Honolulu, and were now in the hands of the people."

There was something to compensate in a measure for the disappointment in not receiving the complete Gospel by the *Morning Star*. She had brought a printing press, and so the missionary and his friends consoled themselves. "We can now print the Matthew for ourselves," said they. They came very near having their joy turned into sorrow, however.

The case which was supposed to contain the press was landed and speedily opened, and there was a small box of types, cases, and other things used in printing, but no press! Oh, what a disappointment! The captain was sure that all had been landed, but Mr. Bingham could not rest till he had gone on board and inquired at the mate. He, however, repeated the assurance given by the captain that nothing remained in the ship. "As I paddled home that evening," says the disappointed missionary, "my heart was doubly heavy from this second disappointment."

The next morning the captain came on shore and informed Mr. Bingham that another search was to be made, and that, in case it should prove successful, the Stars and Stripes should be hoisted. "How great was our joy," says Mr. Bingham, "on leaving the school-house (he had been examining one of the schools) to see the old flag at the masthead." But their difficulties were not yet at an end. They had a press, indeed, with types and other necessaries for printing, but there was no printer. This difficulty does not appear to have occurred to Mr. Bingham till he was brought face to face with it. A *book* was sent telling him how to proceed, but to learn the art of printing in that fashion would have been a tedious and difficult undertaking. Months must have passed before any practical result could have been reached, but the difficulty was met in a way which filled the hearts of the missionary and his people with wonder and their lips with praise. Two days after the *Morning Star* left, a boat arrived which had belonged to a vessel that had been wrecked in some part of the ocean many hundred miles distant from Apaiang. The shipwrecked party tried to find a small guano island which they supposed to be about forty miles from where they were wrecked. In this they were unsuccessful, and after being ten days upon the ocean in the boat, and voyaging some six hundred miles, they reached the island of Maiana. There they rested one night only, starting on the following morning for Apaiang in the hope of finding the *Morning Star*, and obtaining a passage in her to Honolulu. A head wind and adverse currents compelled them to return to Maiana, where they were detained five days. On the sixth day they again started for Apaiang, which they now succeeded in reaching, but to their sore disappointment the *Morning Star* had gone; but there was doubtless an overruling hand in their detention and disappointment, for in consequence of that a printer was supplied for the Gilbert Islands' mission. One of the shipwrecked party was a printer, and he was willing to leave the sea, and settle down to his old employ, an opportunity of so doing being so remarkably put in his way. With reference to his arrival Mr. Bingham remarks—" We love to think that God sent that kind printer to us over the wide ocean to help us in giving the Word of Life to the poor Gilbert Islanders."

The printer, Mr. Hotchkiss, soon got the press in working order, and in a few weeks the Gospel of Matthew was in the hands of the people, and several other books followed, among which were the Gospel of John and the Epistle to the Ephesians. These were printed on note-paper, the supply of printing-paper having been exhausted, and only fifty-four copies of Ephesians and sixty-four of John could be printed; and at this juncture Mr. Bingham's health broke down, and he was obliged to leave the mission for a time.

It does not appear how long Mr. Hotchkiss remained in connection with the mission, but Mr. Bingham mentions it as an "interesting fact that twenty-two years later, in his declining days, he set the types of the six books of the Old Testament, Job to Isaiah inclusive, just printed in one of the publishing houses of Honolulu."

The failure of Mr. Bingham's health led to a long interruption in the work of Scripture translation. A visit to the United States was found to be necessary, and while there, in the summer of 1866, he carried through the press of the American Bible Society in New York a second edition of the Gospels of Matthew and John and the Epistle to the Ephesians of 1000 copies each.

After his visit to the United States, Mr. Bingham's health was still such as not to allow of his living on shore in Micronesia, but his heart was so set on mission work that he qualified himself to take charge of the mission ship, and for the space of seventeen months he was a sailing missionary, visiting and superintending evangelistic work in the Gilbert Islands and elsewhere; and afterwards in 1868, 1870, and 1871 he was engaged at Honolulu for climatic reasons in revising and printing the first three-quarters of the New Testament, and in composing, translating, and printing hymns for the Gilbert Islanders. In January 1872 he began the translation of the last quarter of the New Testament, and that important work was completed in April 1873, and an edition of one thousand was printed in the same year at Honolulu under his superintendence.

Throughout the whole of this great work Mr. Bingham had the help of his devoted wife. Of this he makes grateful mention in the following significant terms:—" During the progress of the translation of the New Testament many suggestions from Mrs. Bingham as to modes of expression were gladly accepted. Many pages of the manuscript were either copied by her or written as an amanuensis, and very material aid was rendered in proof reading."

Mr. and Mrs. Bingham had the great joy of being themselves the bearers of the priceless treasure to the people for whom it had been prepared. Mr. Bingham's health had so much improved that they determined to give the islands another trial, and in the course of 1873 they sailed in the *Morning Star* for the Gilbert Islands, and again took up their abode at Apaiang. Rough work met them on the threshold. The dwelling-house which they left in 1868 had been destroyed and the whole of the mission premises desolated by a savage tribe from a neighbouring island, so that in re-entering upon mission work they had in a manner to begin again at the beginning.

About that, however, we hear no complaints. The dwelling-house was rebuilt, and other necessary buildings were completed in a short time, and the work of the training school and other departments of mission work were resumed; and among these the revision of the New Testament had a place, and was carried on till towards the close of 1875, when a second breakdown in Mr. Bingham's health compelled him again to leave his loved work in the Gilbert Islands, and remove to the more temperate climate of his native Hawaii. Here at Honolulu he went on with his revision work till it was completed in 1877, and during the course of that year the second edition of the New Testament, consisting of 2000 copies, was printed. This edition met with a ready sale at Apaiang and elsewhere. Part of it was sent to Samoa at the request of the District Committee of the Samoan mission, and these were sold by the agents of that mission, who occupy six islands south of the equator, on which the Gilbert Islands language is spoken, and the proceeds of sales, amounting to £118, were remitted to the Hawaiian Board.

In 1880 a third edition was printed in New York by the American Bible Society, and was electrotyped, the proofs being read by their own proof readers. From these plates three more editions have since been printed, making six in all, and there is still a demand. Of 3000 copies ordered from New York by the Samoan District Committee, 2000 have already been sold, and the proceeds of sales Mr. Bingham estimates at about £200. The Gilbert Islanders in the part of the group under the care of the American Board, in conjunction with the Hawaiian Board of Missions, together with those who have resided in the Hawaiian Islands and Tahiti, have paid to the American Bible Society for such portions of the Scriptures as they have received about £392, 17s.

The following statement by Mr. Bingham shows unmistakably that the Gilbert Islanders value highly the Word of Life. They are a poor people, living on comparatively barren islands; and when they leave their homes to labour on Hawaiian or Tahitian plantations, their earnings are obtained at the cost of no small amount of hazard and self-denial. Mr. Bingham's statement is as follows:—

Proceeds of sales, including a donation of 229 dollars 45 cents to aid in printing the New Testament	$2,193 73
Purchased by the Samoan District Committee .	2,090 85
Donation from Samoan missions towards the expense of electrotyping New Testament .	200 00
	$4,484 58

Mr. Bingham's health not allowing of his resuming missionary work at Apaiang at this time, he accepted the appointment of Corresponding Secretary to the Hawaiian Board of Missions, and held that during 1878, 1879, and 1880; and during 1881, 1882, and 1883 he was also protector of South Sea immigrants, especially Gilbert Islanders, for the Hawaiian Government Board of Immigration; and the duties connected with these appointments, together with revising, enlarging, and printing a hymn-book for the Gilbert Islanders, and evangelistic work among the natives of that group who had come to work on the Hawaiian plantations, made such demands upon him, that the work of Scripture translation was suspended for a number of years.

He had finished the translation of the New Testament in April 1873, and on the 16th of August 1883, his fifty-second birthday, he resumed the work of translating the Old Testament; and from that time to the present (May 1887) he has continued to apply himself as closely to that work as his health will allow. At the date of the reminiscences which he has so kindly furnished (February 22nd, 1887), he had translated six books of the Old Testament, viz., Job, Psalms, Proverbs, Ecclesiastes, the Song of Solomon, and Isaiah; and on the above date the last sheet of an edition of 1500 copies of these books had been printed, 500 copies of which had been ordered by the Samoan Committee, and the balance (1000 copies) is to be sent to the central and northern portions of the Gilbert Islands by the next visit of the *Morning Star*, only reserving enough to meet the wants of the Gilbert Islanders resident on the Hawaiian group, and I suppose on Tahiti.

The translation of Genesis has also been completed, and Exodus is in hand, and Mr. Bingham adds the following forecast:—" He hopes that, if the Lord will, he may be permitted to complete the translation of the whole Bible by the middle of 1893 in Honolulu, to print it at the Bible House in New York, and to take it to his people in 1895. He thanks the Lord that his wife is still spared to make many a suggestion which improves the translation. Mr. Moses Kaure, a native of Apaiang, is also with him as an assistant translator and proof-reader. Many of his criticisms on the above seven books of the Old Testament have been most valuable."

Mr. Bingham adds a few words of grateful acknowledgment of the help he received from two of his native converts in the translation of the New Testament which we must not omit. "In this connection," he remarks, "it may be added that Joseph Ekewa and T. Tekea of Apaiang rendered most important aid in the translation of the New Testament. Their names should be remembered among their people as having done for them a great and priceless work both at Apaiang and Honolulu. Joseph was one of the first two who were baptized from among the people. The young man seemed to have been raised up of the Lord at a time when in the beginning of the work of translation, the difficulties of which were such as only those who have attempted a similar work for a barbarous people can fully appreciate."

Mr. Bingham closes his remarks with the following most gratifying statement with reference to the results of Bible circulation and missionary labour among the Gilbert Islanders:—" These can only be fully known to God, but the fact that at least fifteen churches have been established with a membership of about 3000, and that about 9000 New Testaments have been purchased by them within the last fourteen years, and that many of them are being constantly read, are grounds for joy to all who are the friends of the Lord Jesus. To God be all the praise."

THE MARSHALL ISLANDS.

The Marshall Islands consist of the Ralick and Radack chains at the eastern extremity of the Caroline archipelago. They number about thirty islands, but only one-half are inhabited. The people number about 15,000. They speak two dialects, but books printed in the one are intelligible to all. They lie two or three hundred miles to the north-west of the Gilbert group.

The Gospel was introduced to the group in 1857. In December of that year two missionaries from the American Board, the Rev. George Pierson, M.D., and the Rev. Edward T. Doane, settled upon the island of Ebon. We need hardly remark that there was no written language, and that, as in every part of Polynesia, east, west, north and south, the language had to be picked up from the lips of the natives. The first portion of Scripture translated was from the Gospel of Matthew, from the fifth to the eleventh chapters. These were printed on the island during the course of 1858. The work of translating and printing was done jointly by Messrs. Doane and Pierson. Mr.

Pierson returned to the United States in 1859. Mr. Doane translated the twenty-sixth, twenty-seventh, and twenty-eighth chapters of Matthew in 1861, and they were printed in 1862. Mr. Doane also translated the Gospel of Mark, which was printed at Honolulu in 1863.

About this time Mr. Doane seems to have moved to some other island, and he, Mr. Bingham states, was succeeded by the Rev. B. G. Snow, who removed to this island from Kusaie. He continued the work which Mr. Doane had begun. He, according to Mr. Bingham, translated at least Matthew, Luke, John, and Acts, besides revising Mark, previous to his return to the United States on account of failure of health in 1876. The remaining books of the New Testament were translated by the Rev. E. M. Pease, M.D., who came to Ebon in 1877. The earlier translations were also thoroughly revised by him, and an edition of 1500 copies of the entire New Testament was carried through the press of the American Bible Society in New York by him in 1885, Mrs. Pease rendering assistance in proof-reading.

The book of Genesis was translated by the Rev. J. F. Whitney, and 400 copies were printed by him at the mission press on the island in 1877. The translation of the Epistle to the Romans, Mr. Whitney states, was left incomplete by Mr. Snow when he was compelled to leave the mission and return to the United States on account of health. "He had translated the first twelve chapters. This work was left to me; and I finished Romans and translated the Epistles, from first Corinthians through to Philippians. These were printed at the Bible House in New York in 1882, together with the book of Genesis and the three Epistles of John, which I translated after coming to this country." Mr. Whitney is in the United States at the present time, I presume, on account of health.

Dr. Pease, now in charge of the training school of the

Marshall Islands on Kusaie, intends proceeding with the translation of the Psalms and other portions of the Old Testament as his other duties will allow.

I am indebted to Mr. Whitney for the following gratifying information. Referring to books which had been translated by Mr. Snow, and reprinted during a visit made by him to the United States in 1870, Mr. Whitney remarks:—"These, with the Gospels of Mark and John, were taken to Ebon by the *Morning Star* in 1873. They were in great demand: 750 of an edition of 1000 were sold in a few days. The rest of the edition, which was left at Honolulu, was forwarded in 1874, together with a revised edition of the Acts of the Apostles. The demand was so great for these that we ordered a reprint of 3000 copies, a part of which was sent out in 1875, and the rest later. They are nearly gone now. The demand has been constant for these, and more were sold in 1880–81 than any previous year since 1873."

KUSAIE OR STRONG'S ISLAND.

This is the most easterly of the Caroline Islands. Here the Rev. B. G. Snow, one of the pioneers of the Micronesian mission, settled in July 1852. It has a population of about 1200, who speak a language peculiar to themselves. Mr. Snow reduced the language to writing, but we have no information as to any portion of Scripture being printed till 1860. In the course of that year some extracts from the Gospels of Matthew, Luke, and John were printed at Honolulu; and the complete Gospel of John was printed at the same place in 1863.

After ten years residence on the island Mr. Snow removed to Ebon, another island of the same group, and laboured especially for the Marshall Islanders, but continued to give a portion of his time to translation work for those who had been his first charge; and when he was called to his rest in May 1880, he left them a priceless legacy, consisting of all the four Gospels, the Acts of the Apostles, the Epistles to the Philippians, Colossians, 1st and 2nd Thessalonians, the 1st, 2nd, and 3rd Psalms, the book of Ruth, and the Ten Commandments—all of which, I presume, have been printed. "There now remains," Mr. Bingham remarks, "less than four hundred of the Kusaieans, and probably not much more of the Scriptures will be translated for them at present."

PONAPE, OR ASCENSION ISLAND.

Ponape, Mr. Bingham tells us, is one of the largest islands of the Caroline group. It lies about 300 miles to the west of Kusaie. When Messrs. Sturges and Gulick began their work upon it in September 1852, its population was about ten thousand, but a few years later the smallpox reduced the number to about one-half. The missionaries reduced the language to writing, and Dr. Gulick translated the first eight chapters of Matthew, which were printed on the island in 1859. After a residence of seven years on the island, he left, and the work of translating the Scriptures was carried on for a time by Mr. Sturges alone. He completed the Gospel of Matthew, and translated the Gospels of Mark, Luke, and John, the Acts of the Apostles, the Epistle to the Romans, 1st and 2nd Corinthians, Ephesians, Philippians, and Colossians.

In 1865 Mr. Doane returned to Ponape, and since that time he has assisted Mr. Sturges more or less in completing the translation of the New Testament. He translated from Galatians to Revelation, thereby completing that part of the sacred volume. He translated also Genesis, Exodus, Joshua, Judges, and Ruth, all of which, with the complete New Testament, are now being printed in New York. The proceeds of sales so far as reported are £50, 7s. 9d.

THE MORTLOCK ISLANDS.

These are a cluster of islands in the Caroline archipelago about 300 miles south-west of Ponape, and contain about 3000 people, who speak a language of their own, which, however, is closely allied to the Ruk dialect. The Rev. R. W. Logan of the Ponape mission began the translation of the New Testament into the Mortlock dialect in 1878, having picked up enough from natives of these islands who were living near him on Ponape to enable him to translate the Gospel of Mark. The translation was completed in 1879, and printed in Honolulu in 1880.

In November 1879 Mr. Logan left Ponape and settled on the Mortlock Islands, and in a remarkably short time he completed the translation of the New Testament into the language of these islands, Mrs. Logan being his constant copyist; but in the midst of his exhausting labours his health gave way, and he was compelled for a season to leave his work in the islands and try the effect of change of climate. In 1881 an opportunity to go to New Zealand occurred by a small schooner, which he embraced, and proceeded with his family to Auckland, and thence to the United States; and while there he superintended the printing of the New Testament by the American Bible Society in New York, with the assistance of Mrs. Logan in proof-reading. This was published in 1883.

It is cheering to record that Mr. Logan's health has been so far restored as to allow of his return to his work among the islands. He is now stationed on Ruk, a cluster of islands within an immense lagoon, about the centre of the Caroline archipelago, having a population of 10,000.

"Whatever portions of Scripture," Mr. Bingham remarks, "he may hereafter translate will doubtless be in the Ruk dialect, with the hope and expectation that the translation will suffice for the Mortlock Islands, and other islands adjacent to Ruk on the north and west. If his health is spared the Rukites will doubtless soon have large portions of the Scriptures in their own tongue."

Mr. Bingham closes his notes on Bible translation in Micronesia as follows:—"At least three more languages in Micronesia remain to be reduced to writing—that of Vuleai, Yap, and the Pelew Islands. Who will undertake to give the people of these islands the Scriptures in their own tongue? Will the Spanish priests who have recently landed on Yap?"

Mr. Bingham leaves his question unanswered, meaning doubtless to imply a strong negative. Romish priests don't trouble themselves with Scripture translation. May the God of the Bible—the God of mercy—interpose, and raise up a goodly band of men of the stamp of Bingham, and Logan,' and Sturges, and others to carry the light-diffusing and life-giving tidings of salvation through the Lord Jesus Christ to every group and island where men are found, till the darkness of heathenism shall all be scattered, and the light of the knowledge of His glory cover all, as the waters cover the sea. Towards that blessed issue all is tending, and in due time it will assuredly come, for the mouth of the Lord hath spoken it. The Lord hasten it in His time.

The following remarks by the Rev. J. F. Whitney have come into my hands since this chapter was written. They will form an appropriate sequel to the above account of Bible translation in Micronesia. "In translating the Bible," Mr. Whitney writes, "we have always felt constrained to be as exact as possible. There is of course a limit to the time one may consistently spend in searching for an expression by which to translate some idea foreign to their language and thoughts, but I have often spent hours, and even a whole day, on one word; sometimes one important verse would involve more study than a chapter at other times. The question is not what would have been written had the writer been in our time and place? but what is written, and how can it be most nearly expressed in this new language? It is not what would Jesus have said had He walked by the lagoon shore of our coral island to the natives who would have thronged to listen? but what did He say to the assembled multitudes on the shore of the sea of Galilee?

"In all the poverty of language there is sometimes a great richness of expression. Occasionally an idiom will carry one over the English to the Greek or Hebrew, and bring out a meaning and beauty which could not come to any one without a knowledge of the original. So our experience has often been delightful, and while handing the water of life to the thirsty we have found a cooling drink for ourselves. It often occurs that a passage translated into another tongue suggests some new phase of truth unthought of before, but as we search back we find it was there though not seen. With the people it is ever a new revelation; and as the language is becoming recorded in the words of Scripture, it is pleasant to think that while the Scriptures are a saving power as they enter into their lives, so must they be a conserving power to the language itself. It is the Word of God that we thus seek to send forth; and it will not return to Him void, but it will accomplish that which He pleases, and it will prosper in the thing whereto He sent it."

CHAPTER XXII.

THE MARQUESAS.*

As stated in an earlier part of this work, the first party of missionaries to the islands of the Pacific, who sailed from England in the *Duff* in 1796, were instructed to attempt to commence missionary operations on three groups of Eastern Polynesia — the Tahitian, the Tongan, and the Marquesas. How these instructions were carried out, and with what results in the case of Tahiti, and that of Tonga, we have seen; and this work would be incomplete without some information with reference to the third— the Marquesas. That group is the most easterly of the Polynesian Islands. It lies to the north-east of Tahiti, distant about 500 miles, extending from 7° 51' to 10° 25' south latitude, and from 138° 48' to 140° 29' west longitude. There are six or eight islands, larger and smaller, containing as was supposed in early days a population fully equal to that of the Tahitian group. That was Mr. Ellis' opinion half a century ago. The principal islands

---

* A word of explanation. The reader will notice that the Marquesas Islands lie to the south of the equator, and belong to Eastern Polynesia, and that that being the case, our chapter on them occupies an anomalous position in this work. The explanation is that for many years they have, as a mission field, been occupied by the agents of the American and Hawaiian Mission Boards; and on that account it seemed natural that our notice of missionary work on them should follow the chapters on the parent mission, the Sandwich Islands, and its other offshoots in Micronesia.

of the group were discovered in 1595 by Alvaro Mendano, a Spanish navigator, who was proceeding from Peru with the view of forming a settlement in the Solomon Islands. In honour of the Marquis Mendoza, Viceroy of Peru, and patron of the expedition, Mendano gave to the group the name it still bears, the Marquesas. We must not stop to notice the visits of later navigators to the group, but pass on to give a very brief notice of the islands and their inhabitants, and the efforts that have been made to bring the people under the influence of Christianity.

Mr. Ellis tells us in his "Polynesian Researches," vol. iii. p. 310, that the group is inferior in extent to the Tahitian group. "Nukuhiva, the largest, is much smaller than Tahiti, and probably not more than fifty miles in circumference. The mountains are lofty, bold in outline, and either clothed with verdure, or adorned with plantations: cascades roll over the sides of the mountains, and streams flow through the valleys. The land capable of cultivation, however, is comparatively small, as the islands are not protected, as most others in the Pacific, by coral reefs. The sea extends to the base of the mountains, and thus prevents the formation and preservation of the low border of prolific alluvial soil so valuable in the Tahitian and other islands to the westward. The shores are rocky and precipitous, and a level beach or a good landing-place is seldom met with. Deep, wide, and extensive valleys abound in the islands, and in these the natives generally dwell. The vegetable productions of the islands correspond to those of other islands in Eastern and Central Polynesia; and the breadfruit is found in perhaps greater perfection than in any other island of the Pacific."

The natives, physically considered, are among the most perfect specimens of the human race. They are somewhat lighter in colour than most of the other islanders, and both men and women are of the handsomest type.

Such are they physically, but what about their character? Alas! that forms a melancholy contrast. But enough will come out as we proceed to give the reader sufficient insight into that without any particular description, so we will proceed to give a brief outline of the efforts that have been made to impart to the Marquesans the blessings of the Gospel.

The first attempt was made in 1797. In June of that year the *Duff* visited the group, and the Rev. W. P. Crook was left on Tahuata (Santa Christina), and remained on that island about twelve months; and after being about seven months on the island of Nukuhiva, an opportunity of proceeding to England offered, which he embraced. His object was to confer with the Directors of the London Missionary Society as to the best means of establishing an efficient mission on the islands. Very little of course could be done by a single individual towards embracing the groups. The original intention was that Mr. Crook should have a fellow-labourer, but the individual who was chosen to be a second to him declined to remain on the islands after being on shore a few days. Mr. Crook went to England with the expectation of returning shortly, but the capture of the *Duff* by a French privateer, and the disasters which befel the Tahitian mission in the early years of its history, prevented any further efforts being made to occupy the group for more than a quarter of a century.

In the meanwhile the Gospel had taken root in the Tahitian group. The long dreary winter had passed away, and the seed sown in tears was being reaped in joy. Many of the Tahitians, once as deeply sunk as the Marquesans, had now been raised to a new life, and were ready to leave their homes—now really peaceful, happy, and pure—to go and live among the savage cannibals of the Marquesas, in order to impart to them the precious blessings of which they themselves had become possessed. So, early in the year 1824, Mr. Crook, who was now identified with the Tahitian mission, accompanied by four native Tahitian missionaries—two from the church at Huahine, and two from the church at Tairabu of which Mr. Crook was pastor—proceeded to the Marquesas, where, though he had been absent twenty-seven years, he was recognised and welcomed by some of the people. One of the teachers died during the voyage, and the remaining three were placed under the care of a chief named Iotete at Santa Christina, who engaged to protect and support them. Mr. Crook remained with them for a month. "Their prospects of usefulness," says Mr. Ellis, "were at first encouraging, but the wickedness of the people was so great, their conduct so violent and alarming even to the Tahitians, whom they threatened to kill and devour, that they were obliged to leave."

Further efforts were made to occupy the group by Tahitian teachers, with much the same result, viz., failure. At length the missionaries were forced to the conclusion that the state of the people—social and otherwise—was such that the hope of occupying it by Tahitian teachers alone must be given up. In 1833, American missionaries from the Sandwich Islands commenced a mission on the island of Nukuhiva, but they were also obliged to abandon the attempt for the same reasons as their predecessors.

The Directors of the London Missionary Society, loth to abandon the group, appointed two missionaries, the Rev. George Stallworthy and the Rev. John Rodgerson, to make another attempt to establish a mission upon it. They sailed from England in October 1833, and after spending a few months at Tahiti they proceeded to their destination, accompanied by the Rev. David Darling of the Tahitian mission, and several Tahitian teachers. They settled at Santa Christina, and entered upon their work with a measure of encouragement. After remaining with them about twelve months Mr. Darling returned to Tahiti, leaving the young missionaries and their native assistants being kindly treated by the people, but with little to encourage as regards the object of their mission; and such were the profligate habits of the people that Mr. Rodgerson deemed it unsuitable to remain among them with his wife and children, and returned to Tahiti. Mr. Stallworthy, being a single man, held on alone, braving dangers and trials such as fall to the lot of few missionaries in these days; and in 1839 he was joined by another unmarried missionary, the Rev. Robert Thomson, one of the party who accompanied John Williams when he returned to the islands from England in the brig *Camden* in 1838.

Before the arrival of Mr. Thomson two Romish priests were conveyed to the island by a French frigate, and stationed in the same bay where Protestant missionaries and teachers had been at work for so many years. Mr. Stallworthy pointed out to the Commander, Admiral Du Petit Thouars, that there were other islands unoccupied, and other districts of the same island, and respectfully remonstrated against their being landed there. The Admiral, however, would not listen, but informed Mr. Stallworthy that it was his intention to establish Roman Catholic missionaries on all points, and it was soon manifest that the French Government had an ulterior object in view, to the carrying out of which the landing of priests was only a preparatory step. In 1839 ten additional priests were landed at Santa Christina, five of whom afterwards went to Nukuhiva, and some time after Admiral Du Petit Thouars took forcible possession of the group in the name of the King of the French. Before that took place Messrs. Stallworthy and Thomson, in concurrence with the opinion of the missionaries in Tahiti, felt it their duty to retire from the group. This they did towards the close of 1841, and the Marquesans were once more left in darkness in as far as Protestant teaching was concerned, and the darkness was of long continuance.

The resumption of Protestant mission work in the group was brought about in the following manner. A trading vessel called at the island of Fatuhiva, on board of which was a native of the Sandwich Islands named Puu. When the vessel sailed he was left behind sick. He was received into the family of Matunui, an important chief, who treated him with great kindness, and after a time gave him his daughter for a wife. His superior knowledge greatly surprised the poor ignorant Marquesans, and when questioned as to how he came by his knowledge, he told them that he had learnt all from missionaries. This led his father-in-law to conceive the idea of embracing the first opportunity that might offer of going to the Sandwich Islands to beg for missionaries to come to his land and teach him and his people. His brother chiefs approved of the plan, and early in 1853 the wished for opportunity occurred, and accompanied by his son-in-law he proceeded to the Sandwich Islands. The interesting errand on which he had come was made known to the missionaries, and his request presented to them was to the effect that at least one white missionary might return with him to his land, but if that could not be, he would take two or three Hawaiian missionaries, and wait till a foreign missionary could be sent to him. The Hawaiian Board regarded the call as from God, and after due deliberation it was determined to send two native pastors, James Kekela and Samuel Kawealoha, with their wives; and two native teachers, Lot Kauaihelani and Isaia Kaiwi, and their wives; and the Rev. B. W. Parker was appointed to go with them, and assist them at the commencement of their mission. Mr. James Bicknell, a decidedly Christian young man, resident at Honolulu at the time, volunteered to join the mission. He was a native of Tahiti, but his parents were English. He was afterwards ordained a missionary to the Marquesas, and laboured faithfully in that group for several years.

A vessel was chartered to convey the party to their destination, and bring Mr. Parker back to the Sandwich Islands. So Matunui returned to his island home in something like triumph. A warm welcome was accorded to him and the mission party, and work was commenced under promising circumstances. The results were not so satisfactory as might have been expected. The people were kind, and some impression was evidently made, but there does not appear to have been decided conversions. For three years the labourers toiled on amid trials and privations many and great; at the end of which time a call reached them which they regarded as a message from God. An old chief from the island of Hivaoa visited them, and begged that at least one of them would remove to his land, and teach him and his people the way of life. Three of them went to the island, and after a careful survey of the place, and holding intercourse with the people, they were satisfied that it was a far more promising field than Fatuhiva. Mr. Bicknell, who was one of the deputation, decided at once to remain, and the other two resolved to join him as soon as they could get their goods brought from the old station. After a time they succeeded in this, and commenced work in their new sphere. Hivaoa is one of the largest islands of the group. It is twenty-two miles in length, and seven in breadth. Three stations were commenced on the island, viz., at Paumau Bay, Hanahi, and Hanamana; the mission entered upon a new stage of its history, and the prospects were brighter than they had ever before been.

Such was the state of the mission in 1857 when the *Morning Star* arrived at the Sandwich Islands. Letters had been received there from the missionaries labouring in the Marquesas, giving an account of their work, and begging that supplies of clothing and other necessaries should be sent to them with the least possible delay, as they were in great destitution. No time was lost. In one week from the time of the arrival of the *Morning Star* at Honolulu she was ready to sail for the Marquesas. One Hawaiian pastor, Kaukau, and his wife, went to reinforce the mission, and the Rev. J. Emerson and a Hawaiian named Namakeha went as a deputation from the Hawaiian Missionary Society. The visit was an exceedingly interesting one to all concerned. The missionaries, so long cut off from intercourse with Christian lands, and having been reduced to such straits for the lack of necessaries, hailed the advent of the *Morning Star* with great joy. The visitors, too, shared fully in their rejoicing, being specially glad to witness unmistakable indications that success was at length crowning missionary labour on the Marquesas. In their heathen state the people had been incorrigible thieves; even clothes could not be hung out sufficiently long to dry without being stolen. Now, nothing was molested, and locks and bolts were no longer needful; and the call was loud for missionaries from almost every island. "We want American missionaries," the people were crying out, "right from the Sandwich Islands"—meaning that they did not want Popish priests. One chief urged his claim on the ground that "drunkenness, theft, and war are the passion of my people." "Send me," he said, "missionaries, that these evils may be removed, and we will protect and feed them." And a chief of Fatuhiva said—"Three long and almost fruitless years did the missionaries labour among us with much endurance; the wedge has entered, the Gospel has taken root, it will grow. God will not forsake Fatuhiva."

A meeting of the mission was held during the stay of

the *Morning Star*, in the course of which a service was held which must have gladdened the hearts of all present, especially the resident missionaries. A notable part of the proceedings was an ordination, and the person ordained to the ministry of the Gospel was a native of the Marquesas! John Kaiwe, the first decided convert to Christ in the group, was judged a fit and proper person to be set apart as a preacher of the Gospel to his countrymen—a marvellous thing surely when all the circumstances are taken into account; and a native chief named Pohuete, who for two years had given evidence of a change of heart, was baptized, and added to the church. Of this man even the heathen bore testimony. "He is really another man," said they, "unlike his former self, and unlike us."

So far but little progress had been made in educating the Marquesans. Five schools were in operation, attended by persons of all ages, but there were no books in the native language; hence little progress could be made. The Hawaiian is a dialect of the same root, so some progress could be made with the aid of books in that language; but the necessity for books in the vernacular was now felt, and it was arranged that Mr. Bicknell should proceed to Honolulu in the *Morning Star* to prepare and superintend the printing of some books adapted to the wants of the mission.

But the time came when the *Morning Star* must take her departure. Her work was done, and the object of her visit was accomplished. "The missionaries," Mrs. Warner remarks, "had been cheered and comforted, and their wants relieved. Many delightful seasons of prayer and conference had been enjoyed, and God's blessing had richly descended upon them. Bidding those they were leaving farewell, with many prayers for God's blessing to abide still upon them, the visitors went on board the *Morning Star*, and set sail for Fatuhiva to land those natives who went as passengers to the meeting." Having landed these, she stood away on her return voyage, having lain at anchor in the different bays sixteen days.

In the following year the *Morning Star* made a second visit to the Marquesas. She sailed from Honolulu on the 16th of March, the Rev. S. E. Bishop proceeding in her as a deputation from the Hawaiian Missionary Society, and several teachers to strengthen and extend the mission. Fatuhiva was reached on the 25th of April, and they had a joyous welcome. Mr. Bishop, referring to that, wrote as follows:—"The arrival of the *Morning Star* was a great event to the natives, giving consequence to their valley and the missionaries stationed there, which called forth a liberality never before manifested by that people. On every side were greetings and expressions of cordial esteem which I had never expected to witness. Hogs, bread-fruit, cocoa-nuts were brought, more than the missionaries and their families could possibly consume. The surplus was sent off to the vessel, and we were supplied in the greatest profusion."

"But," observes Mrs. Warner, "other hearts were glad besides those of the natives. Mr. Bishop and those who accompanied him were no less delighted to meet them, and see evidence that the missionaries had not laboured in vain and spent their strength for nought." The reader will remember that three years passed before much impression appeared to be made on the people at this place. Now the first-fruits had been gathered in. The day after the arrival of the visitors was the Sabbath. About one hundred attended the service. Five new members were added to the church, and the Lord's Supper was observed, making a total of twelve in full membership.

During the stay of the vessel a general meeting was held for the transaction of business. The newly arrived teachers were appointed to stations, and those who had preceded them were found to be contented and happy in their work. And in connection with the report of this visit we find an opinion expressed, the carrying out of which has very seriously retarded the progress of the mission. The notion was taken up and henceforth acted upon "that Hawaiians were better adapted to that field (the Marquesas) than Americans, both from the similarity of the climate and the language to those of Hawaii."

This is not the place to discuss the question which this opinion raises. We may remark, however, that the experience of more than half a century goes to prove its unsoundness, and that the history of the Marquesan mission itself is strongly confirmatory of the same view. I speak with reference to our South Sea missions generally, for there is nothing in the case of the Marquesas materially different from other islands and groups of the Pacific. And in these, one and all, it has been found that European or American missionaries are a necessity in order to the extension and consolidation of mission work. In order to that a literature must be provided, and above all the sacred Scriptures must be translated into the vernacular. And for these works, especially the latter, our most advanced pastors and teachers are quite unequal.

The only white missionary, Mr. Bicknell, who has resided for any length of time in the Marquesas down to the present time, and perhaps owing to the notion we are combating was only a few years in the group, and from the time of his leaving, little or no advance, so far as we are informed, has been made in the translation of the Scriptures or in preparing other books for carrying forward the education of the people.

In a letter from Mr. Bicknell to myself, dated November 24th, 1887, he writes as follows:—"The only portions of Scripture that have been printed are those that I made. The fact is, the mission as yet has not advanced beyond the oral stage. The translations made by me have all been printed, and I suppose are in use among the natives. The translations were the Gospel according to John, the Sermon on the Mount, and the three first chapters of

Genesis. A collection of sacred hymns was prepared and printed; also an Elementary Geography, Colburn's Mental Arithmetic, a tract on the Evidences of Christianity, the Confession of Faith, and Church Covenant."

In the same letter Mr. Bicknell supplies the following information relative to an arrangement by which the Marquesan mission has passed from the Hawaiian and American Boards into other hands. The reader will remember that many years ago the islands were taken possession of by the French, and "being French territory, and so near to Tahiti, the French Evangelical Society thought they could work the missions more cheaply than could be done from here (Hawaii), therefore it was transferred to the care of that society, the Hawaiian missionaries remaining on the islands, and co-operating with the French missionaries."

Of the Hawaiian missionaries three remain, with their wives. They are supported by the Hawaiian Board, and constitute a link of connection between that and the French missionaries, but when they pass away the connection will cease, as no more will be sent. Two of those now on the islands are on Hivaoa, and the other on Uapou. Each has a church under his care, but as no report had been received at Honolulu for some time when Mr. Bicknell wrote, he was unable to give the number of members in the churches.

"The French Government," Mr. Bicknell tells us, "have established day-schools. Both the French and Marquesan languages are taught. There are also boarding-schools. The French would prefer to teach in their own language. We do not know whether they have printed any books in the vernacular. A regular government has been organised, wars are suppressed, taxes are levied, and roads made; also, one of the uninhabited islands has been set apart for the segregation of lepers."

We are not informed as to what has been done by the French Protestant missionaries in the way of preparing educational and other books for the Marquesans, or what progress has been made in the translation of the sacred Scriptures. As Protestant missionaries we may feel assured that they will not lose sight of that essential work which has been so long neglected. Had three or four American missionaries been in the field since 1853, when the Hawaiian Board took up the mission, the translation and printing of the Bible might have been completed years ago, and in that case what a different record in all probability should we have had to make to-day. However, it is useless to indulge in regrets over past mistakes. It is cause for thankfulness that the mission is now in the hands of competent men, and we trust they will do their utmost to get a Marquesan version of the Bible into the hands of the natives with the least possible delay. A substantial consolidated spiritual work which will endure is an impossibility without the Bible. From the Hawaiian missionaries who remain in the group the French Protestant missionaries will be able to obtain most valuable help in translating the Scriptures, and in almost every department of work. Their long experience, and their eminently Christian spirit, if we may judge from the testimony of one of them, written many years ago, will render them invaluable helpers. The good man to whom I refer wrote as follows:—"God sent us here, not man. He has preserved us, our wives and little ones, in perils by sea, in perils among robbers, and in perils by war. He has given us influence and favour among the people, so that our names are sacred, and our persons safe. He has made us mediators between bloodthirsty and vindictive foes. He has drawn numbers from the *tabus*, and from all heathen orgies, and made them our docile pupils. Above all, He has given us *souls*. There is a church here, there are Christians, saints, &c." The occasion of the writer expressing himself in this emphatic manner was, if I remember rightly, the discussion of a proposal to give up the mission, and he spoke in his name, and I suppose that of his brethren, to the effect, that they were determined to continue in their work, and depend upon the providence of God, whether those who had sent them continued to support them or not. The mission was not abandoned, as the reader has seen, and we may hope that all danger of its being abandoned is at an end now.

In the Annual Report of the Hawaiian Evangelical Association for 1887 we find the following brief reference to the Marquesan mission:—" From our missionaries at the Marquesas we have no late reports. At last accounts they were still working on in faith and patience under the French administration of the government."

And so we close our notice of the Marquesan mission. There is so little to record that belongs directly to the subject with which this work specially deals that it may be questioned whether it is entitled to occupy a place in this volume. I feel that there is some force in the objection; still our survey would have been incomplete if it had been passed unnoticed. There would have been a missing link. And there is something to record. A beginning has been made. The Marquesans have a portion of God's truth in their hands, and we may hope that it is only a question of a few years, and the great work will be done. The men who can do it are now in the field, and they will no doubt apply themselves to it with the earnestness and diligence which its importance demands, and in due time we shall have the missing link supplied, the blank filled up, and the Marquesans numbered among the many islands and groups throughout the vast Pacific on which the people are reading in their own tongues the wonderful works of God in His own Book.*

* For the facts embodied in the above chapter I am indebted chiefly to Mr. Ellis' "Polynesian Researches," his "History of the London Missionary Society," and Mrs. Warner's "History of the *Morning Star*."

CONCLUSION.

In concluding his work, "The Students' Guide," the author, the Rev. John Todd, writes as follows:—"It is a solemn season with a man who acts from conscience, when he comes to close his book, and bid his reader adieu. His motives may be good, but it is in the nature of humanity to err.... At any rate, he is about to send a book out into the world, which, whatever may be its fate, has given him the opportunity of doing good; and under that responsibility the writer must continue."

With some such feelings as those expressed by Mr. Todd the writer of this book now bids adieu to his readers. He has spared no pains to make the work as accurate and comprehensive as he was able, and he has conscientiously striven to make the book in a measure worthy of the great subject of which it treats; still it is in "the nature of humanity to err," and I suppose it is also in the nature of humanity to fall short of its own aims and ideals. Great as has been the labour involved in the preparation of the work, it has been thoroughly congenial, and in the course of a long life no more pleasant hours have been spent in literary work than those which have been occupied in the preparation of this book. I seem to have lived my missionary life over and over again while collecting and arranging the records of Bible translation and Bible circulation in the many fields which have passed under review in the course of the work. It is a great joy to me, as it will be to every lover of the Bible, to think of the immense amount of work accomplished and in progress in the vast fields now embraced by the combined efforts of the British and Foreign and other Bible Societies, and the many Missionary Societies which in conjunction with these are working together for the good of man and the glory of God. What mighty influences and agencies have been called into operation! How vast are the results already realised; and how incomprehensible to any but the Infinite mind will be the outcome of these in their ever-widening flow in the future ages of the world, and in the interminable beyond!

To the God of the Bible, the Father, the Son, and the Holy Spirit, be glory, and dominion, now and ever, world without end. Amen.

INDEX.

Adams, Rev. T., 71
Aged, type for, 48
Aitutaki, 20
Allan, Rev. W., 102
Alphabet, 33
Ambrym, 187
American Bible Society, 252, 267
Amos, Mr., 71
Anderson, Rev. Dr., 250
Andrews, Rev. L., 246
Aneiteum, 132
Aniwa, 128

Baker, Rev. W., 202
Barff, Rev. C., 37, 41, 54
Barff, Rev. J., 13
Bereans, 74
Bible, changes wrought by, 51, 92, 93
Bible missionaries, 41
Bible, joy on receiving, 29, 70, 73, 89, 193, 249
Bible, sale of, 17, 45, 52, 60, 62, 129, 144, 166, 196, 268
Bible Society, British and Foreign, 7-11, 44, 72, 177, 233
Bible Society, Scottish, 150
Bible text-book in schools, 75
Bible, value of, 34, 74, 81, 92, 93, 95, 138, 180, 197, 231, 253
Bicknell, Mr. J., 282
Binding of Bible, 7
Bingham, Rev. H., 244
Bingham, Rev. H., jun., 247, 261
Bishop, Rev. A., 247
Bishop, Rev. S. E., 286
Boothroyd's version, 43
Bourne, Rev. R., 22
Bowels, 33
Bownell, D., 66

Broughton, Bishop, 105
Brown, Rev. G., 215
Buchanan, John, 66
Buddle, Rev. T., 117
Butler, Rev. John, 112
Buzacott, Rev. A., 28, 39, 41, 199

Calvert, Rev. J., 77, 83, 88, 102
Cargill, Rev. D., M.A., 76
Chalmers, Rev. J., 225
Changes wrought, 51, 59, 93
Chisholm, Rev. A., 13
Church Missionary Society, 104, 111
Civilisation, 105
Clark, Rev. E. W., 247
Claxton, Rev. A. E., 51
Commerce, 60
Committee, translating, 43
Completion services, 45
Conscience, 33
Cook, Captain, 55, 65, 125, 132, 154, 168, 238
Cooper, James, 66
Cooper, Rev. E. V., 17
Copeland, Rev. J., 126, 148, 159
Cosh, Rev. J., M.A., 177
Creagh, Rev. S. M., 192
Crook, Rev. W. P., 6, 279
Cross, Rev. W., 71, 76

Daniel, Rev. —, 71
Danks, Rev. B., 219
Darling, Rev. D., 280
Davies, Rev. John, 2, 66
Davis, Rev. —, 71
Definite article, 35
Deputation to Fiji, 97
Dialectic differences, 78
Dialects of Hervey Islands, 2

Dibble, Rev. S., 245
Doane, Rev. E. T., 270, 273
Duke of York group, 215, 222
Dwight, Rev. E. W., 241

EASTERN and Central Polynesia, 1
Ebon, 272
Eimeo, 5
Ella, Rev. S., 45, 159
Ellis, Rev. W., 4, 8, 12, 208, 243, 278
Emerson, Rev. J., 284
English language, 101
Epi, 186
Eramanga, 154, 188
European missionaries, 96

FAITH, 33
Faté, 168
Fiji statistics, 97
Fiji version, 76
Fison, Rev. L., 92
Fletcher, Rev. W., B.A., 101
Fotuna, 124
Foundry Boys press, 150
Fraser, Rev. R. M., 186
Free Church of Scotland, 135
French Evangelical Society, 288
French oppression, 196

GAULTON, S., 66
Geddie, Rev. Dr., 126, 134
Genealogies, 34
Gilbert Islands, 262
Gill, Rev. George, 31, 172
Gill, Rev. W. W., B.A., 27, 225
Gill, Rev. W., 31
Gordon, Rev. G. N., 155
Gordon, Rev. J. D., 160, 162
Governor of New South Wales, 106, 108
Gray, Rev. W., 152
Green, Rev. J. L., 15, 16
Green, Rev. J. S., 247
Gulick, Rev. Dr. L. H., 256, 273
Gunn, Rev. Dr., 127

HALL, F., 112
Hall, W., 105
Hardie, Rev. C., 41, 157
Harper, S., 66
Hazelwood, Rev. D., 85
Heart, 33
Heath, Rev. T., 41, 128, 147, 156
Heaven, 33
Helps in translating, 43
Hervey Islands, 27
History, Scripture, 41
Hobbs, Rev. J., 117
Hongi of New Zealand, 107
Horsley, Rev. J., 91
Hotchkiss, Mr., 265
Howe, Rev. W., 12, 32
Hunt, Rev. A. E., 235
Hunt, Rev. J., 80, 101

IDIOMS, 35
Inglis, Rev. Dr., 135
Intemperance, 95

JAGGAR, Rev. —, 77
Jehovah, 32
Johnston, Rev. S. F., 148
Jones, Rev. J., 192
Joseph, Rev. T., 13
Joy over the Bible, 29
Jubilee at Fiji, 87

KELSO, Seth, 66
Kelynack, Rev. Dr., 97
Kemp, J., 112
Kendall, Thomas, 105, 112
King John, 105
King's letter, 256
Kipling, Rev. G. A., 117
Krause, Rev. E. R. W., 31
Kusaie, 272

LA PEROUSE, 37
Langham, Rev. —, 90
Lawes, Rev. F. E., 62
Lawes, Rev. W. G., 55, 60, 231
Lee, Professor, 112
Leigh, Rev. S., 114
Lifu, 199
Logan, Rev. W., 274

INDEX.

London Missionary Society, 1, 20, 39, 54, 66, 132
Loomis, E., 244
Lyth, Rev. R. B., 80, 89

MACDONALD, Rev. A., 41
Macdonald, Rev. D., 165, 178
Macfarlane, Rev. Dr., 202, 225
Mackenzie, Rev. J. W., 177
Macnair, Rev. J., 161
Mangaia, 23
Mare, 189
Marquesas, 277
Marsden, Rev. S., 11, 104, 107, 113
Marshall Islands, 270
Martin, E., 83
Massacres, 17, 106, 158, 164
Matheson, Rev. J. W., 148
Maunsell, Archdeacon, 116, 132
Mbau dialect, 80
Mellor, Rev. T. W., 88, 119, 139
Michelson, Rev. O., 183
Micronesia, 255
Mills, Rev. W., 41
Milne, Rev. P., 183
Missionaries, 41, 96
Moore, Rev. J., 14
Moresby, Captain, R.N., 230
Morris, Rev. G., 14
Morrison, Rev. D., 175
Mortlock Islands, 274
Mosaic institutions, 31
Moulton, Rev. J. E., 74
Murray, A. W., 39, 100, 133, 170, 226
Murray, Rev. C., M.A., 187
Murray, Rev. W. B., M.A., 187

NEGATIVES, 35
Neilson, Rev. T., 149, 161
Nettleton, Rev. J., 89
New Britain, 225
New Caledonia, 213
New Guinea, 225
New Hebrides, 78, 124
New South Wales Auxiliary, 57
New Zealand, 104
Nguna, 184

Nicholas, J. L., 108
Nihil, Rev. W., 192, 201
Nisbet, Rev. Dr., 46, 147
Niua, 128
Niue, 53
Noble, Isaac, 66
Nott, Rev. H., 6, 10, 32, 33
Nova Scotia, 134

OBOKIA, 241
Ormsond, Rev. J. M., 23

PARKER, Rev. B. W., 252
Paton, Rev. J. G., 129, 148
Patteson, Bishop, 201
Paulo of Samoa, 54
Pearce, Rev. A., 16
Pearse, Rev. A., 232
Pease, Rev. Dr., 271
Pedigrees, 34
Peek, R., Esq., 194
Philadelphia Bible Society, 249
Pierson, Rev. Dr., 270
Pitman, Rev. C., 23
Platt, Rev. G., 39
Pomare, King, 5
Ponape, 273
Popery, 83, 119, 210
Powell, Rev. T., 48, 134
Pratt, Rev. George, 46, 56, 59
Press from Foundry Boys, 150
Psalter for aged, 48
Pundits, 43

QUARTERLIES, Fijian, 80

RABONE, Rev. S., 71
Races, Bible for all, 34
Raiatea, 22
Rarotonga, 20, 24, 29, 33
Reformed Presbyterian Church, 135
Reid, Rev. R., 97
Richards, Rev. W., 245
Rickard, Rev. R. H., 210
Robertson, Rev. H. A., 164
Rogerson, Rev. J., 280
Roman Catholic priests, 19, 210
Rooney, Rev. J., 220

Rossenmuller's Commentaries, 43
Rotuma, 99
Ruk, 274

SABBATH in New Zealand, 109
Sale of Bibles, 17, 45, 47, 48, 52, 60, 62
Samoan pastors, 56, 100
Samoan version, 37, 47, 49
Sandwich Islands, 238
Savage, Rev. E. B., 235
Saville, Rev. A., 16
School, Bible in, 61
Scott, Rev. J. T., 235
Scott, Rev. H., 235
Scripture history, 41
Sharp, Rev. W., 236
Shelly, W., 66
Shemites, 34
Sheppard Isles, 184
Sleigh, Rev. J., 205
Snow, Rev. B. G., 256, 271
Stair, Rev. J. B., 42
Stallworthy, Rev. G., 172, 280
Stephenson, Rev. W. G., 70
Stories, Bible, 34
Strong's Island, 272
Sturges, Rev. A., 256, 273
Sunderland, Rev. J. P., 45, 136, 151, 192, 226, 232

TAHITI, 1-17, 21, 39, 69, 70
Tanna, 146
Tasman, 65
Thakombau, 95
Thanksgiving services, 45
Thomas, Rev. J., 70
Thompson, Rev. R., 281
Three Hill Island, 185
Threlkeld, Rev. L. E., 21

Thurston, Rev. A., 244
Times, London, 254
Tonga, 65
Tongoa, 184
Translating, mode of, 41, 42, 58, 77, 80, 139, 204, 252, 275
Translations by native pastors, 56
Trust, 33
Tucker, Rev. —, 71
Turner, Rev. Dr., 47, 49, 100, 147, 170, 174
Turner, Rev. N., 70
Turner, Rev. P., 71
Turner, Rev. W., M.D., 236
Tutuila, 37

UVEA, 208

VEESON, George, 66
Vernier, Rev. F., 18
Versions, 43, 59
Volkner, Rev. C. S., 119

WARNER, Mrs., 285
Waterhouse, Rev. J., 100
Watkin, Rev. J., 70
Watsford, Rev. —, 80
Watt, Rev. W., 149, 187
Webb, Rev. A. J., 93
West, Rev. T., 71
Whitmee, Rev. S. J., 48
Whitney, Rev. J. F., 271, 275
Wilkinson, James, 66
Williams, Archdeacon, 117
Williams, Rev. J., 20, 28, 37, 42, 54, 100, 146
Williams, Rev. T., 76, 97
Wilson, Rev. —, 71
Wilson, S., 40
Woon, W., 70

www.ingramcontent.com/pod-product-compliance
Lightning Source LLC
Chambersburg PA
CBHW030817230426
43667CB00008B/1255